THE FASCIST:
HIS STATE AND HIS MIND

AMS PRESS
NEW YORK

THE
FASCIST

His State and His Mind

by

E. B. ASHTON (PSEUD.)
(ERNST BASCH)

NEW YORK

WILLIAM MORROW & CO.

Library of Congress Cataloging in Publication Data

Basch, Ernst, 1909–
    The fascist: his state and his mind.

    Reprint of the 1937 ed.
    1. Fascism. 2. Corporate state. I. Title.
JC481.B32 1972   335.6   72-180386
ISBN 0-404-56101-2

Reprinted by arrangement with William Morrow & Co. , Inc. , New York.

Reprinted from the edition of 1937, New York
First AMS edition published in 1972
Manufactured in the United States of America

AMS PRESS INC.
NEW YORK, N. Y.   10003

1716858

TO

MY EDITORIAL ADVISERS

This book was completed in the early autumn of 1936. Therefore, the reader will find no reference to more recent developments (Hitler's Second Four-Year-Plan; Mussolini's re-making of the Italian judicial system; and, most conspicuous, the dénouement of the Spanish rebellion as a move of Fascist and National Socialist machtpolitik)—although every one of these tends to support the theory of Fascism advanced in the following pages.

E. B. A.

CONTENTS

WE HAVE JUST HELD A PRESIDENTIAL ELECTION. THE campaign, a bitter one, was fought with a denunciatory fervor that painted mild liberals as dangerous radicals and cautious conservatives as die-hard reactionaries. This, of course, is nothing new in American history. Still, an inventory of the political smear-words of 1936 will disclose an unusual fact: there was one epithet— not mere billingsgate but a word with a definite meaning —which *every* group in our political arena hurled at its opponents. Democrats and Republicans, "Lemke-ites," Socialists, and Communists, men whose points of view are otherwise as different as Heywood Broun's and Mark Sullivan's, tried to pin this one on their respective enemies—"Fascism."

This is more than strange; it is unprecedented. Here is a distinct political system, which several European nations have put into practice, about which facts are known and reports available—and yet, in this country, the exponents of diametrically opposed political philosophies are being earnestly accused of fostering that very same system. Furthermore, every casual conversation about it is apt to show an amazing divergence of interpretations. Today it is no rare occurrence to hear two intelligent and well-informed Americans give exactly contradictory definitions of Fascism. Radicals, for the most part, call it a capitalist dictatorship. Those old-line rugged individualists, however, who still think laissez faire is a synonym for freedom, might well believe they are expressing the essence of Fascism when they call it an anti-capitalist dictatorship! Many people, offhand, would say that primarily it means a vicious class rule. But those who have been able to observe it somewhat more closely will probably insist that its main actual achievement is, on the contrary, a leveling of class distinctions. A vast literature has been written on the subject, but despite it we continue to use a term—applying it to our own everyday political life—without being able to agree on what it means.

If the discussion were purely academic, this would not be of such moment. But we do not know whether it is academic—nor how long it will be. Only a few months ago a great American novelist shocked us out of our complacent satisfaction that "it couldn't happen here." Then, right after Sinclair Lewis's gruesome fantasy, Lawrence Dennis published a glowing picture of a "Coming American Fascism," under which the élite of our one hundred and twenty millions would take charge and lead us into a happier future. Between these viewpoints there is not the normal difference of opinion separating a protagonist from an opponent of a theory, but an ideological fog completely enveloping the American public. We feel that Fascism must be fundamentally unpopular, or our politicians would not all be so eager to put its label on their adversaries. On the other hand, should we not be alarmed over the fact that virtually all political groups in this country are incessantly discovering Fascist tendencies—in others? At present, we can be fairly sure that none of these cries of "Beware Fascism" is either given or taken quite seriously. But, after all, when a number of people habitually refer to each other as thieves, would it be surprising if at last one or the other took to stealing? Franklin Roosevelt, Alf Landon, and William Lemke, our three potential "people's choices" of 1936, were all equally "against it"; which would appear to leave us reasonably safe. Yet what did Landon and Lemke partisans say Roosevelt stands for, and Roosevelt and Lemke partisans say Landon stands for, and Roosevelt and Landon partisans say Lemke stands for? Are we not putting the cart before the horse—with all the excitement over whether it can't happen here, before we can even make out what "it" is?

To provide a foundation for the work of others who may eventually undertake to clarify the issue, this book has been written. It purports to be nothing but a sketchy attempt to start an analytical structure on the basis of present, available material. The Fascist background of philosophy and political science has advisedly been kept out of the discussion; it is a sufficiently involved task to analyze Fascism as it is, without delving into its intellectual ancestry—which here, because of conclusions we shall reach, would have to be extended far beyond the range of writers from Hegel to Pareto that is usually mentioned in this connection. Neither has the wealth of contemporary writing on Fascism been discussed or quoted; this was thought unnecessary, since, whenever possible, the deductions of this study were based on such premises as may be assumed to be generally known: on unquestioned facts, or on traits too general to escape open-minded observation.

As to sources of facts, it seems to me that the objective press of the world has given out surprisingly accurate and comprehensive information about Fascist developments. By "objective press" I mean those newswriters who, without renouncing their own point of view, still consider it their prime duty to *report* facts—not to color them or to omit what does not fit into their particular picture. I am not prepared to argue about things that are obvious. If, for example, American ace reporters, after touring Europe in 1936, describe Germany and Italy as "seething" with political unrest, they are welcome to their opinion. It is not within my province to point out that they are the exact counterpart of their most heartily despised colleagues—of the type that makes periodic predictions of an impending rise of the Russian people against the Soviet dictatorship. To that brand of journalism—and to its unfortunate readers— applies that saddest of Hitler jokes, of the last two German Jews' hushed conversation in 1966: "And I tell you, they won't last another six months!" In both cases, of anti-Communists as well as of anti-Fascists, these wish-fulfillment dreams by men to whom information of the public was entrusted have proved the greatest obstacle in the way of the dispassionate appraisal indispensable to intelligent opposition. I have tried to provide leads for such an appraisal. May following them prove helpful to those who will some time make a complete and exhaustive analysis of Fascism, the twentieth century's strangest political phenomenon—and most misused catchphrase.

THE FASCIST:
HIS STATE AND HIS MIND

CHAPTER ONE

THE ARGUMENT OF FASCISM

Appearances and How to Exploit Them

WITH AMAZING FORCE THE ADVENT OF FASCISM HAS stirred the Old World out of its post-war political lethargy. The Italian trial-balloon was not taken very seriously at first. Acute observers, however, soon began to realize that here was a new political faith, which, in the very crudeness of its outer aspects, had all the requirements for a tremendous appeal to men in masses. Upon the ordinary citizen it conferred simple tasks and no responsibilities, and it gave him always something to look up to. It provided for a swift and efficient discharge of governmental functions. It possessed the charm of restless activity, and it was intensely and naturally nationalistic, which is always more attractive than a nationalism whipped up only for special occasions. In Mussolini it was fortunate enough to find a genius who made its first venture a success in both domestic and foreign politics. Therefore, when Germany (considered a stronghold of democracy since 1918) went completely Fascist, and half a dozen other European governments began to operate on more or less similar lines, the world

3

could not but wonder if this, perhaps, might be the cure for what ailed it.

In addition, the new creed soon displayed the proselytizing zeal of the true apostle. At a very early moment Mussolini said: "Fascism cannot be exported." But then he hailed the conversion of Germany with genuine enthusiasm—so genuine, in fact, that it has since caused Il Duce more embarrassment than he used to relish in international relations. Today there is hardly a country where, at one time or other, spokesmen of Fascism have not sought to convince the people of its intrinsic values. On grounds of theory and of practice, because of political and economic troubles, racial unrest and spiritual dissatisfaction the word has been spread that our century needs, and is bound to achieve, a novel frame of community life—and that Fascism is it. How well the Marxian lesson has been learned: that all one has to do to get something accepted as desirable is to describe it as inevitable!

Out of these two components, world misery and Fascist propaganda, grew what may be called the Argument of Fascism—the violent and determined advance of a new political faith against a slow thinking, slower acting and badly disorganized opposition. The opponents tried to make up for their inefficiency in fighting by a righteous indignation. But, for one thing, it is hard enough nowadays to detect the difference between the rights and the wrongs of a political issue; for another, there has never been much use in doing so; for a third, the Fascists are masters of righteous indignation themselves. So the argument soon became heated and—in countries where democratic instincts were not very deeply rooted—somewhat one-sided. A general confusion as to what Fascism really meant, wanted, and stood for, did not help to ease the tension. The emphatic anti-Socialist attitude of the movement led to its being labeled a bodyguard of capitalist interests. The anti-Jewish drive in Germany resulted in Fascism being commonly associated with anti-Semitism, with which, in principle at least, it has nothing to do whatever. Unpunished outrages committed by its followers brought the charge that it condoned crime as a matter of general policy. Frightened conservatives declared that they could not see anything to distinguish this new Bolshevism of the Right from the old Bolshevism of the Left. It was only in the great democratic nations that the public began comparatively soon to concentrate upon one fundamental point: the Fascist abolition of what used to be considered the inextinguishable rights of liberty and equality of Man, rights won in a long and painful struggle for such trophies as England's Magna Carta, France's Declaration of Human Rights, and our Declaration of Independence and Bill of Rights in the Constitution of the United States.

The Fascists countered first with an attempt to show what they offered instead. What is usually cited for that purpose is an impressive record of achievements in Italy since 1922. It is true that Italian party rule after the World War had made a pretty thorough mess of the country in general. It cannot be denied that materially

the first Fascist decade brought an enormous advance—
although, of course, it will never be possible to prove
that it could not have been accomplished in some other
way. But beyond question Italy, for centuries a pictur-
esque country of dirt, vermin, thievery, and dolce far
niente, now has a reputation not only for color but for
clean hotels, clean trains and a notable absence of pick-
pockets; has attained leadership on the Continent in the
manufacture of automobiles; has built an exemplary
commercial oversea and air fleet; has reclaimed the
Pontine marshes—now a site of model cities—and the
scugnizzi and lazzaroni of its sidewalks, who have become the best track athletes, riders, fighters and racing
drivers in Europe. The presumption of credit for all that
must necessarily be in favor of Fascism.

The second convert to the new faith, however, proved
not so good an example in this respect. In Germany
trains had always run on time, and cleanliness had always been one of the most attractive qualities of the
country. Industry, sport—every aspect of material progress had been on an extremely high level from the start.
Under the Republic the nation had gone through an
amazingly fast process of recovery from a state of near-
elimination—until, with the depression, the basically
unsound borrowing policy which had financed the boom
brought the country to the verge of economic collapse.
This, and outside pressure intelligently exploited by
first class propaganda, precipitated the National Socialist victory. But it would hardly have justified any Nazi
claims of credit for eventual improvements; and, as a

matter of fact, few such claims were put forward. As unquestionable achievements of German Fascism, however, we might list (1) national unity and co-ordination, (2) success in foreign politics. Today it is the vogue to call the first a prerequisite to the acquisition of world-political power. There the advocates of national concentration often seem to be entirely oblivious of the fact that, for instance, the British Empire and the United States managed to become important in international affairs despite their highly decentralized systems of government, to which the existence of an independent and carefully encouraged opposition is essential. However— every nation is free to select its own national virtues, and there is no reason why it should not choose the elimination of political strife. About the National Socialists' success in foreign politics there can be no doubt whatever. It was brought about by the unbelievable incompetence of European statesmen, who year after year stubbornly refused to the German governments they liked what they later did not dare but grant the government they loathed. As a potential third achievement may be mentioned economic recovery, although it is as yet impossible to judge this properly. An immediate upswing was manifest during 1933, and again to some extent in 1935-36. But developments in general have been too confused to say whether that upswing was not purely artificial, and might not ultimately prove damaging to real recovery. Politically, at any rate, internal unification and external success cannot be denied.

The price of these achievements: abolition of representative government, of individual liberty, of the rights of free speech, free assembly, a free press and free religion, and of the principle of equality before the law. (It must be noted that, for the purposes of this investigation, these terms will have to be understood in the sense they have come to have in democratic countries. The word "free," for example, has recently acquired a very different meaning in Germany, and any German editor will, with utter conviction, call the German press of today entirely free. This, of course, is only a question of terminology, which has to be settled before going more deeply into the subject.) The question—and the answer is not nearly so axiomatic as it might appear!— is whether the result is worth the price. The Fascist says that all those discarded ideas may be summed up in the two words, Liberalism and democracy. He contends that both, having had ample opportunity to prove themselves, have failed miserably. He says that the function of government is to get results, to look after the well-being of the nation, and not to quibble over how to go about it. He thinks that the participation of the individual in the process of governing can neither do him any good, nor have any ultimate effect except to slow up the government machinery, and that therefore it should be abandoned. He is convinced that individual liberty is a worthless catchphrase, that the guarantee of equal protection under the law is necessarily detrimental to the community, that the duty to think in a group is infinitely preferable to the right to think individually. And it cannot be emphasized too strongly that at present these convictions are shared wholeheartedly and sincerely by hundreds of thousands of the most cultured, erudite and intelligent men and women; whether in Italy, where five centuries ago began the finest realization of absolute individualism of all time, or in Germany, where the Nazi's favorite classic poet, the revolutionary Friedrich Schiller, erected the image of Marquis Posa to the immortal memory of the struggle for freedom of thought.

A herd, however, is no argument—certainly not for a movement which despises majorities. It may serve to establish a certain tolerance, or may lead to certain conclusions on the suitability of various system for various people, but it can never change an honest conviction. Therefore, the unanimity in Fascist countries is seldom cited in preaching the gospel of Fascism elsewhere. Indeed, a very careful selection had to be made in choosing points for use in propaganda abroad. Little effort has been devoted to advertising Fascism in general on the strength of its accomplishments in Germany. Success in foreign politics is, of necessity, a matter for home consumption. Bragging in public is tabooed by good taste as well as by a sort of caution so long as one is not yet definitely stronger than one's neighbors. Talking too much about national unity may also produce quite undesired reactions, nor is German economic progress yet conspicuous enough to be proclaimed otherwise than perfunctorily. Besides, the National Socialist revolution had certain unlovable highlights which were not particularly suited to advertising purposes—from traditional Jew-baiting to the most serious impairment of international security—and which, fortunately, were quite absent from the Italian test case. Il Fascismo, accordingly, has been broadcast all over the place. Being a born propagandist the Fascist is convinced that anybody will believe anything if it is repeated often enough. This explains a strange fact: that the increasing industrialization and efficiency of Mussolini's Italy were even seriously advanced as reasons why the successful system should be desirable for the United States, already over-industrialized and over-efficient to the extent of about ten million unemployed.

The Fascist evangelist is well aware, however, that no example will quite overcome a resistance which has its origin in inherited ideals—moral, social, political or religious. He knows, too, that the principles of democracy, to which Fascism is diametrically opposed, are the inherited ideals of, for instance, the vast majority of the American people. Recognizing fully that he cannot make a people give up or exchange such ideals by pure persuasion, he sets out to shatter their beliefs, and for this purpose, as a rule, cleverly employs a simple but ingenuous reasoning. If, in the course of a discussion, the convinced democrat shows indignation at the Fascist suppression of his most beloved principles, the Fascist replies by calling him a hypocrite. The democrat asks why, and the Fascist starts to enumerate dozens of instances in which democratic practice has been quite inconsistent with democratic theory. The United States, in particular, offers many such examples. The Southern negro is put forward as justifying the treatment of the

Jew in Germany which an obviously hypocritical American public dares to condemn. The Darwin trial in Dayton, Tennessee, is a case of state interference in the teaching of science, the Scottsboro case a flagrant denial of equal protection under the law. That American businessmen exert political pressure upon their employees, and that Communists are not particularly welcome to government positions, are facts quoted to prove the largely fictitious nature of this country's much extolled political liberty. And all that leads up to a triumphant question: With what right do we presume to reproach other nations for taking the honest step of discarding principles which, though still receiving lip-service in America, are not observed here either?

This logic usually meets with remarkable success. Taken aback, the defender of democracy can think of no adequate reply to the accusations, which are flung into his face with an air of outraged innocence, and he often begins to worry that there may really be something fundamentally wrong with his convictions. At once hardly anybody realizes the gigantic fallacy. To use a very drastic example, it is exactly as if, because the United States has a great many gangsters, we could not criticize a country where murder and banditry were legalized and made into pillars of the state! In other words, it is as if crime were not a reason to enforce the law but to abolish it; as if immorality were not a reason to seek to raise the moral level but to remove the moral standard; as if violations of the principles a people has stood for through generations were not reasons to fight for a closer adherence to these principles, but on the contrary were reasons to abandon them altogether.

It is the twisting sophistry in the *presentation* of this argument that often stuns opponents into silence. Once they are able to visualize the underlying principle clearly they must see, of course, that it is too ridiculous to need serious refutation. At this point, however, the anti-democratic attack frequently receives unexpected but powerful support from the ultra-democratic side, which, in a two-party system, is usually the party just out of power. In this country, for instance, today more than ever, the Outs are apt to cry over alleged usurpation of governmental authority by the Ins, and to magnify all kinds of incidents until they can be sold to the public as cases of suppression of constitutional liberty —or God knows what. In this connection the word Fascism has been used frequently and impressively. In Republican newspapers one could read day after day that the United States was suffering under a dictatorship, and find Franklin Roosevelt likened to Hitler or Mussolini. It is not the purpose of this book to comment on the policies of the present administration or on their relation to those of the one-man-rulers in Europe, but this much may be said: it would prove an enlightening experience for the men responsible for this trend of political discussion to try a change of atmosphere for a while and broaden their views by assuming the leadership of an opposition party in a truly Fascist country. Most critics of this type entirely fail to appreciate with what a howl of delight their statements are greeted in the genuine Fascist ranks. They would be appalled if they realized to what extent their "warnings" tend to weaken the people's already shattered confidence in democracy. These wails have exactly the effect the Fascist intends to produce with his method of pointing out sore spots in the democratic system. Only they are much more effective. For the man in the street is likely to conclude that, when even these enraged democrats fall in with the chorus of vituperation, what the Fascist takes such pains to tell him must really be true: democracy itself has failed. And, not caring to fight for a lost cause, he either grows indifferent or goes and joins the nearest colored-shirt movement.

Whether, and at what point, undemocratic practices and developments in a democratic country constitute a "failure of democracy," and whether and why democracy has "failed" in other countries, is quite another question that will be discussed more explicitly later. As far as they concern the Fascist argument itself, a few principles may be stated at this point. First, even a really "failing" democracy is no Fascism. Fascism is positive and uncompromising, and though it may, of course, use any conceivable *name*, it can never exist within a democratic *structure*, a fact which the super-zealous defenders of democracy had better find out before it is too late. Second, because a Fascist country may have achieved certain extraordinary results it does not follow that another country should adopt the same system, unless her problems *and* the political disposition of her people also happen to be the same. Third, the fact that democratic ideas are not always lived up to in practice is no reason for discarding them—just as no Fascist would admit that the validity of his theory depended on its application in every practical instance. Finally, the clever, opportunistic change in the Fascist argument in various countries should present the decisive weapon to the democratic defense. Here—as in England —Fascism appears on the scene as a new gospel of salvation from economic and political distress. That is how the inside missionaries dress it up and how one hears it explained by the official representatives of the Fascist powers. In those countries, on the other hand, the Fascists used to work on the theory that, regardless of material advantages or disadvantages, democracy and Liberalism were conceptions alien to the people and therefore doomed to extinction. This contention contains a great element of truth—but it works both ways! We may concede that in Germany and Italy the present "dictatorships" are not dictatorships in the adverse sense of the word, but political structures wholly expressive of the German and Italian peoples' basic inclinations. But in this country democracy is native—bound to the people by ties too old and strong to be severed by the mere appeal of any intruding movement. To borrow a Nazi phrase: democracy is rooted in American blood; and to each of its principles more American lives have been devoted throughout the centuries than to all the Fascist ideals put together.

What yet remains to be dealt with, however, is the core of the Fascist argument, the spearhead of its demagogic attack, the point that is hammered at until millions lose breath and reason—the "Communist menace." It worked exactly like the discovery of the "Yellow Peril," which around 1900 brought forth violently "Aryan" philosophies in countries where race consciousness at best had never been more than a mild traditional arrogance. Communism is something which, for one reason or other, vast numbers of people happen to dislike intensely. Intelligent exploitation of this dislike may well bring them into the fold of a different movement, which soberly observed, they would dislike just as much, if not more. Before bringing this argument into play, therefore, it is necessary to build up the bogey which, it is hoped, will frighten them out of their wits. Hence the furious cry of the menace of Communism. Again, just as with the assertion of the failure of democracy, the attack received the most gratifying support from the quarters of the attacked. The Communists were extremely pleased to hear that they had been able to stir up something so powerful and so dangerous. This was especially true in countries where Communism so far had been conspicuously harmless. As a rule, where the Communists were really a political factor, they realized the necessity of applying the only intelligent tactics for a party (or a nation, for that matter!) which intends to seize power by force, if need be, but is not strong enough yet: to talk war inside and peace outside—to point out your strength to your comrades and your weakness to your enemies. But in countries where they had not yet been able to gain any footholds worth mentioning, the Communists fell back on the old technique of boasting. They claimed a following, an organization, a power, which they could not hope to possess for a long time—on the principle that frightening an enemy might be a good way to win a friend. So they were delighted with the Fascist battle cry, convinced that if they were pictured as dangerous long enough, they might become dangerous after all. That a belief in the existence of a Communist menace might drive a considerable part of the masses into the Fascist camp, was so utterly unthinkable for those realists that it did not even enter their dangerous minds. And they set out gallantly to fight every group that could have been useful in fighting Fascism, as Fascism in disguise bribed by capitalist money. It always seems to be the good luck of Fascism that its foes should kill each other off.

This still does not explain why majorities should recoil from the Communist Utopia and turn to the castor-oil-and-black-jack-reality of Fascism. The real reason for the success of the "wolf, wolf" propaganda method is a matter of technique: Fascism profits from conjuring up a choice between itself and Communism, because people will disapprove of various aspects of Communism, while Fascism, before seizing power, shows them nothing to disapprove of. It is the ancient trick of the magic cap—and, far from being limited to the presentation of Fascism as an alternative to Communism, it permeates the entire Fascist argument. Everybody knows today what democracy means and stands for. The aims and demands of Communism, too, are a matter of public

record all over the world. They have been discussed and
attacked and distorted, but the general ideas are fairly
well realized in a fairly accurate form. With Fascism
it is different. A nation seldom really finds out anything
about Fascism until Fascism is in the saddle. Before
that time the people see flags and colored shirts and
storm troops and lusty scrambles with political enemies.
What is behind all that is a myth. At most a few nationalist catchphrases which later on are quickly forgotten.
This is the main source of the Fascist strength. Fascism
can attack all the weak points in the position of its
opponents, while able to interpret its own away as political moves, transitory drawbacks without deeper significance. In that way the Nazis overcame the doubts which
the civilized classes in Germany had about Hitler's Jew-
baiting campaign. In that way they explained their industrial affiliations to the workers and the socialist
planks in their platform to the subsidizing industrialists.
The real features of the structure behind those tactical
attitudes and temporary appearances are shrouded in
mystic darkness. That makes the idol attractive. It is
glittering and plastic, though apparently firm—and it is
expedient. It is perfect for the leitmotif of Fascist policy:
first power, then program.

The same tactics are pursued in every country. And
in every country the effect is the same: the Socialists
oppose the thing as capitalistic, the democrats as tyrannical, the conservatives as revolutionary. None of them
realizes that the shrewd tacticians of Fascism are simply
playing off one adversary against the other in building

up their own argument—not a logical one, perhaps, but one most effective. And whenever the Fascist feels himself cornered by unfavorable conclusions drawn from Fascism in Fascist countries, the emphatic nationalism of the doctrine offers an easy way out: "Yes, but here we wouldn't do it that way!" Convincingly pronounced, it will catch anybody. The helplessness of the anti-Fascists is due to the fact that they have never met an opponent who did not shout every detail of his political creed to the four winds as soon as he made his entrance. They do not know how to deal with this strange and terrifying foe who never explains his standpoint beyond the most commonplace generalities, who takes the greatest care *not* to announce a program, and who deliberately removes intellectual conviction from his political armory. They do not realize that to make it possible for them to combat Fascism their way, they will have to bring it up (the Fascist will say down) to their level. That their only chance to refute Fascism is to define Fascism. That they cannot fight it unless they know what it is all about. That the argument of Fascism can only be met with success by reversing the usual process, by doing exactly what the Fascist would be expected to do but, for good reason, never does: find out and show what Fascism means where it prevails, what it would mean elsewhere, and whether and why it must necessarily have the consequences which so far only a rather superficial observation has led us to connect with it.

CHAPTER TWO

WHAT IS FASCISM?

Premises and Their Consequences

DURING THE LAST WEEK OF OCTOBER, 1922, A MIDDLE-aged Italian revolutionary and former Socialist, by the name of Benito Mussolini, directed, from his private headquarters in Milan, the "March on Rome" of his private army. Consequently appointed head of the government, he became in due time creator, prophet and personification of Fascism.

And what is Fascism?

To discover that, we shall first have to choose between two possible lines of approach. One of these is easy, popular, and productive of conclusions that will inevitably be as fallacious as they will be pleasing to the individual investigator. The other is frankly difficult, requires an adaptation to totally unfamiliar intellectual and emotional premises—but in exchange seems to provide a chance for us to know what we are talking about. The first is the customary way of analyzing Fascism from one of our traditional points of view—whether that of what is generally called democracy or that of Communism of the Moscow pattern. The conceptual tangle that usually ensues if the topic of Fascism is brought up in our drawing rooms or in the political arena, is the outcome of this kind of reflection or "analysis." We all have our predetermined points of view, in the terms and on the premises of which we undertake to appraise Fascism. We are seldom bothered by the possibility that the *basis* of our appraisal may be open to question. Of course, in these days of wishful thinking, we cannot expect people to start out from the assumption that their personal convictions are wrong—although many ancient philosophers applied this method of reasoning with conspicuous success. But what might have been done—in fact, what must be done now, if we want to avoid the continuous misunderstandings so fatal to the average discussion of our subject—is to admit that the *bases of political thought may be truly relative.* We must realize that in public life, too, one man's meat may be another man's poison. That conceptions axiomatic to us may be not professedly but actually meaningless to others—or may, also not professedly but actually, connote something entirely different.

This is not a question of bias. It is a question of the applicability of terms and premises. True, our authorities on Fascism went about their task with all fairness—but unfortunately it is a task for which fairness and the most acute analytical intelligence are insufficient. Tackling Fascism with no other equipment, the non-Fascist scientist will have just as much chance of success as the theologian who would try to obtain, not an opinion on, but an understanding of Buddhism by investigating it fairly and intelligently in the spirit and in the terminology of the Protestant Episcopal Church. The essential relativity, of course, is not as obvious in the field of political thought as in the field of religious belief; and, accordingly, it is all too little realized as yet that *in both cases the ultimate issue is entirely a question of irrational personal preference,* insoluble by logic or deliberation—whether it concerns Man's conception of his relation to God or his conception of his relation to the community of his fellowmen. Very probably, our constant neglect of this relativity is due to a subconscious misinterpretation of the principal maxim which liberals and Marxists alike inherited from eighteenth century materialism: that "all men are created equal." There seems to be a widespread belief that, because of this biologically undeniable fact, all men must also be equally suited to a universal "ideal" form of government or community life. And it also seems that the most unbiased and most scientific analysts are simply incapable of omitting this pseudo-axiom from their reasoning. Be that as it may, it is a fact that in almost every known investigation of Fascism the subjective measures applied were thought to be objective. The results were easy to anticipate: unanimous condemnation from every angle—of public practice, theory, and morals—and later unanimous surprise at, or professed disbelief of the fact that an apparition conclusively proved doomed by the most scientific logic actually seemed stronger and more vigorous each time one looked at it.[1]

There *is* another way to go about it. The first step is a realization of the subjectivity of *any* analysis. Then— once we admit that we can only analyze subjectively— we should attempt to do so from the point of view of the thing to be investigated, and not from one essentially incompatible with it. Thus we may hope to arrive at conclusions which will stand the test of actual events. Should they be false, their inconsistency with known

[1] Conservatives, remembering what happened to their predictions of a speedy disintegration of Soviet Russia, showed a little more reserve this time—but it is surely not without irony to see the Communists commit, in their critique of Fascism, exactly the same mistake they had so justly ridiculed when others made it about the U.S.S.R.

Since they defined Fascism as a dictatorship of finance capital, supported by the petty bourgeoisie and "such backward workers as can be successfully deceived" (Strachey), the fact that a majority of labor in a country went permanently Fascist would either cast a most unwelcome reflection upon the workers' intelligence, or prove that they could prefer, from the Marxist point of view of material well-being, their slavery under Fascism to their freedom under democracy. To escape from this dilemma, the Communists seized upon the application of force in Fascist regimentation, using it simply to deny any conversion of large parts of the working masses in Fascist countries, and to assert the existence of a "seething revolutionary unrest"—contentions which every newspaper correspondent able to see beyond the Communist underground movements themselves would be forced to deny, however reluctantly. As a matter of fact, the failure of Communism to find a place in its dogmatic structure for the Fascist phenomenon without distorting it, may be the first definite evidence of a *logical* inadequacy of the Marxist-Leninist system of political thought. Heretofore opponents, scornfully rejecting that system on principle, had always found it difficult to disprove by cold logic.

facts will appear somewhere without any doubt. The method of analysis need never interfere with our personal mental reservations. It involves neither conversion nor acquiescence. It means only that if we, as non-Fascists, want to assert and justify effectively our stand on *our* premises, we shall first have to realize Fascism not from our point of view but from its own. That is to say, we have to find out what Fascism means to Fascists —not to any imaginary "objective" observer. And to do that we must learn to discard our superiority, pocket our convictions for the time, and accept, if only for the sake of argument, Fascist pronouncements at their face value. It will not do to dismiss peremptorily, as opportunistic hypocrisy, everything that will not fit into our mental pattern—a course which, to cite a warning example, was largely responsible for the helplessness of German democrats in the face of the Hitler tidal wave. We must find out whether a thing will fit into the *Fascist* mental pattern, and if it does so we must use it as a contributing factor to our understanding of Fascism.

Another mistake—usually made by the most conscientious observers—should be noted here. Fascism as a movement professes a deep contempt for logic and "materialistic" reasoning. Time and again Fascist leaders have made statements that were conflicting or obviously wrong—and, cornered, explained that Fascism had to be "felt" and could not be measured with the yardstick of cold theory. Now if this were true, what we want to do here—analyze Fascism on its own premises—would be impossible. It is not true. We shall soon find abundant proof that Fascism, though it may scorn logic as a weapon, is itself strictly logical in all its aspects. Moreover, it has a definite set of doctrines: a clear-cut and exclusively Fascist dogma—though it often disclaims it. But—and here lies the danger—because of this official anti-dogmatic attitude it is impossible simply to base conclusions on every general statement from a sufficiently authoritative source. More often than not this will lead us into startling paradoxes—and both Fascists and anti-Fascists would react alike to our bewilderment: the former with "we told you, our spiritual impetus cannot be scientifically dissected," and the latter with "you see, they are nothing but liars and hypocrites."

With a little discrimination, these pitfalls should be avoidable. For instance, it should be reasonably clear that if the head of a Fascist state writes an essay for publication about Fascist ideology, this will be a better basis for deduction than a statement for the foreign press by his minister of propaganda. Furthermore, after thirteen years and four years, respectively, of experience with the Fascist and National Socialist totalitarian states, it should be possible to do almost completely without specific statements and explanations from Fascist sources—except, of course, as fact-materials and in matters of terminology. It should be possible—without resorting at all to the rather cheap trick of confuting a movement, that disavows logic, with illogical words of its exponents—to take the facts (which we know) and try to fit them by our logic (which Fascism disclaims) to the large and generalized tenets proclaimed by every

Fascist movement (though we may disbelieve them). It is only in this way that we can possibly find something like a theoretical structure of Fascism—which the Fascists themselves say does not exist. *They* don't need it. But we, liberal or Socialist, yet always materialistic opponents of a mainly mystic creed—we do need it. And if we make it easy for ourselves now—by saying in complete agreement "there is no such thing; it is all hokum and tyranny, or capitalist exploitation"—then we shall find it increasingly difficult later to convince others who may surprise us by succumbing to the Fascist spell.

To begin with, we shall have to recall a few uninteresting but necessary fundamentals. Ever since Man became a political animal, there have been two opposing views of the relation between a community and its members: one that puts the state above the individual and the other that puts the individual above the state. This, of course, is an issue that will never be settled. It is no more possible today to find a logically convincing argument for one side or the other, than it was possible ages ago for mankind to choose definitely between the individualist political philosophies of the early Hindu and Chinese nations and the collectivist ones of the Roman republic and the conquering Islam. The Greeks were probably about equally divided—with Plato's communistic collectivism and Epicurus' often so sadly misunderstood individualism as poles. These classifications, of course, can only attempt to state fundamental trends and have to be taken with a grain of salt. In practice, mostly, the contrast between the two basic *conceptions of the state* has been all but completely obscured by the historical consequences of race, state form, economic conditions, and other given influences.

First, in numerous cases, absolute monarchy changed the meaning of the term "state" from a community of citizens to Louis XIV's famous "l'état c'est moi"—thus cutting short at the outset any discussion of its aims and functions. Genuine absolutism, disowning principles like supremacy of law or inviolability of tradition, actually bases the entire national life upon the will of the ruler, whether he be thought of as divine, like the Roman Emperor, or as merely divinely inspired, like the Christian absolute monarch. Such a system is really not, in the strict sense of the word, a "political" one. It creates no polis. It expresses no relationship between a group and its members, only the power of one individual over all others. It signifies a distinction, not an interrelation. In a state identified with a single exalted individual, the conceptual connection between the community and the other individuals is dissevered and no more speculation is possible about their relative importance.

The second and, up to the present time, most important element to becloud the issue of individualism versus collectivism, is the oligarchic system of "rule by the few." Originally meaning government by a few men, later broadened (by addition of the principle of heredity) into government by men eligible from a few families, it finally led to the creation of the "ruling *class*," membership in which could be acquired by birth, office, wealth, or in any other way. The extremely interesting result was that most communities actually practiced a double political system. The relation between the state and the "upper class" was built on individualistic lines; that is, in relation to the privileged few the state was conceived as a device to serve and protect the interest of the individuals, otherwise not interfering with their activities as long as they adhered to their self-made rules of the game. For the lower class the system was collectivistic—in relation to them the community did not visualize itself as subordinate, but rather as creditor and master. It granted them protection of the law, but only in exchange for a claim on their services and on unconditional submission to regulation of their lives in a manner that to some people may seem natural by habit but becomes strangely significant in comparison with the respect accorded the upper class by the state. The most striking example of this double standard over the last hundred years has been the industrial section of the United States. There being no legally recognized nobility, wealth and economic position became the deciding factors. "Business" was the guiding star, indicating the steps to be taken. Business was to be safeguarded and independent, a privileged judge of its own affairs. Members of the lower class, which included everybody who made his living not by *doing* business himself, but working *for* business, were not only not supposed to consider the state as their servant, but were understood to be under a definite obligation to the community not to attempt to better their conditions *as a class*. Individually it was different—as soon as any one of them managed to get "into business" for himself, he was held entitled to its privileges and allowed to enjoy to his heart's content his new opportunity to step on those below him.

Quite naturally this kind of communal set-up, even if triumphant in practice, was scarcely presentable in theory. The spread of education, and the resulting self-consciousness and power-consciousness of the masses, made hereditary privileges less and less suitable as bases of political doctrines—whether garbed as inherited office, inherited nobility, or inherited wealth. Therefore, crowns slowly became symbols instead of sources of power, aristocracy ceased to be a serious political aim after the days of Alexander Hamilton, while plain plutocracy as a theory never even found a champion in the political arena. Practically all political systems of the last century recognized—with certain general exceptions as to sex, race and religion—the equality of citizens in relation to the state. In some conservative European countries traces of discrimination could be found up to the World War—as in the Russian and Prussian class-differentiating election laws. Those, however, were definitely remnants of the past, saved by tradition; the general trend toward equality was unmistakable. But, sharply separating the doctrines in the field, the old rift suddenly gained new importance—individualism versus collectivism.

The practice of the synthesis of the individualist conception of the state with the so-called "liberal" system of representative government and civil liberty came, in the last century, to be known under the name of "democracy." It meant that government existed only to serve the interests of the people, to be determined by them or their elected representatives, and that it should be carried on according to the will of the majority, should safeguard civil liberty and strive for what has always been the slogan of liberal individualism—"the greatest good of the greatest number." How this might be accomplished in the realm of economics, for instance, could obviously only be a question of economic and not of political theory. That the economic doctrine of laissez faire, a main point of modern capitalism, came in the course of time to be completely confused with the popular conception of democracy, was an unfortunate and utterly unwarranted development. The blame for it rests on the economists of the nineteenth century, who meant to increase their own importance by constant meddling in questions of purely political theory. As a matter of accuracy, it must be maintained that democracy, expressing a conception of the state and a theory of political government, has nothing whatever to do with any economic point of view. It is logically as possible for it to exist in connection with socialism as with capitalism. It is a system of representative self-government of a people, and its one and only axiom is that the community exists only to serve the interests of its members.

In opposition to this view has stood, since the beginnings of community life, the ideology of collectivism. Thereunder, the community is no longer merely the sum total of the individuals. By addition of an imponderable element, it gains life and an aim in itself. Its purpose is no longer to benefit its members; on the contrary, the sole natural function of each individual member is to serve the interests of the community. The final goal is not widespread individual, but unified collective well-being. Whether the collectivists talk about the "classless society" of Marxism or the "organic conception of the state" of Fascism—they always mean some "a priori community," beyond analysis, and consisting of a number of human beings *plus* an irrational something which changes the mass of people into a superior organism claiming exclusive allegiance.

It was only natural that the rising *economic* movement of Socialism should have grasped the collective idea for its political expression. After all, Plato had shown how to combine the two schemes more than two thousand years ago. The Socialists advocated an economic system which—by making the community sole owner of property or means of production, without allowing private profits or needing private initiative—brought the possibilities of economic friction between individuals down to a near-minimum. Furthermore, they planned to abolish nations and recognize only mankind. Therefore, they could afford to substitute an idealized conception of the community for the sum total of its members without having to fear resulting injustice, hostilities, or the necessity of undue sacrifices. The position of the community as the one and only employer brought about, anyway, the dominating influence of the state, which democracy dreaded. In practice it meant nothing but a broadening of the collectivist lower class of the "double standard society," so as to include the individualist upper class as well—which seems a much more innocent way to put such a change than "dictatorship of the proletariat" or "expropriation of the expropriators." Thus, for some time, Socialism and Communism (for the purposes of this discussion the theories of the Second and Third International may be considered as one) figured prominently as the only modern exponents of a collectivist theory of state and government. They were opposed by a variety of parties and movements, widely divergent in their political denominations and beliefs, but united in two respects: in an individualist conception of the relation between the people and the community, and in the intention, emphatic or reluctant, to achieve their purposes by democratic means. Until suddenly the world realized that in unimportant little Italy another system of collectivism was in the making—most definitely subordinating the individual to the state, but preserving private property, private profits, private initiative, and with a decided aversion to internationalism: Fascism.

When it took over the reins of the Italian government in 1922, Fascism was a party, and a purely opportunist one at that. It had a backbone of war veterans, a following made up largely of disappointed Socialists like Mussolini himself, a riotous nationalism as a distracting means of popular ballyhoo, and *no* program. Instead, it had a very capable leader with a level head and a flexible mind. In 1922 and 1923 he averted the imminent collapse of the Italian political system. In 1924 he saw that this alone would not overcome the resistance of the parliamentary groups which had at first entered into a coalition government with him, and that there was trouble ahead. He decided to wipe all other parties off the map. He proceeded to do so. And then only did the necessity of creating an entirely new system of government become apparent. There were two major points to be considered. First, the resentment of the vanquished prohibited the continuation of representative government—and government by decree could only be founded logically upon the thesis of the supremacy of the state. On the other hand, it was desirable that economically everything should go on as before. An actively socialist program was, therefore, out of the question. The two considerations were put together—and the new *Capitalistic Collectivism* was born. Fascism is nothing else. From those two premises evolved, step by step, the whole Fascist ideology. There is not one point of the dogma, not one feature of the movement that cannot be traced to either of its two basic sources: collectivism—i.e., supremacy of the state over the individual; capitalism —i.e., preservation of private property, production and distribution, and the profit motive.

The first characteristic of the new combination to be noticed by the outside world was its intense and aggressive nationalism. This was generally held to be due to the inherent trend of modern capitalism toward appropriation of new consuming fields and new natural resources. Actually, however, it can be much more easily traced to the collectivist element in Fascism. It is the equivalent of the first consequence of applied individualism: in which Man's tendency to further his personal interests is so sanctioned as to become the motivating force of communal life. That this tendency, in large measure, would seek satisfaction at the expense of other individuals, was quite understood. From collectivist premises, the same process of reasoning leads straight to the conclusion that the dynamic impulse of every community—and, therefore, of all the individuals comprising it—must be the tendency to further the collective interest, which also is largely possible only at the expense of other "basic units." Realization of the fact that such furtherance of collective interests involves a risk of conflict is the basis of every national feeling—democratic no less than Fascist. The difference is caused by the fact that the Fascist state is not blessed with those natural checks which, in a democracy, keep a sane and essentially pacific national consciousness from turning into an aggressive and dangerous national furor. The state as an end in itself is not in the unfavorable position of the state which is only a device to serve the best interests of its citizens—and which must always be afraid lest they develop the idea that it might not be to their best interests to die for their servant. In the Fascist state, where the individual has no right to exist except in his function as part of the state, his own personal good is of no importance whatever to the good of the community—and, since the good of the community can be realized only in comparison with units of the same kind, international greed is the feature in which its exalted status was bound to find its natural expression.

It was equally natural for this exalted position to produce a sort of religious worship. When intensified by a touch of superhuman glory, the irrational appeal of patriotism will always bind a people faster than any theory, however convincing. Quite obviously, on the other hand, to a majority of the individuals, most "liberalist" or even Socialist ideas will sound highly reasonable from a material point of view. Therefore, it was necessary for Fascism to take a stand not only against material reasoning, but against any reasoning—as far as the state was concerned. The state would have to be accepted as a priori, as an axiomatic end in itself—Man could fulfill his destiny not as an individual but only as part of the higher unit.

Perhaps it might be just as well at this point to leave the explanation of these rather difficult points to a higher authority. The section on "Fascism" in the present *Enciclopedia Italiana* has been written by no less an expert than Benito Mussolini himself:

"To Fascism the world is not this material world, as it appears on the surface, where Man is an individual separated from all others and left to himself, ruled by a law of nature causing him through his instincts to lead an egotistic and momentary life of pleasure. Man in Fascism is individual, nation, and country all at once, and is thereby a party to the moral law which binds individuals and generations together into a tradition and a mission, and which, in suppressing the instinct of a life enclosed in the short cycle of pleasure, bases a higher life, beyond the limits of space and time, on duty. . . .

"Fascism is a religious conception of life, in which Man is seen in his inherent relation to a higher law, to an objective will that transcends the individual and raises him to the consciousness of a spiritual community. . . .

"According to its anti-individualist attitude the idea of Fascism is for the state, and for the individual insofar as he coincides with the state. . . . It is against classical Liberalism which had its origin in the force of reaction against Absolutism, and which has reached the end of its historical function, since the state has changed in the consciousness and will of the people. Liberalism negates the state in the interest of the single individual, Fascism affirms the state as the true reality of the individual. It is for the only freedom which can seriously be considered—the freedom of the state, and of the individual within the state—because, for the Fascist, everything is in the state, and outside of the state nothing legal or spiritual can exist, or still less be of value. In this sense Fascism is totalitarian, and the Fascist state is unity and synthesis of all values and gives to the whole life of the people its meaning, development, and forcefulness." 1716858

This is the credo of the new "religious conception of life." It will be noted that but for the restriction of the community to the state, instead of its embracing all mankind, the whole thing might very well be taken from a catechism for Communists. The anti-individualist set-up is the same in both cases. The difference evidently comes in at a later point. In fact, it does not come in until the question arises of what to do with the splendid self-submerging spirit with which the new movement has imbued a people. Who shall determine the "objective will" of the "personality of a higher order"— which is the Fascist state? The Communists propose to do it by majority vote of elected representatives. But as majorities today have a dangerous leaning toward Socialist ideas, this might imperil the second pillar of the Fascist system—the capitalist element. Therefore— and *only* therefore, as follows without any trace of a doubt from the early history of Italian Fascism—it was necessary to replace representative government and majority rule with the principles of (1) *hierarchy*, and (2) *authority*—government by appointment, and decision by command.

Hierarchy: The democratic idea of how government should be constituted was altered in a singularly thorough and complete way. Instead of (to take an extreme example of a democratic structure) having the people elect many little representatives who elect fewer and bigger representatives who elect and control the top fellows who run the country, and of making every representative responsible to the men who elected him, the Fascists simply reversed the process. They put up a single supreme head of the state; he appoints a few big officials, each of whom appoints a great many smaller ones, and so down to the mayor, judge and county clerk of the remotest village, and every official is responsible not to the people whose affairs he administers but to the official who appointed him.

Authority: The method of making governmental decisions was changed from vote to command—even the overwhelming desire of those immediately affected carries no weight against the order from above. Likewise, theoretically, no unanimous agreement of subordinates may hold out against the decision of their immediate superior. He may have an advisory body of experts for every question, but the decision is his, and only his—and so is the responsibility.

The two principles cover every field of communal activity. There is nothing to interfere with them—no consideration for coming elections, no dreaded public opinion, no appeal to the courts. Whether the judiciary may ever decide any issue concerning governmental activities against the state, has not been authoritatively decided in either Germany or Italy. The question simply did not come up. And that leads us to the third principle which completes the famous trio of Fascist qualities: *discipline*. This appears to be a matter of course. Control of positions by appointment and decision of questions by command should alone suffice to insure ready obedience. The Fascist idea of discipline, however, is much more comprehensive than that to which we are accustomed. It involves an unswerving purpose of mental co-ordination, of surrender of individual consciousness, and of devotion, without reserve, of every activity of body and mind to the collective will. Fascist discipline means the complete voluntary adjustment of an individual to a group, the change from an independent human mind to an intellect capable only of working in a group and through a group, and towards a goal not chosen individually but always common to the whole community. It comes perilously close to the conception of the Robot—and nobody could be blamed for calling it so outright—but there is a difference, though it may be hard for a non-Fascist to perceive. The co-ordination is really not only natural, but voluntary; by some miraculous process the order *does* become not only the collective will of the community, but the real individual will of every particular member. For the Fascist the function of making up his mind has simply been removed from his brain. He has to wait until he gets his mind made up from above, and then he keeps right on going and concentrates all his energy and intelligence on carrying out this will—his will. Which, as is easy to see, he will do much better and more efficiently than a democratic individual could in his place—first, because he has nothing else to worry about, and second, because the ready-made-up mind is of course made up much straighter and more decisively than if he had done the job himself.

Naturally, this degree of co-ordination cannot be achieved at once. Neither in months, nor in years. To make it completely genuine would take generations of careful breeding, selection, elimination—exactly what the Germans, with their usual resourcefulness in long-range planning, now seem to be considering in earnest. For the present, it requires continuous organization and propaganda, and, moreover, constant supervision, control, correction. It is particularly important that any heretic, any dissenting voice, should be segregated from the flock of the faithful. The Germans found concentration camps useful for that purpose. Italy transferred the recalcitrants to volcanic islands—islands of beautiful scenery but which offer no chance to spread the poison of opposition. From these practices our anti-Fascist optimists jubilantly inferred that but for the brute force employed by their governments the German and Italian people would gladly cast off the Fascist yoke. In the opinion of this writer, the inference is deplorably wrong. According to the bulk of available non-Fascist information, there can be little doubt that in Germany as well as in Italy the co-ordination under the present régimes is overwhelmingly voluntary, and that the system is quite in keeping with the people's own ideas and expectations. What seem to prove this most convincingly are the very incidents which we like to interpret as incipient insurrection. Our anti-Fascists point with glee to the German Church dispute, or to the restiveness that was noticeable in many parts of Italy during the Italo-Ethiopian War. Now it is a fact that the campaign in Africa was a particularly unpleasant affair—to be fought in tropical mountains, in a climate laden with disease and against desperate opponents rightly suspected of a kind of cruel, primitive guerrilla warfare most terrifying to civilised soldiers. It is also a fact that nothing short of this stark horror has been able to evoke any signs of general displeasure with the Fascist régime in Italy during the thirteen years of its existence. Does this not strongly tend to dispel the illusion that the Italian people are essentially opposed to the system? And is it not an even stronger argument against the anti-Fascist thesis, that in Germany none of the Nazi outrages has met with any noticeable resistance, while the religious issue—at first probably thought quite insignifi-

cant by most Western observers—has been in the head-
lines now for over two years? Even if we assume (cor-
rectly, by the way) that this issue touches a particularly
vulnerable spot in most Germans, the turmoil created by
the comparatively slight interference with their freedom
of religion is a pretty strong indication that the complete
loss of all their personal and political liberty, against
which hardly a word of protest was forthcoming, cannot
have affected them very deeply. What we consider their
disfranchisement obviously did not strike them as being
that at all. And in any event, it was not the government's
retort to trouble brewing in the populace.

No; it is not fear of being overthrown which forces
Fascist governments to suppress individual opinion—it
is the fundamental conception of their system. Fascism
cannot authoritatively effectuate the superiority of the
community over its members and at the same time recognize the possibility of their dissenting. If, by virtue of
the conception of a state, its goal as well as the means to
achieve it are determined from above, recognition of
the possibility of legitimate differences of opinion about
either would lead the structure itself ad absurdum. It is
neither because of arbitrary despotism nor because of
apprehension of popular revolt that Fascist administrative agencies are empowered to arrest a citizen, seize his
property, throw him into jail, or deport him to an island
—all without court, trial, or possibility of appeal. This
power is a logical necessity to the very existence of the
Fascist state. We have seen that its principle of hierarchic authority is the direct consequence of the combina-

tion of collectivism and capitalism: it does not dare to let the people use the power of the first, for fear they might upset the second. The next principle—discipline, with all that it implies—is the result of the combination of collectivism and hierarchic authority: if the conceptually superior community is to have its will determined in a specific manner, this determination cannot be open to questioning by the very individuals who are conceived as its inferiors. That is the reason why the Fascist state *has* to abolish personal liberty. It has to be hierarchic, authoritative *and* disciplined—like the Catholic Church, from which it took structural principles, if not neighborly love. It has to be infallible and exclusive, leaving no room for any ideas outside of the officially approved trend. It has to be constantly on guard for suspicious moves or signs of individual activity in its ranks. And it has to remove the sore spots, instantly and without fail, lest they become centers of infection which might necessitate the application of force and bloodshed.

We have said before (anticipating a conclusion we shall reach in a later chapter) that the Fascism of the German and Italian people seems predominantly genuine. In other words, that in the Fascist countries of today there is virtually no opposition irrespective of what their governments do to suppress it. But the point is, *if* a Fascist government meets opposition, it *cannot* tolerate it. If it did, it would leave itself in a permanent state of suspense prohibitive to its normal functioning. That is the main difference between the workings of the Fascist and the democratic state. The latter invites criticism. It needs it; it is an essential part of its system that there should always be an opposition to point out mistakes and to provide a real choice for the people's right to choose their government. Under Fascism, where the individuals do not direct the state but where, on the contrary, the immovable will of the state directs the individuals, opposition is not only useless but intolerable. It would refute the axiomatic authority of the superior organism on which the whole system rests. To Fascism, every single critic is a danger. He jeopardizes not the continuation in office of the government but its logical foundation—which does not make the danger any less real. To stifle it in its very beginning, the whole mentality of the people and of every single individual must always be kept in line. Every mental and physical activity must be brought under the dominating influence of the state. That is why there can be no freedom of speech, of the press, of peaceful assembly, why science, arts, trades, professions, sports, everything must show the Fascist coloring. That is the reason for the totalitarian state. If the foundation of the Fascist community is to be firm, every thought and every act in every field of human endeavor must be imbued with the same spirit and reflect the same collective will.

That this will is determined by a single leader, without participation of any of the other individuals constituting the Fascist state, makes no difference. It is nevertheless meant and understood not as the will of the man on top, but as the will of the "higher unit." This distinction is no hairsplitting but a matter of deep and real importance. It is one of the main points of support for the structural theory of the Fascist community: the "organic conception of the state" (of which more in our following chapter). In particular, this interpretation of Fascist leadership bears out the contention that, however great the resemblance in many instances, there is a world-wide difference between Fascism and absolutism. The absolute monarch, as ruler by the grace of God, was in himself a denial in toto of the collectivist conception of the national community. He was most emphatically *not*—as is the Fascist leader—the directing and governing organ of the state. Quite the contrary: the state was nothing but the instrument through which the monarch chose to exercise his God-given power. Whatever state features or functions an absolute kingdom might have had, it had not by virtue of its conception as state but by the king's volition. Even if he went as far in benevolence as to consider himself the "first servant" of his people, this was not due to the character of his office but to his own free will and personal moral sense. There was no integral connection between the wearer of the crown and the other individuals. He was *substantially* different— whether he treated them well or badly, his subjects were, in reality, mere objects of his pleasure. They executed his orders or exercised the rights he had had the grace to grant them—but they had no organic relationship to the state, which was simply the visible manifestation of the power inherent in the crown.

Fascism is altogether different. The Fascist leader, while probably less restricted in his actual power than any monarch in history, is dogmatically just as much in the service of the national community as the humblest of his followers. And the individual, for the very reason that theoretically he exists only through his relation to the state, is not a state subject but a living and integral part of the state. He may have less to say than a medieval serf, but as far as the *substance* of the state is concerned there is no difference in value between the individual on top of the Fascist pyramid and the one at the bottom. The latter carries out the will of the state, the former determines it; but it is never given or received as his own, as was the case with the royal command—he is always pronouncing the will of the entire community.

It is certainly difficult for anyone schooled in democratic thinking to accept this distinction. Accordingly most observers fell into the error of branding Fascism as a black reactionary movement advocating a return to seventeenth century viewpoints and ideas. For the liberal, who measures progress with the yardstick of the civil liberties list, it must necessarily mean a move backwards. But it is precisely he who should take a leaf from the Fascists' book and realize that—whatever may be contended afterwards in the political arena—the first step to victory is a complete and thorough understanding of the opponents' ideas; and that it does make a difference whether he is just being deceived by the Fascist application of medieval methods, or really right in picturing Fascism as a movement to revive the dark ages. Actually Fascism is nothing of the sort. While the Fascist state does away with practically all the rights

of the individual secured in the last one hundred and
fifty years, it is essentially the most up-to-date political
structure of the world—composed of the most recently
developed economic system of modern capitalism and
the old but also only recently revived state conception
of collectivism. The abolition of progressive achievements is only the extremely logical result of the combination of those two extremely modern elements. One
cannot combine them otherwise. To have collectivism,
capitalism *and* civil liberty is impossible. One of them
has to go.

The modern capitalistic democracy cut out collectivism. With the principle of "the greatest good to the
greatest number" as leitmotif, it built a government "of
the people, by the people, and for the people," creating
elaborate safeguards for the individual and converting
the state into a corporation with the citizens as stock-
holders. The Marxian "socialist democracy" (which the
U.S.S.R., since the beginnings of its "proletarian dictatorship," has proclaimed as its eventual goal and now
seems about to establish in earnest) aims to dispense
with capitalism. It calls for a combination of the collectivist conception of the state, as supreme over the
individuals, with representative government, majority
rule, and respect for equality before the law and every
kind of personal freedom compatible with the economic
principle of universal employment by the state. Fascism,
based on collectivism and capitalism, had to abolish
civil liberty. It is as modern as either one of the others
and, while the shortness of its evolution made its structure seem arbitrary, it was nothing but consistent.

CHAPTER THREE

THE POLITICAL STRUCTURE

"The Party"

HIERARCHY, AUTHORITY, AND DISCIPLINE ARE THE THREE pillars of the Fascist state, justifying Mussolini's pet phrase, "stato armato." Which does not mean "armed state," but rather "militarized state"—a state which in its most peaceful functions shows a warlike spirit, where mailcarriers and dishwashers think of themselves not as postal or hotel employees but as soldiers in a great army, marching to victory on their particular "front" under the command of an invincible leader. People in other countries have often scoffed at the Fascist custom of turning a relief drive into "The First (second, twenty-sixth, ad lib.) Winter Battle" or an employment gain into a "Victory on the Labor Front." Yet this militarization of civil life is more than just a drawing-card for a goose-step-loving public. It is the expression of a state of mind, of the "one-of-my-kind"-feeling in the Fascist community—stato armato.

The backbone of the militarized state, its reservoir of disciplined human and intellectual resources, is "the Party." It is also the only remaining political element in the state. *Personal political feeling,* the consciousness of the interrelation between the individual and the group, does not of course vanish under a Fascist régime. It is, in fact, immensely intensified. Only personal political *activity* is eliminated—the expression of individual differences of opinion over affairs of the group. Fascism, while bringing political life in the state to an end in one sense, is perpetuating it in another—while extinguishing *individual influence upon* the state, it is stimulating *collective interest in* the state. For the citizen his voluntary participation in public life in an optional direction is replaced by compulsory participation in a prescribed direction—but it remains participation in public life all the same. And machinery for this new form of political activity is provided in "the Party."

What is "the Party"? Everybody knows that (regardless of the obvious phraseological anomaly of a "single-party-system") neither the Fascist Party in Italy nor the National Socialist one in Germany would fit the definition of a "political party" as used in other countries. We know, however, that the National Socialists were a real political party before they came into power. It seems, therefore, not that the wrong word was chosen for the matter, but rather that the object changed its character after it had been termed. Accordingly, it is not just the Fascist Party as such but a more narrowly circumscribed phenomenon which we now have to deal with: the Fascist Party in the Fascist one-party state. In the preceding chapter we have seen why the "totalitarian state" cannot tolerate opposition, least of all political opposition. This involves the necessity of exterminating the existing opposition parties. Simultaneously, however, the political group which by parliamentary or other means has established the Fascist state, undergoes a change of function. It stops being a political fighting machine because there is no more need of political fighting. As soon as the Fascists assume control of the government, they have to give up the belligerent attitude towards the rest of the population *as such*. The very collectivism of their doctrine does not permit recognition of separate groups of citizens—not even for the purpose of attacking them.[1] But, just as the soldiers of a victorious army, occupying annexed lands of the defeated enemy, are not fighting their new fellow-countrymen any more and yet continue to exercise undoubtedly military functions, so the victorious Fascist party remains definitely political and aggressively Fascist. Its new aims are the perpetuation of the victory by peaceful but energetic penetration of the bottom of the national pyramid, as well as a zealous, and jealous, watch over the top.

Thus the Party evolves into, as the official description

[1] The National Socialist rule in Germany does not refute but confirm this: whatever attacking the Party does is directed either —as in the case of the Jews—against a group which under the official dogma does not share in membership of the community, or —as in the case of Marxists or "political Catholics"—against ideas and their exposition; but never against any distinct group of the German people themselves. The line may be hard to discern but is clearly drawn: before seizing power the Fascists fight with the non-Fascists for possession of the state, afterwards they fight against inimical ideas for possession of the non-Fascist souls.

of the Italian "Partito Nazionale Fascista" has it, a "civil militia, at the orders of the Leader, in the service of the Fascist state"—a militant and, to a large part, military body for essentially non-military purposes. This seeming paradox has been the source of much international friction. Every Fascist Party has its strictly military formations; and it is evident that, in case of war, these huge masses of enthusiastic men trained in soldierly discipline and often thoroughly schooled in the technique of warfare would be of tremendous advantage to their country. The Italian conquest of Ethiopia, for which the Italian General Staff employed about twice as many "Blackshirts" as regulars, has proved that amply. Still, the Fascist Parties' bellicose potentialities cannot alter the fact that their basic functions are truthfully peaceful. Of course these large numbers of civilians who have received complete military training might come in handy if an armed conflict should occur. But fundamentally, the Fascist leaders really and truly want their Party soldiers only for home work—and are personally quite outraged at the world's disinclination to believe that. They are absolutely sincere in their protestations that they need the Party as well as its military organizations for domestic politics. They do—and although other countries may be justifiably nervous over the ease with which this tool of national politics could be converted into a weapon for international aggression, the sole reason for the militarization of the Party is the desire for a permanent and reliable *political* instrument with sufficient strength to crush any possible internal opposition at any given moment.

This logic of political materialism, however, must not lead us to suppose that Fascists, too, see in their Parties primarily means of suppression. In the "religious conception of life," which is Fascism, the Party has definite and immensely important *constructive* functions. It is, as Hitler termed it, the "bearer of the political will of the state." The old liberal "corporation state" had found the natural expression for its underlying theories in a division of government into three separate branches— legislative, executive, and judicial; creating a system of mutual checks expressly designed to prevent excesses of state power, and to keep the community well within the limits of its dogmatic purpose to serve the interests of its members. Obviously, the Fascist state—"unity and synthesis of all values," the basic unit of a religious conception of life—could have no use for a system based on the supremacy of the single individuals. Another structure had to be found for its manifold aspects —and it had to be consistent with the theory of the state as a living organism, as the one organism of supreme importance that relegates every individual to molecular insignificance. Thus evolved what will presently be discussed in detail: the "organic conception of the state." From it arose an entire new political technology—in which such institutions as government, or army, or judicial structure, were no longer thought of as instruments for a purpose but as live organs, visible manifestations of the superior being which is the state.

One of the most important of these manifestations grew to be the Party. It became equal in importance to government itself, though with a totally different purpose and realm of action. Just as the army represents the strength of the Fascist state toward the outside world, so the Party represents its inner strength—its political will, its energy, its determination, its spiritual forcefulness. It is an army not for military but for political, not for foreign but for domestic use; an army which is not independent but at the unconditional disposal of the leadership common to all—and which embodies not a governmental function of the state but its Fascist spirit.

This answers the question—sometimes asked in Europe—of why, having served their original purpose to establish the Fascist states, the various Fascist Parties have not been disbanded. In other words, whether Fascism would not work just as well in a no-party state as in a one-party state. The point, at first, seems well taken. But again the collectivist dogma—of the state, a pure abstraction, as supreme purpose of living for the individual—interferes with a seemingly logical solution. It is the doctrine of the communal organism which more than any other needs a living image to inspire faith and fealty. It is confronted with the very practical danger that, unless backed up by a powerful and immortal influence within the state, the abstraction may lose its spell over the people, and at some given moment—for instance, after the death of a Fascist Leader—leave the Fascist authorities not only in a minority but even without recruiting possibilities for their service. This is a danger threatening every abstract collectivism, as demonstrated by the only large-scale attempt on the socialist side—Soviet Russia, which also had to resort to perpetuation of the Communist Party in order to perpetuate the fundamental idea of the state. It seems that no system can maintain a supremacy of a community without employing an organized minority—to keep alive, by persuasion, propaganda, or force, the collective feeling of the majority. A royal family inspires the imagination and the loyal instincts of the subjects by its mere existence. A democracy, as long as it is working, will by its system of government alone tend to be constantly revived and confirmed in its democratic character by the people, who rule it in their own interest. The collectivist state, on the other hand, needs both a collectivist nerve-center and a collectivist nerve system: a source from which to draw incessantly new collectivist spirit, and channels to distribute it throughout the community. The Fascist Party in the Fascist state is both: a huge reservoir of absolutely reliable human material, and a living guarantee for constant and sincere Fascist unanimity of the people as a whole.

Neither one could be secured by even the most drastic application of the unlimited powers of a Fascist *government*. The function of the *Party*, therefore, is to make it unnecessary for the government actually to invoke these powers at all. To this end the Party mobilizes two weapons: organization and propaganda. The first is essential—the mass of men and ideas forming the Fascist state cannot remain amorphous: nor could any of the three basic principles of the system be applied to a community not organized to the nth degree in its every function. The second is supplementary in theory: that is, it is indispensable as long as any part of the community, however small, is not yet in the desired state of completely "natural" and unshakable Fascism—which, of course, may make the use of propaganda necessary for a long time to come. In both fields, at any rate, Fascist activities in recent years opened unthought-of perspectives. The world stood gasping at what was accomplished by those brain-combinations of Machiavelli, Ignatius de Loyola, and Phineas Taylor Barnum. To cement their new conception of community life in the consciousness of the people they employed all the binding and directing devices that, in the past, political, religious, social or economic organizations had worked out in lieu of state power—and which government, so far, had disdained to use because they seemed not only alien to any known function of government but also detrimental to its authority and detached position. The fundamental dualism of Government and Party in the collectivist state allowed its masters to use *every* kind of influence on men and masses—and it was only a combination of power like this that could give real effect to the theoretical omnipotence of the community.[2]

As usual, there is nothing vague or haphazard about the Fascist methods. Their application is governed by predominantly practical considerations of need and efficiency, but they also have a thoroughly sound and logi-

[2] See Appendix A, p. 299 ff.

cal theoretical foundation. The doctrine, according to which the Party in every Fascist state conducts its campaigns, is based upon the "organic conception of the state." Therein the community, the basic unit of the collectivist dogma, is seen as an organism comparable to a human or animal body, with the various public and semi-public institutions taking the place of organs and the individual community members that of minute particles of protoplasm. As a figure of patriotic speech, this has been heard before. It has never amounted to more than that—probably because it was felt somehow to be at variance with the individualist way of thinking. To Fascist thinkers, however, it came naturally and they began to draw conclusions, and to use them to delineate in theory the scope and direction of the hitherto unknown political practices employed by the new system.

One: Just as every cell in a living body is strictly confined to its own function and has no business in any other organ, while the organism as a whole has an interest in everything concerning any one of its cells—so the active interest of the collectivist state in the citizen is infinitely more comprehensive than that of the citizen in the state. The individual's interest in the group—like that of the protoplasmic cell in the human body—is a vital matter for him but cannot be expressed otherwise than through his own limited "organic" function. The group, on the other hand, though not at all dependent upon the single individual, has an interest in as well as power over every least important aspect of his life. In consequence *Fascism*—and this is its decisive reversal of traditional doctrine—*does away with the old distinction between public and private life.* The individualist state was an association of free men, formed for definite purposes: "that to secure these rights, governments are instituted among men, deriving their just powers from the consent of the governed." Accordingly, it was held that the institution's each and every action was the active concern of any one of its sponsors—with the rights to vote, to petition, and to "sue as a taxpayer" providing the means to enforce this concern through all three departments of government. The state, on the other hand, should concern itself with the affairs of its citizens only insofar as they themselves permitted it; only what was expressly designated as subject to community influence or regulation was a matter "clothed with a public interest"—and everything else was "private right," removed from state action and reserved to the individual's own judgment, will, and discretion. Fascism, denying Man's individuality, and demoting him to a mere part of the basic unit Community, had to reverse this process: actions of the state were removed from the influence of the individual except in the realm of his own particular organic function—while the influence of the state was extended to the entire life of the citizen, without any reservation of "individual rights" to interfere with it. Logically all this follows already from the very basis of collectivism, but the introduction of the organic conception of the state makes it inevitable. Any doctrine based upon this concept must require complete elimination of any kind of privacy—of any sphere in which the rights of the state should not prevail. Its acceptance by a people means that they concede the right of the community to interfere in all of their affairs, barring only those in which the higher unit should specifically declare itself not interested.

Two: There can be little doubt that a protoplasmic cell could not satisfactorily fulfill its biological functions if it were endowed with an independent personality. Kidney cells Nos. 360754 and 789645, suddenly able to consider themselves and act as separate units instead of infinitely small particles of a human body, might well endanger the health of the whole organism. The same applies to the individual members of the collectivist state. And since these are not, like cells, wisely created by nature without the power of independent thought, the state's authority must prevent their use of this power from interfering with their essential collectivism. Its task is plainly and simply the welding of a few millions of separate human minds into one, infinitely complex, composite national mind. This is the meaning of the movement's emblem—the bunch of thin, fragile rods bound together into the "fasces," symbol of strength and power. And therefore it is not sufficient, as the ancient autocratic state would have done, to supervise the individual citizens strictly and to punish misbehavior. The Fascist state, in order to effectuate its organic character, has to rule its members from inside out. They must be so conditioned that a mental process divergent from the proclaimed collective thought not only does not occur, but is *psychologically impossible.*

The individual who does not happen to be born into this "collective state of mind," has only two ways of acquiring it: either he must be brought up to it as a child, or later his whole life, in all its everyday aspects, must be so tied up with the group that he has no chance to develop an independent personality. This alternative determined the two main directions of political activity in the totalitarian state: a) collectivization of youth, and b) collectivization of adult life.

The first was perhaps the most far-reaching of all the Fascist innovations. "Suffer the little children to come unto me." In the past, only the Church suspected the potentialities of that message; now the Fascist states have realized them fully. Again, the Soviets were somewhat ahead of them but, lacking perhaps the stimulus of need, their youth policy was neither as forceful nor as consistent. It was Mussolini who first saw *and* exploited the tremendous advantages of being able to mold generations from the very start, to influence them at a time when the mind is open and the soul thirsty. Ordinary schooling—even though the Fascist orthodoxy of its teachings, of course, will always be guaranteed by strict and constant supervision—is no good for this purpose. It is out of school that a child receives his strongest impressions. To dominate these is the main thing, to catch the children in playtime, to guide them in the desired direction when they think they are just having fun. And so the aim is pursued with the whole resourcefulness of an omnipotent state. Games, competitions, camps, outings, marching with flags and music, youth homes in every city and all over the country, badges and uniforms to wear, regulation belts and camping knives to carry, solemn oaths to swear—a paradise for children is created, slowly, imperceptibly exterminating individualities, arousing a deep, inbred, collective feeling. Slowly, imperceptibly, the ties between child and family are severed, to be replaced by unquestioning allegiance to the superior organism of the Fascist community. An inscription over the entrance of Hitler Youth headquarters reads: "We were born to die for Germany." The organization is their training camp for the permanent war—spiritual and, if need be, real—they will have to wage for the state. Balilla, Hitler Youth—they sound like accessories, yet they really form one of the cornerstones of the whole system.

"Fascism takes Man from his family at six, and gives him back to it at sixty." (Mussolini.)

As soon as the young Fascists leave the youth organization to take their place among the grown-ups, Fascism immediately takes hold of their new relationships. Work and after-work, both must be organized, so that no one will escape from the collective consciousness of the youth movement into adult individualism. No one may work or play outside of the spiritual framework of the Fascist community. Here, as in the youth policy, a distinction arises between the citizens' working activities —which make up the economic life of the nation and have to be materially regulated—and the rest of their daily doings which must be spiritually controlled. The first field is subject to administration. That, like every public activity in the Fascist state, it will be administered by Fascists in the Fascist spirit, is a matter of course. But, although in German and Italian practice most of the organizations utilized for the purpose are listed as Party groupings, that regulation is a government and not a Party function. What remains, however —the citizens' leisure—cannot be effectively controlled by the regular means of any government, however powerful. Collectivization of this field, therefore, is up to the Party.

For the bulk of the population, this function is discharged with the help of the device known as "After-Work Organization." The decree founding the "Opera Nazionale Dopolavoro" dedicated it to "promoting, for intellectual and manual workers, the healthy and advantageous employment of the free hours, by means of institutions directed to develop their physical, intellectual and moral capacity." The aims of this organization are manifold: to improve the health, physique, and morale of the members of the working classes by taking them out of saloons or brothels into the fresh air of playgrounds or the countryside, and by providing free medical, hygienic, and vacationing facilities; to improve their minds by offering means for artistic and professional education; to increase their national consciousness by stimulating interest in old culture and folk-lore; to cement their loyalty to the régime with gratitude for what it did for them. All these aims are worthy in themselves and would justify all kinds of measures taken for their realization. To the Fascist After-Work Organization, however, they are only agreeable by-products. The essential, fundamental, dogmatic reason, the reason why *any* Fascist régime will have to develop some like organization, is the necessity for spiritual control of the leisure time activities of the working population. To insure complete submersion of the individual, the community must not only dominate his development as a child and what he later does to earn a living, but—even more important—what he does aside from working for a living. If, as in Italy, this offers an opportunity to improve the general level of health and education, so much the better. But even if, as in Germany, the workers have already taken up most popular sports on a large scale, and such non-political organizations as concert and theatergoers' leagues, educational associations, employer-sponsored recreational schemes for employees, are already very much in evidence, the Fascist state will still be obliged to take all those over, to transform them into Fascist institutions, and to see that every man, while spending his leisure time in any way he might reasonably desire, does so not individually but in constant connection with the community.

What the After-Work Organization and its various appendices did for the plain people, was accomplished in the higher social levels by means of another process —for which the German word has now, I believe, been internationally accepted—"Gleichschaltung." In Germany itself the term has lately acquired the rather too narrow meaning of ousting Jews, and has also been misapplied to private business with which, in its correct sense, it has nothing to do. Originally, it meant simply to give effect to a more or less obvious consequence of the "organic conception of the state": that no grouping of individuals within the state can be run on other principles than those of the "higher organism" itself. Since political groups had lost the right to exist, and economic groups were subjected to comprehensive regulation of a different kind, the natural objects of this activity were non-political and non-business, that is, purely or predominantly social associations. They were the ones that had to be brought in line with the reigning spirit, and to guarantee this co-ordination, their executive positions had to be filled by men of trusted loyalty to the régime. This procedure was called Gleichschaltung. Superficially resembling the "spoils system," as practiced in the United States, it differed from it in two important aspects. First, in this country it is generally admitted that—except, perhaps, for cabinet posts—the offices involved could be run just as well by members of the defeated party, and that the general idea of patronage is to reward faithful partisans. In the Fascist state this consideration plays no part at all—at least in theory [3]— and the reason for the universal replacement of non-Fascists with Fascists is really a dogmatic need for unity of spirit. Second, the field affected by Gleichschaltung is not only wider than that of patronage, but essentially different. The American spoils system is strictly confined to certain administrative jobs. The Fascist state,

[3] In practice, of course, Gleichschaltung became the most gigantic spoils system ever known.

however, can much more safely leave a lukewarm Fascist in an important government position than let a social organization remain unco-ordinated, no matter how innocuous it may seem. This has been proved to be so in many practical instances [4] and is, moreover, thoroughly logical: authoritatively conducted government machinery is rigidly disciplined anyway—so that, as chief qualification for office, technical ability may sometimes be allowed to supersede Fascist spirit. But an unco-ordinated organization, concerned with individual interests which are not subject to other discipline, would constitute a serious threat to collectivism itself. Gleichschaltung, therefore, reached into every field previously considered as "private"—society, sports, arts, professions. And the reason why it affected so many seemingly purely economic bodies (cf. the "Fascist associations" of civil servants, lawyers, physicians, actors, traveling salesmen and so forth) is that these exert, from pre-Fascist times, not so much influence on the conduct and conditions of their members' work as upon their social and "private" lives—which is just where the state, lacking direct means of control, must depend on the Party to enforce the communal interest and produce the essential collective unity of spirit.

It may be argued that only in Germany did co-ordination go to such extremes—that Italy stopped far short

[4] In Germany, the army, the Foreign Office, the economic departments of the government still abound with capable "holdovers" whose lack of sympathy for the régime is an open secret—but no bowling club has been allowed to continue under non-Nazi officers.

of the mark. There is a good enough reason for that. Here, as in every field, Fascism proceeds according to the demands of the situation. Superior progress in a country in any field calls for a more thorough organization.[5] Italy, with a great cultural heritage but a comparatively low scale of modern civilization, economically dependent on a rather outmoded agricultural process, with undeveloped industry and a predominantly ignorant and indifferent population, did not, of course, need the same degree of control as Germany—whose highly educated, highly specialized, politically experienced people had, in the short time since their disastrous defeat in the World War, regained a leading place amongst the nations in almost every field of human endeavor. Also, whenever a people is not yet wholly ready to conform, co-ordinating devices must be more stringently applied. Mussolini, once the Fascist state was established, found little opposition or intransigence—and practically no organized one (the difficulties of "Italianizing" the Trentino and the annexed parts east of the Adriatic were caused by national and not political resistance). In the Germany of 1933, on the other hand, the opposition to Hitler not only nominally outnumbered his following, but its strength centered in large and powerful organizations which no government could afford to ignore and which could not be abolished without seriously jeopard-

[5] "We were the first to assert that . . . the more complicated the forms assumed by civilization, the more restricted the freedom of the individual must become." (Mussolini, Grand Fascist Report, 1929.)

izing the welfare of the entire nation. If the collective idea, at that time, was to gain any secure foothold among the German people, it was imperative to co-ordinate those bodies—or, wherever this was impossible, to create organizations to replace them. Again, it cannot be emphasized too strongly that Gleichschaltung is not fun but dire necessity. Fascism never organizes just for the sake of organizing. It organizes only because and insofar as it is necessary for arousing and preserving the Fascist spirit in the populace. To formulate a general rule: Fascism must co-ordinate every field of human activities which might breed opposing, or even only deviating ideas—either individualism or collectivism of a different stamp than the Fascist formula. It is obvious at a glance that there are few such fields which need not be included in the list.

How completely the Fascist practical methods are ruled by principles of efficiency, becomes even more apparent in the Party's second means of fulfilling its function: propaganda. There—viewed from the outside—the Germans left their Italian predecessors standing at the start. In his early days Mussolini, though he knew their value, had no high regard for purely advertising activities. His objective, at that time, was the coup d'état, not conversion of the majority. He seized control of the government, supported only by a relatively small but determined and reliable minority, in a rather short campaign carried on with a good deal of violence and very little systematic ballyhoo. For the next two years he headed a majority coalition, and had to fight a minority against whose attacks, under the parliamentary system, even a further increase in his following would have been of no avail. And when, at last, the establishment of the totalitarian state gave him complete power, he organized it thoroughly—and felt no actual need for propaganda then either; for he soon gained the genuine confidence of most Italians and those who were still antagonistic were either too intelligent to be convinced, or too stupid to be influenced, by propaganda. So it was not until he noticed the astonishing exploits of his German facsimile that he even thought of taking press censorship out of the police department and putting it with other forms of propaganda under a special Ministry. Internally, even after that, this agency concerned itself with little but the control of newspapers and radio, directing the general line of the news supply of the country—while all other propaganda was left to the Fascist Party, the proper agency, to be administered at the discretion of its national or local functionaries when- and wherever necessary or advisable.

In Germany the situation had been entirely different. The Nazis came to power not in a rush but after a long fight that had been bloody and not without severe setbacks before the final victory. In this victory the ingenious application of every campaign trick in the bag had played a very large part. When the new rulers seized the reins, they knew themselves still opposed by about half of the population—and they knew that of their own followers many were merely opportunists, and many only under the spell of a deluge of previous propaganda. If the necessary co-ordination was to be accomplished without further struggles, the nation had to be put into a state of trance, until the structural changes had gone into effect.

Evidently, propaganda was needed here not as a corrective, to be applied in judicial doses wherever Party authorities noticed a slackening of collective spirit, but as a concentrated assault upon the mentality of a nation, as a high-pressure treatment relentlessly hammering upon all the conscious and subconscious reactions of the multitude. For such a purpose, the loose and disconnected ordinary propagandistic activities of a Fascist Party were clearly insufficient. So, immediately after Hitler's ascent to power, the direction of National Socialist propaganda was taken from the Party and handed to a specially created department of the Reich's government, with virtually a free hand to delimit its own competence and to draw upon all the resources of the state. And now Dr. Goebbels, who up till then had hardly been known outside of the Fatherland, showed his real mettle. He drugged the Germans in a way that had never even been attempted in history. He hypnotized a whole people, one of the most civilized, intellectual, and discriminating ones of the world, right in Central Europe and surrounded by democracies, into a frenzy of blind, dumb and reckless obedience. Day and night, his office poured forth "popular enlightenment" through newspapers, magazines, radio, movies, theater, opera, vaudeville, and parades. He was the first politician to find out that people do not get tired of parades. He set up a schedule of compulsory parading holidays that made workers in other countries pale with envy. He administered to Germany the medicine of the late Roman emperors—with the one difference that, bread being outside his jurisdiction, he gave only circuses. His success was complete; his instinctive showmanship triumphed over every obstacle of time, space, or fatigue.

In between Hitler's high-voltage propaganda engine and Mussolini's low-voltage one lies normalcy—the principle being always not to spend more effort on any one activity than is required by the circumstances. One thing is certain: that to the Fascist state propaganda is not an instrument for a particular purpose—as, for instance, a government bond sale or a re-employment campaign—but a normal and permanent feature. It becomes one of the regular all-time activities—of the government, if necessary, but always of the Party in its function as "essence of the state." Of course, one cannot set up the same kind of a pattern for its propagandist activities as for its organizational campaign. Political propaganda, to be successful, has to take into account so many intangibles of popular psychology that no theoretical scheme will ever cover all of its practical possibilities. Propaganda is an art—and, as in any art, an ounce of genius is worth a pound of rules. Still, there are certain general principles which may be assumed to apply in a majority of cases—and which yield important leads for a further investigation of the Party phenomenon as such.

In the first place, Party propaganda is always carried

on by spectacles. Even without the paradomania of Dr. Goebbels it is one of the major objects of the Party *to be seen.* To impress the rest of the people with its strength, its unity, its patriotic devotion. So the Party stages events. A review of the militia, a review of the youth organization, the opening of a waterway, of an automobile road, of a factory, the christening of a ship or the distribution of prizes to prolific mothers—everything serves as an occasion to turn out the black, brown, blue, or purple shirts, to have them march in seemingly endless columns, and to have the population look on in awe. The effect is twofold. First: though there are differences in degree in the susceptibility of people in various countries to flags, martial music and the like, there are few individuals in any country totally immune to a quickening of the pulse at the sight of a sufficiently impressive goose-stepping display. Second, and more important: there is nothing that will so convince an individual of his insignificance, of his essential "molecularity," as to let him face—either alone, or as one of an amorphous crowd—the controlled force and precision of a disciplined body of enthusiasts. The dread of absolute helplessness as an individual as well as the instinctive desire to share in the power represented by the pageant will exert tremendous influence on any man of not more than average individuality. The ground thus prepared, a skillful management of the intellectual diet of the population—including not only what people read daily in the newspapers but also what they read in books, see in the movies, hear over the radio—serves to wipe out slowly any still extant individualist convictions, by starving them. A conviction needs nourishment to stay alive, and not many humans are capable of producing it all by themselves. That is one of the main reasons why Fascist publicity never, not even when it might do so successfully, engages in argument with divergent doctrines beyond assertions of generalities and a rather crude type of vituperation. Argument, no matter what its outcome, will give food for independent thought—which is the very thing Fascism strives to extinguish. Only isolation from *discussion* of undesirable trends as well as from these trends themselves will force any not extraordinarily intelligent individual to succumb.

Then, after the two basic forms of propaganda—impression and information—have taken care of the majority of average character and intellect, those who are neither stupid enough nor weak enough to give in to them are subjected to the third, more subtle and more insidious method of inducement. Ceaselessly the Party and all its members work on individuals who may not yet be wholly converted. The available weapons range from conversational hints to the most terrific moral and economic pressure. There is an unlimited number of threats and promises to use, of fears and hopes to arouse, of interests and sentiments to play on. Whether the obdurate is to be ostracized by his acquaintances or to be dropped from his job, whether the convert shall be advanced socially or aided economically—there is practically no harm which the Party cannot inflict on those it frowns upon, and nothing it cannot do for those in its good graces. In fact, it is almost never necessary actually to resort to strict measures. In nearly every individual the slightest hint, coupled with the dread of the Party's imminent action and with the consciousness of its inescapable presence, will suffice to cause any change of color desired. And—which seems to contradict every known experience—the practical psychologists of Fascism did as good as prove that, in their case, pressure did not produce resistance. That on the contrary a man, who at first might have given lip service to a hated creed only under duress, did eventually, in most such instances, under continued influence turn into a sincere and believing Fascist. That there is only one explanation for this—that the Fascists are right in their contention, that for the people of their countries their system is "natural" and therefore inherently right—is an inference that will have to be taken up in detail later. In any case, supposing this basis of Fascist thought to be correct, the scheme is flawless in theory—and in German and Italian practice it has shown itself capable of producing a one hundred per cent conformity in human material that no neutral observer would ever have considered auspicious for experiments of that kind. What did the trick is the combination of organizing campaign and propaganda—and its application by an impersonal, immortal, and omnipresent force, unhampered by the formalities restricting the government of even a Fascist state, yet backed by its entire power.

The internal set-up of a Fascist Party is quite simple. Its structure and operation must of course be as consist-

ently hierarchic and authoritative as those of the state
to which it is supposed to impart its morale. That leaves
only two fundamental problems to be solved in one way
or another: the question of ultimate responsibility, and
the question of succession.

The first is a most lucid example of a cleavage between Fascist theory and Fascist practice. To begin with,
it requires a re-definition of our conception of public
responsibility. The Germans combined the three principles of hierarchy, authority, and discipline, and called
the compound the principle of "responsible leadership." The term will confuse the observer accustomed
to the language of democracy—until he realizes that
what is meant here is not the responsibility of a leader
to his followers, but his responsibility to *his* leader.
Otherwise, being responsible means the same in both
cases: that the leader can be removed from his leadership by whomever he is responsible to. What this could
be said to mean for the top of the hierarchic pyramid,
has puzzled everyone, including the Fascists themselves.
Ecclesiastical hierarchies have an easy way out: they
make their heads responsible to a deity whose absence
from this concrete world of affairs is a guarantee
against practical complications. In Fascism the "superior organism" of the state takes the place of this abstract supernatural—but its popular conception is so
tied up with concrete things, like "crown," or "people,"
that even in a country very much inclined toward collectivism it will be hard to dematerialize it completely.
So in Italy, Mussolini, as Head of the Government, has

kept himself legally responsible to the King—and Fascist doctrine, which could never allow that responsibility to become practical, has at no time attacked it in theory. Hitler, on the other hand, has repeatedly proclaimed himself responsible, not to the shadowy abstraction of the "German nation" which is otherwise being extolled as the all-important superior unit, but to the "men and women of the German people." And this responsibility is what he attempted to express by having the people pass on his policies in a series of plebiscites. Of course, had these "elections" been uninfluenced, they would have presented the strange spectacle of a Fascist state resurrecting the previously carefully extinguished individual judgment of its members, in order to have them pass on its own (according to the dogma essentially superior) collective judgment—a procedure that would have been not only full of potential dynamite but also completely anomalous. It was avoided by a careful preparation of the plebiscites, guaranteeing, in fact, that the collective will, as proclaimed by authority, would be confirmed by a heavy vote. This made for the double anomaly of a compulsory "vote without choice" as basis for an authoritative, anti-vote system—but at least it was not immediately dangerous to the régime. Both the German and Italian treatment of the question prove that Fascism has not, as yet, reached the point where, in consistency with the dogma, the abstraction of the state could be set up as the sole recipient of the Leader's responsibility—as, for instance, the heads of ecclesiastical hierarchies are responsible only to the deity itself. Both

Fascist states, so far, have found it necessary to inter-
pose, between their Leaders and the superior organism,
some concrete medium holied by tradition—like a
"monarch by the grace of God," or "The People" in the
sense of the sum of the individual citizens. However,
while this is a very interesting phenomenon, and might
lead to startling conclusions about the psychological
bases of collectivism, its practical importance is nil. The
fact of Fascist discipline will always prevent any show
of ultimate responsibility from becoming more than a
phrase—for all practical purposes the supreme leader
of a Fascist state is irresponsible.

The second problem, that of regulating the succession
to the leadership, is practically much more difficult but
theoretically simpler. It is clear that perpetuation of the
Fascist idea, the principal reason for the continued
existence of the Party, will also have to be the starting
point for any approach to the question. In Italy, Mussolini worked out a fairly airtight scheme for Fascist
control over the choice of his eventual successor. Following the example of the Catholic Church's College of
Cardinals, he utilized for the purpose a supreme representative body of the Party, membership in which he
himself controls absolutely: appointments to the "Grand
Council of Fascism" are to be made only by himself or
by the Crown at his suggestion. Should he die or resign,
his successor will be selected by the Crown out of a list
submitted to it by the Grand Council. Of course, if Mussolini himself during his time in office should desire to
designate someone as his successor, he would always be

able either to change the law, or to give enough power to the man he favored to enable him to hold his own later against any attack. But if he should step out without having shown any preference, the choice, while limited to a score of men in his complete confidence, is to be *made* as such by a third person in a traditionally exalted position—which will naturally provide less chance for any jealousies to break into an open struggle for power than if the possible rival aspirants were left to fight it out amongst themselves. In Germany, Adolf Hitler has not yet said anything about the succession to his "Leader—and Chancellorship"—whether or not he has done so in a secret testament is not known. He appointed Rudolf Hess as his personal deputy in Party affairs—and, though Hess does not seem to be ambitious, this might well lead to a repetition of the lesson which Stalin, after Lenin's death, taught the U.S.S.R. on the relative importance of government and Party control in the totalitarian state. On the other hand, Hitler's administrative and military lieutenants seem to hold stronger positions, as compared to the Party machine, than it was the case in Russia. So in Germany, at least for the present, a vacancy would seem to involve grave risks of a struggle of the diadochs. In Italy, as far as can be said today, that danger is virtually non-existent—quite aside from the fact that Mussolini, from the very start, was either more fortunate or more clever in subduing potential diadochs than his German disciple.

He also had a luckier hand in dealing with the biggest practical problem of "running" a Fascist Party—

that of maintaining it, in terms of the quality of its membership, as the "élite" of the Fascist state. This habit of describing a Fascist Party as an élite, or at least an intended élite, did not actually originate with the Fascists themselves. It started when the first Fascist converts in democratic countries tried to explain the one-party system to their countrymen—and only later was it seized upon in the Fascist countries, as a good slogan and convenient argument. As a matter of fact, it is a great error and responsible for a good deal of confusion. A Fascist Party is emphatically not supposed to be an élite in the sense of a group of individuals of some kind of qualitative excellence. The only quality in which it must be superior to the rest of the population is the quality of Fascism: meaning, chiefly, discipline and collective spirit. The Party is the concrete symbol not of a moral or other superiority of the Fascist state, but of its Fascism. It should be composed of neither the best nor the most able nor the most influential part of a nation but of its *most Fascist* part. It represents not the élite but the *essence* of a Fascist state. In fact, most "born leaders" will not last very long in a Fascist Party, unless they happen to have started it themselves, because they will run afoul of the requirements of discipline and unquestioning obedience. And most of the people who do belong to some social, financial, or intellectual élite, will not stand up either—because the very consciousness of their real superiority in any one field will make them doubtful about a selection that is based on premises which they cannot reasonably admit as valid, and that summarily dismisses all their claims to be élite per se. Of course, a large percentage of the able, influential, and ambitious members of a community will find their way into a Fascist Party as soon as they realize that there is no possibility, outside of it, of utilizing their capacities and gratifying their desire for success. But just as the Church of the Middle Ages, although it attracted most of the men of this type, was not, even then, a body based on personal ambition but on personal humility, so the Fascist Party is based not, as some of its apologists want us to believe, on an individual "will to power" of "élite members," but on the qualities of individual obedience, discipline, and unconditional self-sacrifice for the good of the whole. Of course, during its struggle for power, every Fascist Party will try hard to gain as many members as possible among the rich, well-born, and able. But it does so only in order to use the influence they wield for its own purposes, and after it has reached its goal—or even before that—it will quickly get rid of whomsoever does not meet its other requirements. The decisive things for the Party as a whole, as well as for every one of its members, are never position, influence, ability, or any other quality admitting a person to any pre-Fascist type of élite—they are always and exclusively the specific qualities of Fascism.

To maintain these at a level sufficient to insure performance of the Party's functions is the task of its leaders. Two kinds of action are necessary for the purpose: limitation of membership, and weeding out of those who do not, or no longer, measure up to standard. Both were introduced into practice by the Communist Party in Russia, and later taken over by the Fascist powers. The first is an inevitable consequence of the one-party system— no group destined to bear the holy flame, to perpetuate the political spirit of a state, could be composed of more than a comparatively small number of its citizens. Equally obvious was the equitable way to execute the measure: after the Party had reached the appropriate numerical strength, admission to its membership had to be closed to adults in all but exceptional instances, and thereafter its ranks had to be filled only from its own youth organizations. Thus the Party is protected from a further influx of opportunists that would be disastrous to it and to the state; and what new members it needs are guaranteed to have gone through a long and thorough Fascist education. In practice, of course, the fact that these young men and women have been in the Fascist youth organization for a number of years does not guarantee that they have really acquired the degree of discipline and collective spirit which the work of the Party demands. It is also certain that of the men who got into the Party before it closed its doors, a great many are in no way fit to belong to either the élite or the essence of the Fascist state. The remedy has also been developed by the Soviets: the "Party purge." The U.S.S.R. made this a regular procedure to be applied at fixed intervals. Mussolini had a general purge once, soon after the March on Rome, but later preferred to let the threat hang over the Party membership and to have cases necessitating the expulsion of individuals dealt

with by Party courts. Hitler, clearly more by accident
than with premeditation stumbled into his unfortunate
"blood purge" of June, 1934—but has besides an elaborate permanent judicial apparatus within the Party
quietly and continually proceeding with the removal of
undesirable Party members. Neither the German nor the
Italian method of purging has the confidence-inspiring
publicity of the Russian model, but they are scarcely
less extensive and strict, and the rules applied to the
membership are the same in all three countries: organization discipline and collective spirit, which means not
only esprit de corps among Party members but particularly the untranslatable German Volksgemeinschafts-
geist—the realization of an integral, organic solidarity
with all other members of the nation—or, in short, loyalty to the collectivist idea of the country.

As a matter of principle, so far as is consistent with
the rules about limitation and "purging" of its membership, a Fascist Party will be open to all citizens of the
state who give their unqualified support to the Fascist
régime. At first, this really fundamental rule of every
one-party system will sound most inconsistent to many
people—who will probably cite, as refutation of the contention, the sad case of the German Jews. But—recalling
that this is not an investigation of particular Fascist actions from the point of view of law or ethics, but of
generally Fascist practice from a point of view of political, and specifically of Fascist theory—it will become
clear that the skepticism is unfounded, as soon as we
make the necessary distinction between exclusion of a

group from admissibility to the Fascist Party and its exclusion from the national community as such. The latter, which is the case with the German Jews, may be an ethical outrage or a violation of national and international law—but when it comes to studying the political system of a nation, who can say whether or not a group "belongs" to it except the people of that nation themselves? Would anyone contend that our Southern commonwealths should not be called democracies before the passage of the Fifteenth Amendment, because the negro slave population was not admitted to citizenship? Two principles must govern the treatment by political science of any such case: first, that the question of where a political community should draw the line of its members, can only be decided by that community itself; second, that this decision will have to be the basis of every investigation of its affairs, regardless of whether it appears right or wrong to the hypothetical "objective" observer. This is the more so because that question is one of state practice but not of state theory. It may be a question of theory in another respect—of economic theory, like the Communist restriction to proletarian workers, of race theory, like the German restriction to "Aryans," or simply of international law, like the fact that one country acknowledges every person born within its borders as a citizen while another does not. But the theoretical structure of a state can be based only on its own decision as to who is to compose it—and a student of the structure will have to accept the premise without question. In other words, the definition of membership adopted by a community must not be confused with its political set-up.

Consequently, whenever a Fascist state pronounces a certain group as "outside the nation," or as "inhabitants" as opposed to citizens, the fact that members of this group are barred from the privilege of joining the Fascist Party does not justify the conclusion that the Party is not open to the entire community. It is—emphatically so—and that group does not count because it is no part of the community. On the other hand, every bona fide citizen who is technically admissible and sufficiently Fascist will be welcome to the Party—whether he be poor or rich, obscure or prominent, illiterate or intellectual giant. As a matter of fact, the obliteration of class distinctions in politics is one undeniable accomplishment of the Fascist states. This also may surprise those who are still mistaking Fascism for a movement of reaction—but it will be confirmed by everyone with a first-hand knowledge of German and Italian conditions. It is absolutely essential to Fascism that the single Party should not only be open to everyone but should know of no distinctions between its members except those of Party rank which are only to be earned by conspicuous Fascism and service to the community. Therefore, every Fascist Party takes considerable pride in having made it possible for the lowest-born to rise to the heights of leadership, and in having done the utmost to clean out the traditional vestiges of social and economic snobbery. The former accomplishment is a matter of record. While over here, in the Horatio Alger country, people fell into the habit of scoffing at Hitler as a "former house

painter," the roster of Fascist and National Socialist
sub-leaders presents a unique variety of men from all
walks of life—from royal princes and reigning dukes
to ex-laborers and tenant farmers. Neither can there be
any doubt about the Fascists' success in their drive for
social re-orientation. Today German Junkers may vent
their inherited anti-Semitism in quasi-official Jew-baiting, but they will be very careful before attempting to
assert a feudal superiority over any small peasants or
lowly farmhands—who may well have a lower "Party
number" stamped on their membership cards than the
aristocratic lord of the manor. Industrialists, who can
often get rid of an individual obstreperous employee on
the pretense of his being engaged in Communist activities, will first make quite sure that he holds no Party
commission—nor will any of them refuse to stand at
attention in line with their five-dollar-a-week workers at
plant ceremonies and humbly salute any of their "followers" who might chance to hold a position in the Party
hierarchy superior to that of the boss. And no fashion-
able hotel or night club will ever refuse admittance to
even the most unpleasant individuals in Party uniform,
or in mufti—because nowadays one cannot tell a man's
status in the important part of the community from the
way he looks, talks, or behaves. All our ideas to the contrary notwithstanding, this "democratization" of social
life under Fascism is real—and it is not even surprising.
It is just good Fascism. The community is superior to
any one of its parts—and no quality distinguishing any

of the parts can be held superior to the quality of Fascism which distinguishes the Party.

The strange but unmistakable effect of this principle is the disintegration of a community pattern that has always been contrasted with the state: "society." Society —not in the narrow sense of groups listed in Social Registers or frequenting the haunts and resorts of fashion, but in its widest conception as the total of non-political and non-economic human relations—was widely felt to be the real, aboriginal group set-up, over which that of the state was artificially superimposed. Society disregards the state—cutting across state lines as well as splitting the state unit into self-conscious factions. Its challenge to the influence of the state over the individual is the more effective in that it is so wholly vague and indefinite, and its ramifications—if unchecked at the start—are virtually impossible to control. That this is eminently unsatisfactory to a doctrine elevating the state to a superhuman plane, is self-evident. That Fascism directs a tremendous effort toward control and co-ordination of the social life of the individuals, we have seen before. But that—whether with premeditation or not—every such move of Gleichschaltung in behalf of the movement extolling the state aims at disrupting the other structure; that every move for organization within the framework of the state tends to weaken the social framework; that the establishment of the totalitarian state, as the completely political group structure, inevitably spells the doom of the a-political structure of human society—these consequences have often been sensed but seldom been conceded to be parts of the Fascist pattern. But parts of it they are, without question. Their logic is inescapable: it is a prerequisite to any realization of the superior place which the state holds under the Fascist dogma that there should be no group structure existing beside, and independent of, and therefore incompatible with, the state. Nor does this only apply to clearly defined structures: since the dogma demands that the Fascist consciousness shall prevail exclusively, every other type of group mentality, and especially the hazy kind of social and "class" instinct, is an obstruction which it is imperative to remove. For the making of a Fascist nation, as distinguished from the setting up of a Fascist form of government, it is not enough to issue decrees and create organizations that will fit its ideological frame—it is necessary first to destroy the structure of society that will not fit it. The tearing-down process must precede the Fascist Party's permanent constructive tasks: it must uproot in the people not only individualist trends but also any state-disregarding social consciousness before it can replace it with the uniform collective mentality based on and enclosed in the Fascist state.

CHAPTER FOUR

THE ECONOMIC STRUCTURE

Economic Leadership Principle or Corporate State?

FROM OUR DEFINITION OF FASCISM—AS THE COLLECTIV-ism of a capitalist community—we were able to deduce its general principles as well as a more detailed outline of its political body, the Fascist One-Party State. For a survey of Fascist economics, however, the definition, as it stands, will not do. Collectivism is a psychological phenomenon, the attitude of a group toward itself, and there will hardly be any doubt about its interpretation as a term. Capitalism, on the other hand, is a conception so muddled by a hundred years of strife and propaganda that only a thorough airing will make it acceptable as an unequivocal foundation for any practicable system of political economy.

The term "Capitalism" originated long after the system—just as did the term "Socialism." The latter, as a theory, was championed by Plato and Thomas More, while credit for coining the word is still being disputed on behalf of various nineteenth century economists. Capitalism, in fact, has never, even by its critics, been exactly defined as a system—it always constituted a given and inherited state of affairs, which had to be attacked or justified rather than explained. Really to define a doctrine of capitalism seems possible only in antithesis to socialism. In a socialist economy, all means of production and distribution of goods would be owned and operated by the community, which would remunerate the individuals who do the actual work. Therefore, in the ideal capitalist economy, ownership, production and distribution of all goods would be strictly private, the profit motive serving as incentive, and the individual work involved in any process would be paid for by the owner of the goods at that particular stage. In theory, each system is uncompromising and does not admit the introduction of any features of the other. In practice, however, there has never been a complete capitalism—nor a complete socialism. The most nearly complete capitalist economy in history—that of pre-Roosevelt America, abhorring state railroads, state power plants, state factories—knew publicly owned lands and forests and a public monopoly in carrying the mails, both definitely socialist traits. Neither do we know of an example of consistent socialism. The U.S.S.R., even if we suppose the extermination of the kulaks to be complete, still maintains competition between various collective enterprises—which directly contravenes the principle of universal communal ownership.

What we know today in economic practice are intermittent stages, with elements derived from capitalist as well as from socialist sources. It is really quite unjustifiable to call any one of our present economic systems capitalist. They are only predominantly capitalist, since no really consistent capitalism could stand for any publicly owned means of production or distribution of goods.[1] However, the idea that we live under a capitalist system is so firmly established that we shall have to use the term itself in a less restricted sense: as a system standing *as a rule* for private ownership and operation, but which allows them to be supplanted by public ownership or operation in extraordinary cases, or when the strictly capitalist stratagem does not function satisfactorily. It is this sort of capitalism which we have always known under democracy and which constitutes one of the two primordial elements of Fascism.

It is easily apparent from this definition of a "practical capitalism," that in every democracy it will encounter one inherent logical difficulty which will not arise in a Fascist state. Whether a particular part of a national economy shall be owned and operated privately or publicly, depends, it has just been said, on whether or not private operation is satisfactory. This will inevitably raise the question: satisfactory to whom? Democracy—conceiving "the people," that is, the individuals, as finally destined to receive the benefits of government —is in a quandary when called upon to decide this. A

[1] The Communist method of denying the socialist character of those inroads of "state capitalism," because of the continuing existence of the "class structure" of society, does not remove the logical difficulty. Obviously, in a hypothetical complete "state capitalism," an existing "upper" class could no longer be termed "capitalist"—and Communist doctrine has never been able to decide at what point to draw the line.

business might give a great deal of satisfaction to its owner, and yet very little to its workers who are being sweated, or to its customers who have to pay excessive prices or do not get decent service, or even to investors who fail to get the expected dividends while the men controlling the stock are voting themselves huge bonuses. To draw a line here *in principle* is a problem which no democracy so far has been able to solve. Every one has had to rely for guidance on special aspects of the case under consideration—none of them was able to enunciate a fixed policy. For Fascism, the answer is easy. The abstraction of the state itself being the last and only object of community life, there can be no doubt that its interests must also control the decision whether private operation of any one business has worked satisfactorily. And as the will of the state is proclaimed authoritatively, there can be no dissension about it either. Therefore, while it might be very difficult to define exactly the capitalism of a democracy, the definition of the capitalist element in Fascism is clear and precise: a *general tendency* toward private ownership and operation of means of production, as well as toward use of the profit motive as economic stimulant—the *extent*, however, to which this tendency is to be followed in practice being entirely subject to the interest of the state as determined by its given authority.

On this unequivocal foundation Fascism had to build a practical economic system. It was obvious that this system would have to be developed in quite a different way from the other aspects of the Fascist community. For while a main axiom of political Fascism is the essential unity of all members of the state, in economic life the capitalist premise will inevitably divide the people into two groups: employers and employees. In particular instances the development of modern capitalism may confuse the distinction—from the case of the bondholding director of a company to that of the factory worker who, by possession of a single share of stock, can legally become part owner of the biggest industrial enterprise in a country. But on principle it is evident that in any capitalist economy the population must fall into two classes —Class A, by and large, comprising the men who own goods or their equivalent, and live by selling them, and Class B, comprising the men who work at producing or distributing these goods and live by being paid for such work by the respective members of Class A. This division is essential to capitalism and, therefore, to Fascism. On the other hand, it tends to produce psychological effects very much opposed to the spirit of Fascism, because quite naturally the members of each class develop strong feelings of solidarity which, given favorable conditions, will eventually grow into what is known as the "class struggle." Class struggle within a nation, however, is nothing but the breaking up of the (to Fascism) axiomatic collective body of the national community into two collective bodies violently opposing each other. It is the one development the Fascist state cannot stand for. So its task in the economic field is perfectly clear: it has to set up a capitalistic structure without capitalism's normal class-severing consequences.

In a people of Fascist docility, under normal circumstances and with the unlimited powers of a Fascist government, this is really not altogether impossible (in spite of the storm of protest which any statement to that effect will call forth from Marxists and economic determinists in general). To begin with, the easiest and most reliable method of keeping people from an undesired alignment is to align them otherwise. The desirable line-up is not hard to find, either: if, among the individuals making up a modern economy, one does not like to distinguish between employers and employees, the most obvious other distinction available is between the persons engaged in one trade or industry and those engaged in another. The main idea, therefore, in the organization of each trade and industry, must be to destroy from the start any hope its employees and employers might have of improving their individual economic positions by joining efforts with the employees and employers, respectively, of any other trade or industry. This is a matter of organization, and therefore can be accomplished. Second consideration: in any economic system there must be a method of determining the most important point of capitalist practice—the conditions under which employees shall work for their employers. The general Fascist principles of authority and discipline are no good here. Business cannot be privately operated in an efficient way without at least having a voice in the determination of the largest item of its operating costs; a scheme of compulsory authoritative decision of all questions concerning labor relations would mark every

Fascist attempt at maintaining practical capitalism for failure from the start. The practice of old-line laissez faire capitalism, to have these questions decided (actually, if not in theory) by managerial fiat, will not do either. It would not only be incompatible with the Fascist axiom that the state alone has authority over its otherwise essentially equal citizens, but it would also be practically inconsistent with Fascist policy, since simply to subject employees to their employers' dictum would necessarily revive labor's just extinguished solidarity. Workers, therefore, must have a say in these matters; in fact, they must—at least theoretically—have exactly as much to say as their employers. This, in turn, leads to the last consideration: in practice such equality would almost inevitably deadlock negotiations and provoke industrial strife—of an especially objectionable variety because it would not, like the orthodox class struggle, disrupt only the population as a whole, but also the newly-established separate organization of trades and industries. Besides, it would be impossible in a collectivist community to relinquish the superiority of the whole over any of its parts in any instance. Thus, for practical and dogmatic reasons, it is necessary to reaffirm the *power* of the state to decide authoritatively on any question concerning its members. The state must be made a party to every one of the organizations comprising employers and employees of a trade or industry—with the right (although the *policy* will be not to exercise this right!) to dictate to both elementary parties, regardless of how they may make out among themselves.

Summed up, this blueprint of a Fascist economic structure might read as follows: organization of the national economy into independent bodies along trade or industrial lines; within these bodies equal rights to employers and employees in determining wages and working conditions, with any sort of struggle strictly forbidden and the state installed in every organization as superior authority. It will be noted that what we have here developed, by simple deductions from the fundamentals of Fascism, is nothing but the skeleton of Mussolini's "Corporate State." [2] The economic structure of the Fascist community is quite as logical as all its other aspects. Starting from the two given bases of collectivism and capitalism—and strictly excluding every other consideration, intellectual, traditional, or sentimental, of economics, politics, or philosophy—one can hardly fail to arrive at it as at the natural economic expression for a political system built upon those foundations. And so it was rather surprising that in the entire field of Fascist economics actual developments somehow seemed to lack that inexorability of purpose so evident in all other Fascist activities.[3]

Even Italy, which in the long run adhered rather conscientiously to the corporate blueprint, took an inordinately long time in doing so; and the economic structure of the New Germany seemed not only to differ in result, but at first sight appeared even to represent quite another theory of economic organization than the Italian

[2] See Appendix B, p. 302 ff.
[3] See Appendix B, p. 305-6.

model. The Germans refuse to admit, on principle, that there is such a thing as an inherent conflict of interest between capital and labor. They consider every single business enterprise as an organic whole—a live particle of the economic body of the nation. Within these micro-organisms hierarchic functions are distributed: the employer is to lead, the workers are to follow. This new scheme of labor relations, however, is not meant to enlarge any rights of employers based upon ownership, of capital or means of production. National Socialism, in converting the employer from an "owner" into a "leader" of his business, changed his whole structural position. His business is no longer regarded as a piece of property, to be used, within the law, at its owner's pleasure. It becomes a public trust; and in connection with it the employer has no longer any *rights*, as an independent economic individual and master of his property —he has only state-conferred *powers* which are necessary for the performance of his organic *function*. This function, chiefly, imposes upon him definite and original duties: the duties of the primus inter pares—to lead for the good of the whole, to place, in the exercise of the authority which his followers are to obey, the "common good" above his "individual good." As in every other field, the "leadership principle" in economics represents not a superiority of the leader over his followers, but a division of functions between essentially equal parts, with mutual obligations to be discharged in the interest of the collective body.

To enforce these obligations, the Third Reich established a huge cover-all economic structure (similar to Rossoni's Italian vision [4] of 1923 and 1924): the German Labor Front, "organization of all Germans working with fist and brow." While the concrete details of any employer-employee relationship were supposed to be worked out within each business unit, the Labor Front received complete power to supervise performance of the mutual functional duties, by plant "leaders" and "followers," in the entire field of production and distribution of goods (excepting agriculture and cultural activities, which the Nazis, for reasons of their own, organized separately). In other words, it was authorized to maintain Fascist economic discipline. The full scope of this authority became apparent only when in 1935 the Reichs Chamber of Economics, comprising all German business, joined the Labor Front. Upon this move have been placed all sorts of political interpretations. Doubtless it represents a compromise in the struggle for power between various Nazi groups; doubtless its details are too much the outcome of political wrangling to be of great theoretical significance. Still, it proved one thing convincingly: that, irrespective of who happens to be at the controls, the *idea* of the new economic structure of the Reich is the totalitarian idea—with one communal organ comprehending all economic activities, and without, as a matter of theory, separating the effectuation of national economic policy from the handling of labor problems.

[4] See Appendix B, p. 306.

As a whole, this system seems to bear little resemblance to the one worked out in Italy. Only if we compare the essential features of the two Fascist economies, shall we note a similarity. We have seen that "Corporate State," in nuce, means a state-controlled and exclusively state-subservient economy, organized along trade or industrial lines, based upon capitalist practice, striving to make employers and employees collaborate as partners with equal rights in the interest of production—but recognizing the existence of a contrast between their material interests. Now this is, word for word, the kind of economy constituted by the German system—except that the latter denies *any* inherent capital-labor conflict. The aims of either structure are identical; the Corporate State, too, has the principal objective of eliminating, in the interest of national solidarity, the class division which capitalism is apt to bring about. The entire difference is one of technique. The Italians—though they deplore the contrast between the material interests of employers and employees and seek to avert its natural consequences—utilize it as a means of economic organization. The Germans, on the other hand, organize economic production hierarchically and authoritatively like any other national interest—and consider capital-labor conflicts as irregularities *in fact,* which must be ironed out in practice but have no claim to dogmatic recognition. Each system seeks to overcome the normal capitalist trend toward a class struggle; the first attempting to straighten it out after first using it as a structural implement—the other preferring to remove it right at the source.

The difference in technique, moreover, had its sound historic reasons. In Italy, the corporate doctrine had been developed during a period of world-wide prosperity, and in a country where labor's economic solidarity had only to a very limited extent turned into real class consciousness. In Germany, on the other hand, the old trade union structure had been thoroughly imbued with the ideology of the class struggle, and four years of depression had made the class sentiment of the workers grow by leaps and bounds. To effectuate national solidarity, it was necessary to break labor solidarity completely. The corporate structure came much too close to unifying employees as such to be acceptable. Some other way had to be found to organize national production—in a totalitarian way, preserving the capitalist framework but without disfranchising labor. Hitler's answer to the problem was the "economic leadership principle"—the completely functional form of organization. Denying the employer-labor conflict of interests in toto, undertaking to protect the worker by means of the state's supervisory organs against "misuse of leadership," employing, for practical reasons, a completely different technique from the Corporate State, the National Socialist scheme is equally totalitarian, equally capitalistic in principle but not in essence, equally designed only to promote production.

Both the Italians' long delay in putting their corporate blueprint into effect, and the Germans' complete deviation from that formula, have been hailed in democratic circles, as "failures of Fascism." Nothing, unfortunately, could be further from the truth. We have said before—and shall see yet more clearly later—that even the capitalism of a Fascist state is nothing but a principle of private ownership and management of the means of production, the application of which is entirely subject to the authoritatively determined needs and interests of the community. It follows that the corporate plan, theoretically deduced for a model Fascist economy, will hold good only under model conditions—in other words, in a wholly normal economic situation. Any economically abnormal circumstances will automatically render the formula inadequate. Furthermore, they will dispose of any and every other economic principle; leaving Fascist authorities guided solely by collectivist political axioms—totalitarianism, state supremacy, etc.—and by their own opinion of what, in practice, will be best for the state they are heading. In contrast to its firmness in other fields, this elasticity of Fascist doctrine in the field of practical economics is an essential trait of the whole Fascist system. Leadership, discipline, the incorporation of the state's Fascist spirit into a special movement— none of these features could be discarded by a Fascist leader even if he personally should deem it best for his nation, because they represent either the very essence of Fascism or inevitable results of its realization. Not so the Corporate State. It is definitely Fascist; but it is a laboratory product of political science and strictly a fair-weather proposition—a gratifying achievement if circumstances allow it to be applied, but nothing which a Fascist state would have to feel morally bound to put into practice. The corporate formula, in fact, is not only no hard and fast rule but no rule at all; economically the Fascist state has but one immutable principle: to be unprincipled.

This applies even to the source from which the whole system sprang: modern capitalism. Every Fascist state starts out on a capitalist economy. It continues that way because—in the words of the Carta del Lavoro—it "considers private initiative in production the most valuable and most effective instrument to protect national interests." And it cannot be emphasized too strongly that there is no point whatever in looking for other motives, because the question of *why* Fascist leadership *really* sticks to the capitalist system is wholly irrelevant. The important fact is that the Fascists themselves believe in the validity of the reasoning set forth in the Carta—and that it is impossible to dissuade them. But if, in the opinion of Fascist leadership, national interest should require it, no Fascist will mind the most drastic interference with capitalist practice, whether by regulation or regimentation or—again quoting the Carta—"immediate assumption of control." In conflict with any national need, capitalist dogma is an interest of secondary importance, theoretically acknowledged as sound, but practically unessential. Likewise, a Communist government could never dispense with public ownership of farms and factories but need not, before it conveniently can, introduce the ideal Communist method of compen-

sating the individual according to his needs rather than
according to his work. A capitalist democracy could not
strike out its Bill of Rights but is not less democratic
for reserving to itself the right to impose martial law nor
less capitalistic for maintaining individual public mo-
nopolies. It would be impossible for a Fascist leader to
let class or individual rights interfere with state supremacy. But in the field of economics he can do whatever
he may deem expedient for the welfare of the national
unit—and he need not even shrink from near-elimina-
tion of the capitalist plank of his system. The only condition is that he must give as the motive for his actions
the interest of the state and must not touch the principle
of the desirability of capitalism. Capitalism is a *basis*
of Fascism and, as such, cannot be abandoned publicly
and in so many words—but it is not an essential feature
of the Fascist system, and therefore need not be maintained consistently, or at all, in actual practice. It will
be maintained, if possible and expedient. But it will
always be subject to the interest of the community; and
—which is emphatically not the case with the Fascist
political tenets—its partial or near-complete abolition
does not impair the Fascist character of the state.[5]

[5] When Hitler first formulated this economic opportunism into
a Fascist credo for the relation between economics and the state
—"formerly the nation was there for the government, and government for business; now business is there for government, and
government for the nation"—the world was inclined to dismiss it
as an empty pronouncement smacking of insincerity. When Dr.
Schacht proceeded to demonstrate it in practice, foreign observers
said that was due to Germany's desperate and unprecedented economic straits, and cited it as proof that National Socialism was in

The paradox part of the situation is that the policy which is thus declined in practice but held entirely acceptable in theory—the partial or complete socialization of the means of production—is nothing but the form of economic organization advocated by Communism. And, as everyone knows, it was Communism upon which Fascism, from the very start, trained its guns as upon its chief enemy.

To those who do not believe in the Communist theory of Fascism as a tool of finance capital, this has always been surprising. First, Fascism wrested power not from Communism but from democracy. Second, the Fascists readily recognize—both Hitler and Mussolini have proclaimed it, as well as dozens of German and Italian lesser lights—that Fascism, as a political conception, is really opposed not to Communism but to democracy, the

reality only a crude dictatorship and no "correct" Fascist régime, of which the corporate thesis was held to be the first and foremost criterion. When Italy in 1934 established a government monopoly in foreign trade and practically nationalized the banking business, these actions were put down as emergency measures in preparation for the Ethiopian adventure and as exceptions that proved the rule. But now, in 1936, in the very proclamation of the actual completion of the corporate system, Mussolini announced the imminent passing of Italy's "key industries" into the hands of government. And Hitler, at Nuremberg, explained to the German workers that of course he "could take over all business" but that the resulting elimination of competition would depress the quality of production needed for building German self-sufficiency—the very argument used against socialization in the Carta del Lavoro. And neither in Germany nor in Italy was there an outcry of "Bolshevism!", nor even a sign of surprise at these casual references to the possibility of knocking the capitalist prop from under the Fascist system.

political structure championed by Liberalism. Democracy exalts the individual, while Communism and Fascism both exalt the community. Democracy guards the privacy of economic enterprise as an individual right, while Communism and Fascism both consider it a communal interest—with the Communist state taking its operation into its own hands, while the Fascist one "contracts" it out to individual businessmen. Even the internationalism, which inevitably brings Communism into conflict with Fascist fundamentals, is hardly more "un-Fascist" than the peace doctrines with which Liberalism shackles national interest itself to the anti-war instincts of the single citizen. And yet the political creed which Fascism raves against, the movement which it delights in picturing as "the world pest," as evil incarnate—is not Liberalism but Communism.

If we are fortunate enough to encounter a Fascist capable of carrying a rational discussion of these topics beyond emotional outbursts, and ask him for an explanation of his choice in enemies, he will rarely try to justify it on grounds of the dogmatic antithesis between Fascism and Communism. Most probably he will answer that he does not fight Liberalism with the same fury as Communism, because Liberalism nowadays is doomed anyway. He will quote Mussolini to the effect that democracy has outlived its historical function, that it has lost its vitality, and that it can no more appeal to a healthy and virile people. The inference, that to a healthy and virile people Communism *might* appeal, is one not likely to be drawn by Fascists. Yet it is the key to their whole attitude. For, consciously or subconsciously, they are well aware of the fact that Communism springs from the same collectivist stem as their own system, and that the two points which keep them apart—the Fascists' choice of a national instead of a class basis, and their refusal to have the state, on principle, take care of its productive needs itself—constitute a feeble barrier indeed. And they realize, accordingly, that while their collectivist conditioning of the masses will effectively preclude a conversion to Liberalism, the appeal of Communism might not only prove rationally attractive to the impecunious majority of their people but could also count on finding there an entirely favorable political state of mind.

That is the reason why every Fascist leader constantly fulminates against the Red Menace; why the antagonism of the people against anything ever so faintly suspected of Communism has to be kept at a fever pitch—in strange contrast to the amused contempt in which they are trained to hold democracy. Democracy is something that would not fit their mentality—and this fact in itself is sufficient defense against it. But Communism, as a theory of government, *would* fit them—and therefore has to be constantly guarded against with all the energy, resourcefulness and perseverance of a Fascist nation. This conceptual kinship is also the reason why the anti-Bolshevist tirades are always purposely emotional, and never mention any specific features of Communist doctrine. They are all in much too dangerous proximity to essential Fascist notions to be attacked resolutely—even outright expropriation of property, even the class-angle. The Fascist persecution of Communism and Communists is a phenomenon of purely political significance—and *not*, as the Communists would have it, a class-determined persecution of labor. The Fascists would be glad to take from the ranks of the bourgeoisie alone the number of Communists they must liquidate to deter others from heresy. To do this would indicate precisely what they desire to prove: that their own working population is immune to the poison. Fascists persecute Communists not because they represent labor—which in the Fascist view they emphatically do not!—but because they aim to turn the political consciousness of the people away from Fascist authority, and because their use of a concept of group supremacy similar to the Fascists' own makes their attempt particularly dangerous. Communism must be destroyed—not because it is so incompatible with Fascist conceptions, but on the contrary because it is so close to them. Fascist Red-baiting is not motivated by social antagonism, but by the strictly political necessity of preventing the people from turning to something for which Fascism itself has set the emotional stage.[6]

[6] This does not mean that either present Fascist state is in imminent danger of a Communist upheaval. In the opinion of the writer, the various Communist underground movements in the Fascist countries are simply wasting their breath in the face of the totalitarian machinery arrayed against them. It does mean that if a Fascist community should, by some concurrence of circumstances, cease to be militantly Fascist, there would be little or no chance of its turning toward democracy, but a reasonable chance of its turning to Communism. It means that for people with a

Only if we understand this, can we realize how a Fascist state can be wholly anti-Communist and at the same time pursue policies causing wrath and anguish in capitalist circles (where Fascist discipline has not turned that anguish into a willing acceptance of patriotic sacrifice). *From a Fascist point of view, the problems of Capitalism and Communism are in no way related.* Capitalism—in its Fascist sense—is a structural principle of a national economy. Its governmental regulation is a matter of economic policy in which, in the organic community, no ideological points can be involved. And even if such regulation should actually duplicate measures proposed by Marx or Lenin, that would constitute no reason to relax the opposition to Communism—which is a purely political enemy of the Fascist state, a menace not to its economic structure but to its political control. Today it is the Fascists' arch enemy, because it is the only contemporary collectivist movement with a will to power, with a planned attack, and with the ominous international background of the Soviet Union. If tomorrow the Catholic Church should devote its potential strength to attempts to seize the reins of government in various countries, it would soon reap as much or more Fascist abuse than Communism. On the other hand, if Moscow were to dissolve the Comintern—and if Social-

Fascist mentality democracy is dead and buried—that the choice for the powers of the future, in Fascist eyes, lies only between the two exponents of collectivism (which explains also, by the way, why our Communists so stubbornly refuse to believe that the alternative to their political views can, in practice, be anything but Fascism; they, too, are collectivists!).

ism should again become the purely economic doctrine which it was at the start, without the element of class-solidarity transcending national boundaries—then the Fascists, very likely, would cease to denounce Communism, no matter how they handled their internal economic issues. These are hypothetical cases with little chance of realization. But continually, in Fascist countries, developments of lesser significance are under way which bear the thesis out—developments quite inexplicable and contradictory in themselves until Fascist anti-Communism is realized as being not the loyalty of a capitalist body-guard, but a political system's fight against a purely political menace—a fight for the preservation of a totalitarian concept, without any other significance either social or economic.

The field where this has been most apparent, although least discussed, is agriculture. There, in Germany and Italy, Fascism pursued a policy as out of step with capitalist notions as the Russian system of collective farming.[7] What the Reichsnährstand and the Bonifica Integrale did to land-owners, cannot be called capitalism even by the most doctrinaire Communist. Farming was brought under a system of regimentation—or, more precisely, conscription—to a degree known heretofore only in the Soviet Union. The reform affected large estates as well as small peasant holdings. It was not content with dictating crops (and that, by the way, not by promising benefits in exchange for compliance, but by administra-

[7] See Appendix B, p. 309 ff.

tive ukase backed up by penal force). It broke up farms, qualified the ability of citizens to take up activities connected with agriculture, restricted the rights to own land, to dispose of it, or to borrow money on it—and over any farmer of insufficient zeal in carrying out its policies it held the threat of direct expropriation. In short, it made, as a matter of principle, the right to own farm land dependent on its use in the manner required by the communal interest—thus narrowing the context of private ownership, operation and initiative in the field of agricultural production in a way entirely incompatible with the fundamentals of capitalism.

The reasons why, in agriculture, the Fascists went so much further in restricting the free play of capitalism than they did in industry, are well known and easy to comprehend. The decisive ones are ideological. Land in any form is a more integral part of the national unit than industrial facilities. *The soil is prima facie national substance.* It constitutes the primordial national element of "country" ("Man in Fascism is individual, nation, and country all at once," said Mussolini), which with the people upon it must be welded into an indivisible whole of Blut und Boden, as the Nazis put it. Industry is a national interest only insofar as it produces and employs—and, therefore, must be organized into a Fascist scheme only as much as is made necessary by output demands and by the need to suppress the class struggle. Land, on the other hand, is a national interest in itself. Since it is a means of economic production, its distribution, as far as possible, will continue on capitalist lines; but its private use must be infinitely more integrated into the communal organism than must industry. The emphasis placed on this is much more than a matter of economic planning. It is based upon recognition of the fact that land, for an organic state, has a significance far transcending its economic value—as stable substance supplementing the dynamic national spirit. This emphasis is the more striking, in that Fascism was created not from nineteenth century but from modern, twentieth century capitalism—a system that for some time showed a strong inclination to forget all about agriculture which provided so little opportunity for large-scale financial transactions. That Fascism, in spite of being a product of this same modern capitalism, remembered agriculture, is due to its collectivist outlook—to the realization that land, an element more stable, more enduring than either industry or business, is not to be valued in terms of production only, and must be brought out of the circle of economics into a more intimate relationship with the concentrated energies of the Fascist state.

Of course, there were also other, more practical reasons for agricultural regimentation: chiefly, as has been pointed out by all democratic observers, the rather obvious desire of permanently war-minded nations to be self-sufficient in their food supply. However, the various "battles of the wheat" and related undertakings—although in Italy they constituted the bulk of the agricultural program of the régime—were economic policies, things that were done *with* the reformed agricultural set-up. They differed in no way from the industrial "battles of production" which Fascism carried on completely within the capitalist framework. Farm production, too, could well have been speeded up to any desired extent without the excessive state control employed by the Fascist nations. It was a dogmatic much more than a material necessity which dictated German and Italian farm policies—and which would also have to dictate the farm policies of any other Fascist state: the need to remove the soil, with its tillers, from the play of economic forces to its ancient place as the nation's backbone—because of all communal possessions it alone is imperishable.

Finance is another field in which the Fascist powers committed one act of heresy after another against axioms of capitalism.[8] There, too, actual developments resulted from both practical and dogmatic causes. The hold of private finance over the economic life of a nation has always been a favorite point of Fascist attacks on Liberalism, particularly in Germany. After seizing power, the Nazis did not embark on their widely heralded crusade to "break the thralldom of interest," because any such move seemed sure to upset the precarious bal-

---

[8] Adequately treated, the story of recent German and Italian financial policies would fill several volumes, although most of it is more or less familiar to the public from commercial experience. The salient point is a discovery of Dr. Schacht's: that not only money owned or claimed by a government, but that the very structure of money and finance is a potential weapon of national policy —a distinctly Fascist idea, substantially different from the pre-Nazi German system of currency protection by means of exchange control, from which Schacht arrived at it.

ance of German economy—and also because the banks, the chief "interest slavers," had been among the first to climb on the bandwagon, and promised to be useful allies in the impending fight for economic preparedness. However, the question of taking them over was seriously pondered by a National Socialist investigating committee, and if this had reported favorably, German private banking would now doubtless be a thing of the past. Even so, in both totalitarian states, the steps that remain to be taken to effect a complete nationalization of the "money trust" would obviously be less revolutionary, economically speaking, than what has already been done. The first move was a co-ordination of banking activities amounting to state control of management. Then came inroads upon the capital structure by way of exchanged loans. Eventually this was followed by government acquisition of controlling interests in the banks' stock itself.[9] Today, the directors of virtually all the larger German and Italian banks are, even in capitalist terms, more state employees than agents of private interests. In a very quiet way—and, to the chagrin of the Communists, without so much as touching the class aspect of the situation—capitalism, as an economic reality, under Fascism seems to be on its way out of the financial business.

Thus, in such fields as finance and agriculture, special

[9] In each case, of course, the opportunity was presented by a banking crisis—but America showed in 1933 that a government with an essentially capitalist point of view can handle such a situation without, by accident, emerging as majority shareholder in most of its country's financial institutions.

circumstances have effected a complete revision of the "general tendency toward private ownership and management," our definition of the capitalist element in Fascism. In most other sectors of a Fascist economy the tendency stayed intact. Materially, moreover—at least in the early years of every Fascist rule—businessmen, especially in industry, seem destined to have things pretty much their own way. The Fascist state's main economic interest is increased production—which is also industry's main interest. Pointing to this parallelism of interests, industrial leaders will usually be able to convince a Fascist government that the national welfare depends on the granting of their requests, even at the expense of other economic groups. It is all done in perfect candor and without any sinister implications; it is obvious that nothing provides such an incentive for fast and efficient production as the prospect of ample profits—and so profits will be safeguarded while the bulk of economic burdens will fall on the workers, tending to hold down their wages, and on consumers, forcing them to pay higher prices.[10] This will be the case particularly in industries directly engaged in filling state needs: armaments, mining, building, export industries that bring in foreign ex-

[10] Outstanding among those burdens is the cost of absorbing unemployment. This is an essential undertaking of every Fascist régime—and, if jobless men are to be put to work in private industry *ahead* of existing demands, *somebody* must pay their wages. As Americans have had a chance to observe, democracy cannot evade this fact either; it can only attempt to distribute the burden as equitably as possible—and (as has also been shown here) the surest criterion of success in this attempt is general dissatisfaction.

change. In other branches of business, a much sharper discipline will be maintained over "profiteers" or "unsocial employers"—and should a retail merchant think himself entitled to the same privileges as an arms manufacturer, he would speedily be disillusioned. Under Liberalism they may occupy the same position in the economic scheme; but in Fascism one renders to the state services of extreme importance, while the other is little more than a drone—and therefore will be compelled to toe the mark much more strictly, and even to assume financially a large share of costs which Messrs. Krupp, Thyssen, or Pirelli can easily cast upon their workers or upon the public. It is a frequent logical mistake to infer a Fascist pro-capital bias from the treatment of nationally important industries—although other employers, too, will often derive economic advantages in relation to workers and consumers from the abolition of democracy. And yet, from the point of view of the businessman of today, it is just the trader and industrialist who, under Fascism, would soon be longing for the good old days of economic liberalism with their "free play of economic forces."

For this is the inevitable outcome of every exhaustive investigation of Fascist economics: while, in a Fascist state, labor, agriculture, and the consuming public will have to pay most of the bill, the class that more than all others will lose *rights* that it considers fundamental, will be independent business. The worker—according to German and Italian experience—will get less in real wages, and will lose the right to strike. But in all probability he will find some system of collective bargaining, with government guarantee of the resulting wages and working conditions, embodied in the national economic structure—so that he will have no reason to accuse the Fascist state of a *theoretically* divergent policy from the basic tendencies of organized labor. The farmer will be subjected to strictest governmental regulation as to the growth and sale of agricultural products. But rugged individualism was never one of those, and since an adequate food supply is the basis of the drive, essential to Fascism, toward a self-contained national economy, the material interests of farmers in general will always be safeguarded by a Fascist government. The consumer will almost inevitably have to pay more for his needs, but it is equally certain that there will be some governmental action to keep prices down—and what else did consumers' advocates ever demand anyway?

Only for business will the situation be entirely different. Business is the only economic group that always *had* a real stake in individualism. From corporation executive to street peddler, the independent businessman treasured one thing: the right to manage his own shop. Nowhere, of course, has this been as strongly apparent as in this country. Resentment against the influence of giant combines on the independent "little fellow" led to trust busting. Resentment against labor organizations "telling employers how to run their business" led to a campaign of active and passive resistance that so far, at the cost of an immense intensification of the class struggle, has in many industries all but succeeded in keeping unimpaired the power of management to fix wages and working conditions. Opposition to governmental interference was more than anything else the common denominator for all political theories and beliefs of American business. One has often heard it maintained—and most sincerely—that actual profits were second in importance to the individual businessman's freedom to conduct his own affairs according to his own judgment. To business, in theory and practice, safeguarding the rights of the individual was a basic interest.

Under Fascism, this is out. The "right to run one's own business" is not, as before, only impaired by labor organizations or trusts and cartels—it is officially eliminated by the unanswerable dictum of the state. And the elimination concerns Big Business as well as small business. This has been the sad experience of German and Italian financial leaders who supported their respective Fascist movements during their struggle for power, under the delusion that afterwards they would be running the show. Individually, of course, quite a few members of Big Business did run a considerable part of the show. But the disappointment here referred to is neither that of the General Secretary of the Confederation of Italian Industries (who paid out Mussolini's subsidies before the March on Rome and later found himself cruelly ridiculed by official theoreticians when he ventured to expound old-line capitalism at the 1932 Economic Congress in Ferrara) nor that of the German newspaper tycoon who engineered the political side of Hitler's victory, only to be thrown on the junkheap after a short and inglorious tenure of the Ministry of Economics. The disappointment we mean is that of those "captains" of industry or finance who sincerely believed —without personally expecting special advantages— that Fascism, by removing the threat of Communism and militant labor organization, would put business in a stronger position than before, and that after the Moor had done his duty they could dismiss him. For they found they couldn't. And they found that with the menace of labor domination had gone the independence of business.

True, they might succeed in slashing wages. But while previously, in collective bargaining systems established under democracy, a union might have had certain rights guaranteed by the state, the employer always dealt only with a protective association of employees, definitely private in character and, as a rule, less powerful economically than he himself. Also the choice that confronted him was always only one of making more profit or less out of his business; as soon as yielding to labor demands threatened to make operations actually unprofitable, the employer was always able to shut down with the comforting assurance that his stubborn workers were bound to be much worse off than he. The Fascist state, however, confronts him not only with the workers' syndicates of the corporate system—plain closed shop bodies with the identical purpose of any other union and strengthened, at least theoretically, by governmental maintenance of a balance of power—but also with a comprehensive labor organization that is an offspring of the Party, and the groupings of which are headed by high-degree Fascists with the power of invoking the wrath of God upon any employer whose labor policies should displease them. (The only possible protection is to be sufficiently well connected with Fascists of even higher degree, which is always expensive and sometimes quite impossible.) And if the harassed businessmen should try to ease their labor budget by laying off a few men—to say nothing of closing plants altogether—it would be pointed out to them that their Fascist duty is to keep every man on the payroll as long as they have a cent in the cash register, that the common good goes before the individual good, and that the Fascist state is concerned with conquering unemployment and does not care if they can no longer make a profit.

True, they might succeed in raising prices. But while under democracy industrial co-operation was in general non-compulsory and the individual trade association member was seldom exposed to coercion in matters of plain business policy, the corresponding Fascist organ- ization exercises absolute power over its members in fact as well as in name and, on the other hand, is prone to every hint from economic headquarters in govern- ment or Party. True, some industries will be well sup- plied with government contracts—armaments, re-em- ployment, public works, etc. But should they expect to make as much profit as the gross volume would indicate; or to be in a position to reject an order that did not promise to net any profit at all; or to be able to keep their profit instead of turning most of it over to government or Party agencies for operating expenses—without, nota bene, considering at all the possibility or probability of graft in either one of these double bureaucracies; or should they expect to have a voice in shaping general policies which would not immediately but indirectly affect them, such as agricultural tariffs, or currency management, or foreign policy in general—in any of these expectations they are apt to be grievously disappointed. True, Big Business will be high in the councils of every Fascist government. It can be far too useful to be left out. But as to running the show—they will not have half the influence they had under any good old post-war pseudo-"Socialist" government. From a position in which, although targets of frequent and popular attacks and generally professed distrust, they wielded tremendous actual power, they will step into the place of universally acclaimed front-rank fighters of a battling nation, coddled with flattery and bribed with government contracts—and with the privilege of mending their sinister ways, dropping their backstage influences, and doing what they are told. Moreover, this aspect of the change is never generally known—because some of the victims are too stupid to realize what is happening to them, and the others are too scared of being suspected of non-conformity if they speak out, even in private.

"Gemeinnutz vor Eigennutz"—"the common good before the individual good." For labor, farmers, consumers, for all the groups that were individually helpless, Fascism will accomplish the collectivization they desired and increase their real influence, though they may have to pay for it with loss of economic freedom and a turn for the worse in actual conditions. But independent business—the group that resented interference and domination and treasured "a man's right to manage his own affairs"—will suffer, though it may be sweetened with honors and economic favors, the complete destruction of its very foundation. No matter whether a Fascist government materializes the "Corporate State" or proceeds according to the "economic leadership principle" enunciated in Germany, no matter what its policies may be as to wages, prices and profits: every economic group, workers, farmers and consumers, will find some scheme of collective representation and will, in one way or the other and subject always to the superior needs of the state, have its interests taken care of—and so will traders and industrialists. But "independent business," the great monument of liberal capitalism, will become a contradiction in terms.

CHAPTER FIVE

THE ADMINISTRATIVE STRUCTURE

Fascist Law and Liberty—"within the state"

THUS, SPEAKING EX CATHEDRA, MUSSOLINI DEFINED LIB-
erty: "the only freedom that can seriously be considered
—the freedom of the state, and of the individual within
the state."

Obviously, a non-Fascist reader will need explanatory
notes to the statement. "Freedom of the state" is plain
enough, but "freedom of the individual within the state"
is about as profoundly ambiguous a phrase as has ever
been coined. Not that it is meaningless—far from it!
But its real meaning has nothing to do with what a lay-
man, equipped only with a democratic mind and knowledge of the English language, might conceive it to be.
To such an observer, freedom of the individual connotes
a state of affairs in which, as a rule, men are at liberty
to act according to their individual fancies as long as
they do not break specific laws of the community—
provided, however, that there are certain privileges and
activities of the individual (such as free speech, free
assembly, a free press, or the right to trial by jury)
upon which the community may not infringe at all, not

even by law. Since this interpretation includes already all the restrictions which the liberal would be willing to accept as possibly compatible with the term freedom, he cannot see any sense in the added words "within the state" of the Fascist definition. To discover its meaning he would have to approach it from Fascist premises. Only when we start out with the state as basic unit and relegate, in our analysis, the individual to his role as an "organic part" of this unit, can we possibly perceive how he may be called "free within the state." His is the freedom of the cell to fulfill its organic functions. The cell is free to do whatever it can want—*but it cannot want* anything not desired by the whole organism. As soon as we realize this—though we may have to turn a logical somersault for the purpose—Mussolini's definition does make sense. We have only to interpret it in connection with his preceding sentence: "Fascism is for the state—and for the individual *insofar as he coincides with the state.*" As far as in these words Fascism is "for him," the individual is free. He is free "within the Fascist state"—which phrase, as the entire state is organically conceived, can also be understood neither locally, nor legally, nor ideologically—only biologically.[1]

---

[1] What makes this so difficult for us to comprehend is that again our terminology is inadequate. It is useless to discuss freedom of the individual, as we understand it, in a system *that does not recognize the individual as a basic social unit.* Essentially, the freedom of a social cell and that of a social unit are not comparable. They cannot be thought of in the same terms. Only our indiscriminate use of the *word* freedom, while mentally restricting its *meaning* to a conception which has no validity outside of the individualist

Actually Fascism—this will sound like heresy but is really the key to the whole problem—does not restrict the *freedom* of the individual at all. What it not only restricts but exterminates is his *individuality*. The difference between the limits of liberty as conceived by individualists and by collectivists is not one of degree but one of substance. The collectivist cannot understand how people can talk about a state as restricting the freedom of the individual—when it is so crystal clear, in his mind, that the idea of a free individual disconnected from the state is devoid of any even potential meaning. To him it does not make sense to talk about individual liberty—since individuals, in practice, are so evidently unable to pursue any other course of action than that of the community to which they belong. John Smith, human unit, consists of millions of protoplasmic cells. He could resolve to grant them any degree of individual liberty and it would not mean a thing—because they are essentially nothing but parts of John Smith and committed to share his fate as well as his actions for better or worse. They can refuse to do their part. In that case John gets sick and has to apply medical or surgical treatment, till the mutineers are either working again or cut loose from his body. But no amount of theory can make them susceptible of "individual freedom," because their organic connection with the whole is such that they would be materially incapable of exercising it.

frame of mind, kept us from realizing what the collectivists mean by "liberty within the state." It makes sense all right—only not the sense we are accustomed to.

Of course one might say that the democratic state, which in this view represents individualism, is also in speech and writing continually compared to a living organism. The difference is that—whether we believe it or not—*the collectivists take the comparison seriously.* The source of almost all our misunderstandings is our failure to realize that to them this metaphor is not a figure of speech but an exact picture of their own relation to their community. It may facilitate the acceptance of this psychological phenomenon to remember a few things about our own arguments with the non-Fascist variety of collectivists. What does the intelligent Communist invariably retort to the charge that Communism destroys liberty? That the average man in a modern community cannot be individually free *whatever* its political constitution; that the overwhelming majority have only the choice between accepting as their superior the socialist community of which they themselves are parts, or finance capital to which they are only objects of exploitation; that for the masses freedom today is only possible collectively—as freedom of the group into which the individuals voluntarily submerge themselves. Mutatis mutandis, the Fascist thesis is exactly the same. The Fascist admits of only two alternatives for the individual: he can either become an organic part of a disciplined but collectively free national community—or he can be duped into believing himself a participant in a scheme of popular sovereignty while in reality a few powerful groups and professional politicians are "playing him for a sucker." To Fascists as well as Communists, individual freedom means nothing because they cannot conceive of a possibility of realizing it in practice in a healthy community. Their definition of democracy is "organized contrariness." A state in which liberty for the individual had actually materialized, is as inconceivable to them as an organism whose every cell, instead of functioning in concert with the others, could walk off in a manner and direction determined by its individual license. Obviously, such an organism could not live. Neither, in the opinion of the collectivists, could such a community.[2] They never think of the individual as restricted by the state, but they are constantly aware of the limitations inherent in the very conception of the individual. Human beings, as social cells, are free to do their part. They are free to act according to their personal judgment or desire in whatever the group inferentially, by not taking an active interest itself, refers to them. There, too, they can always act only as parts of the group and its interest must guide them—but they are to act on their own because the group prefers to get a particular kind of thing done by relying on the individual initiative of its components rather than on its own collective action. As soon as the group *does* take a hand

[2] That is why the Fascists have for every democracy either contempt as for a weakling, or open or concealed disbelief in the reality of its democratic nature. The latter attitude, for instance, was behind the reproachful skepticism with which the Germans used to greet official disclaimers of responsibility for the anti-Nazi polemics of the American press—it was quite impossible for them to believe that the government of the unquestionably powerful United States should be unable to control its own newspapers.

in any field, however, there can be no more freedom for
the individual to take a different interest. His freedom
is not restricted but becomes illusory by the very nature
of things. A liberty of action for individuals regardless
of the stand of the community is from the collectivist
point of view a logical impossibility, a pipe dream that,
in the language of Mussolini, "cannot seriously be considered."

Once we have digested this, we can hardly fail to see
the "freedom of the individual within the state" in a
new and convincing light. From here on the going is
easier—because the same logic, which controls the moral
principle of the Fascist individual-state relationship,
will also enlighten us about what translates it into practice: *Fascist government.*

What is government? Traditionally it means the handling of state affairs—according to state principles. The
democratic community, for example, is held to be established by its individual members for the purpose of
benefiting them, principally by providing a protection
of their interests which they could not effect singly.
Danger threatens these individual interests from three
possible sources: (a) from outside—to be dealt with by
the state's armed forces and international policy (including tariffs, etc.); (b) from unsocial individuals
within the group—to be dealt with by the body of the
civil and criminal law; and (c) from the state itself,
whose powers, although given to it "by consent of the
governed," can so easily be used against them. This last
menace led to the world-wide adoption of a principle

worked out while European absolutism reached its peak: the separation of powers. The idea is to keep the authority, which is delegated to the state for definite purposes, within definite bounds by making the state perform its business in three departments. An elective legislature translates the wishes of the individuals—the real masters of the state—into communal policy. An elective or appointive executive branch carries it out. And an elective or appointive judiciary acts as controlling device—supervising the adherence of the second branch to the directions of the first, and often also of the first to the fundamental principles of the system, whether axiomatic or expressed in some sort of "basic law" or state constitution.

That a Fascist state could have no use for this type of structure is obvious. Since it is conceived as an indivisible unit, the dogmatic purpose of the separation of powers—to prevent the association from disfranchising its composing units—is meaningless. Neither could the principle be helpful in governmental practice. Fascist communal policy—the collective will—is determined by an a priori authority; a Fascist leader is the head of his government, not a branch of it. That disposes of one of the three departments. Judicial supervision of any governmental activity also becomes a dogmatic impossibility: observance of the leader-made law by inferior administrative agencies is enforced by Fascist discipline, and protection of the individual community member against state action is a democratic anachronism incompatible with the very foundation of Fascist doctrine. The judiciary, therefore, in the Fascist state found its functions reduced to virtual identity with those of the administrative branch: to enforce and effectuate, among the members of the community, the collective will as proclaimed from above. From an independent arm of state power, the courts turned into agencies of administration—and, with law-making removed into the metaphysical realm of leadership, Fascist government as a whole became a unified administrative structure with the function of insuring and regulating the compliance of individuals with the requirements of the collective interest.

The courts, ministries, commissions, agencies and other bureaus of officialdom together form the means employed to make Fascism a reality at home. Thus the governmental set-up exemplifies better than anything else what German and Italian political scientists called the "tripartite structure" of every aspect of a Fascist state: Leader, "will-bearer," and people. In every field the will of the higher organism is laid down by the Leader, followed by the people, and "borne" by a conducting organ. In politics that organ is the Party, in international conflict the army, in the "battles of bread and production" the respective economic institutions, and in everyday regulation of internal affairs the governmental machinery. Like the other "will-bearers," government is only a weapon in the hand of the collective body, to guard its interests and to assert its power in a particular field of action. As the Corporate State aims at economic welfare, the army at the effectuation of international purposes, and the Party at the spiritual conformity of community members, so government aims at their conformity in fact.

Hand in hand with this re-orientation of the *concept* of government had to go a fundamental change in the standard according to which it is carried on. This standard—the precepts by which courts and administrative agencies are guided in the discharge of their duties— is "the law" of a community. Of course, no modern government could function without any such fixed set of rules to adhere to; and Fascist administrative agencies proceed by no means less according to law than those of a democracy. But—their law not only differs from ours in substance; it is a matter of entirely different import.

Individualist law, viewed as a whole, *is a sum of restrictions which the people*, by application of the majority principle, *impose upon their freedom*—restrictions which are themselves restricted and, if need be, supplemented by certain "praeter-legal" rights of the individuals, whether constitutionally guaranteed or implied from the essence of the democratic system. In Fascism the state is supreme and, as we have seen, swallows the freedom of its individual members by its very conceptions. Logically, therefore, *Fascist law* can only consist of *restrictions which the community*, through the mouth of its leader, *imposes upon itself*—and which in turn are always restricted and supplemented by the *Fascist* "higher law," the communal interest. Under Fascism the individuals to whom the law is addressed are really not

the objects of its substance. The collectivist principle
controls them much more completely and effectively than
any law could. So the laws of a Fascist state are simply
rules by which the state declares itself willing to abide
in its governmental actions. And it *is* bound by them—
until they are repealed, or conflict with the *state's*
praeter-legal right, the collective will and interest, which
is paramount and nullifies impeding rules even if the
state itself has proclaimed them.

What this change in the conception of the law means
for the citizenry is perfectly obvious. In the democratic
community, the individual is subject to the law, which,
however, is not allowed to infringe upon his specially
protected rights. In other words, *the law signifies the
worst that democratic communities can do to their single
members*. In the Fascist state the relation is reversed.
The individual is bound and restricted anyway, by virtue
of the fact that he is a member of the collective body,
to the behavior pattern required by the communal interest and its many synonyms, like "Fascist spirit," "sound
popular feeling," and such. The law, in this relationship,
marks the extent *beyond* which the community—always
without prejudice to its all-overruling interest—has
pledged itself not to enforce its claims: *in Fascism the
significance of the law to the individual is that its observance is the* LEAST *the state will exact from him!* [3] He

[3] This is most strikingly illustrated by the different development,
under the two systems, of the criminal law. In democratic countries its basic maxim has always been "nulla poena sine lege"—no
punishment without previously enacted law to cover the crime.
Over and above that, however, the individual always had a claim

will have to keep within the law as a matter of course; it marks his evident duty toward the state. But not his only one; for, just as in individualist law the praeter-legal—constitutional or "unalienably human"—right of the individual takes precedence over the letter of the law, so in Fascist law does the authoritatively determined collective purpose. If, in any practical instance, this purpose should require anything at variance with or even opposite to the law, the higher unit must nevertheless be served. The law, which is nothing but a standard of normalcy to regulate the universal service to the common interest, can of course not be allowed to work against this interest. If we may be permitted one more relapse into the Mussolinian: "the objective will of the

to the protection of those rights of his which were beyond the jurisdiction of the communal law—for example, to be properly tried by a jury—whether they were expressed by some authority with power to bind the law, or only inferred from the bases of democratic thinking. His freedom could in no other way be interfered with than as the law prescribed—and even then only if he could not successfully invoke any of his *praeter-legal* privileges. Under Fascism, where the criminal law, like any law, can have no other purpose than to protect the collective body, the logical basic maxim became "nullum crimen sine poena"—no crime which will not be punished, whether the law especially provides punishment or not. If the law does not so provide—if, as the legal phrase goes, there is a "gap in the law"—the collective interest which has been violated by the offense steps in and demands atonement, and there is no individual right which the offender could hold against it. Every criminal running afoul of an express prohibition will be punished, but the rights of the state do not end with punishing *law*breakers. The community is entitled to whatever may seem necessary to the protection of its *interest*—of which observance of the law, as it stands, is only one of the more elementary requirements.

personality of a higher order" makes the law, supplements it, and if any conflict should occur, supersedes it.

Practice, in every Fascist country, soon underlined the distinction. They all found it feasible at an early stage to separate the enforcement of the higher law from enforcement of the regular everyday law over which the other was to take precedence. The result was the emergence of the O.V.R.A. in Italy and of the Gestapo in Germany [4]—organizations with the distinct purpose of uncovering and handling such violations of state interest as are *not* violations of ordinary law, and therefore not under the jurisdiction of the regular agencies of law enforcement. Democratic observers usually wax indignant at the fact that these institutions are so vastly more powerful than any ordinary democratic secret police. Their criticism rests on a complete misapprehension. The democratic secret police is simply a secretly operating branch of the regular police force—with no other task than that of the main body: to enforce the law. But the Fascist political police is an institution expressly designed to enforce that part of the collective interest which is *not* law—and with which, consequently, the regular police has nothing to do. That there is much overlapping—for example, that cases taken up by the political police may also constitute violations of ordi-

[4] In Russia the early revision of the entire Penal Law on a basis of "social defense" served to obscure not only the essential distinction between the definite norms of everyday administration and the blanket provisions guarding the proletarian revolution as such—but also the specific function of the OGPU, so that it came to appear as something like a super-police.

nary law and, if so, will often be disposed of as such—must not obscure the fact that essentially there are two entirely different realms of action. One is the enforcement of the law, in cases where there is no praeter-legal communal interest involved, with the procedure of police investigation, prosecution, trial, and sentence, if guilty, to the punishment prescribed by law. The other field is the enforcement of vital communal interests, regardless of what the position of the law may be in a particular instance. There the case, from beginning to end, is in the hands of the political agency; since the idea is to protect the state, little thought is given to protection of the individuals involved—and their treatment is determined not by any fixed standard, legal or otherwise, but by the needs of the situation.[5] The procedure, as well as the administrative purpose behind it, is entirely in a class by itself. Naturally it does not measure up to the procedural requirements with which democracy seeks to make the citizen safe from oppressive measures—for the simple reason that the process serves a totally different purpose. As the snake-bite victim cares little, in cauterizing his wound, if he kills thousands of healthy cells along with the poisoned ones, so the imperiled Fascist state is not concerned with the safety of its citizens, if its own vital interests are at stake. The Fascist community

[5] That considerations of prophylaxis have in most cases led to similar solutions—the concentration camp in Germany, the confino in Italy, the deportation to Arkhangelsk and Siberia in the U.S.S.R.—does not alter the fact that on principle this type of agency is bound by no rule whatever, and free to act entirely as it deems expedient in a given situation.

is interested only in its own safety. This view, which sounds extremely tyrannical to us, sounds entirely normal to people with a collectivist mentality. We, noticing many instances of state disregard for the legality of a situation, fell into the habit of talking about the "lawless despotism" of the collectivist countries. To Fascists, however, these are simply cases of safeguarding a higher interest at the cost of a lower one. They, in turn, speak with contempt of democratic judicial procedure, where an individual, by exploiting his "legal rights," may escape punishment, though he has done irreparable damage to the community. For a state to permit its law to become a possible accessory of crime, is in Fascist eyes the height of "lawlessness"—while closing legal gaps with communal policy is only a logical step in making the legal system serve its practical purpose.

Moreover, the interest of the Fascist state not only supplements and, if necessary, supersedes its law—it must even rule the law where it prevails. This, too, is nothing but a reversal of democratic practice. Every lawyer can see daily how our law, even where no constitutional privileges of the individual are involved, is filled to the brim with individualism. If possible, for instance, our courts will interpret a private contract of doubtful legality so as to let it become effective. Why? Because it is felt that by making a promise each party has created the substance of a legal obligation even though a lack of formal requirements should make it invalid under the circumstances—in other words, that a contract between individuals represents a kind of individual-made law and is not *essentially* different from our law as a whole. And not only our courts incline to this view—we ourselves think always of the law as the manifest warrant of our sovereign rights rather than as the demarcation of our organic functions. Again, we are so engrossed in our notion, that even serious legal thinkers fail to recognize in it a somewhat naïve way of considering our individual humanity supreme over the universe. Again, the Fascists have to show us how a legal system can work the other way around: in *their* Weltanschauung the law—created by the state and construed as a sum of restrictions imposed, for practical reasons, by the state itself on its inherent power—must in every instance and in every aspect of its application *serve the state.* The "objective will" that makes it law must also rule its operation. We have seen that if Fascist law should ever tend to contradict Fascist authority, there is neither cause nor need to wait for formal amendment: the law has legal force only insofar as it expresses the communal will. And if, on the other hand, customary interpretation should vary from the legal purpose, there is no need to mark its overruling: it is equally fundamental that law can only be *applied* in the sense willed by the higher unit.

Thus when German judges adjudicate today "in National Socialist spirit," to the extent of twisting the letter of existing precepts, this is no mere subservience to a political upheaval but an earnest and sincere fulfillment of judicial duty as it is now conceived. In Italy, a practically-minded people brought about this change in administrative and judicial practice without much ado. In Germany, where pre-Fascist legal ideas had penetrated deeply into the official mentality, and where dogmatic issues had always been taken much more seriously than elsewhere, the change took place only with a good deal of theoretical commotion. But it did take place—and the vast majority of the highly conscientious and professionally proud German civil servants adjusted themselves to the new doctrine with surprising ease. Which proves not only that it must have appealed to some emotional chord, but also that it cannot have struck them as so "unjust" and arbitrary as it strikes us. As a matter of fact, what we call "misapplying the law," to the Fascist simply means applying it in accordance with the principles that made it law. As a great German jurist put it: "the will of the state is the soul of the law." The will of the state is incontrovertibly expressed by its leadership—and any opposing legal concept would be "dead," a scrap of paper bereft of the energy that transformed it into an active force.

The main objection voiced by democratic critics against this way of legal thinking is that it contravenes our idea of the citizens' "equality before law." This principle, which under democracy has stood firm for centuries in the face of every class and social differentiation, is a moral postulate very dear to the liberal heart. We are pleased to think that it gives us "absolute justice"—though in fact, of course, it is nothing but the subjective justice of a mass of democratic individuals. Later, in considering the difference between the democratic and the Fascist idea of science, we shall see how, philosophically, the very basis of all individualism tends to vitiate *any* absolute concept: by placing all values— truth, beauty, happiness, justice—on the subjective plane of personal reaction rather than on a pedestal of objectivity. And yet we insist on pursuing absolute values, especially absolute justice. We cherish it as an ideal— although we know perfectly well that even in theory it can never be anything but the expression of what a particular group of human beings feels to be "right" at a particular time. Now this is exactly what the Fascists maintain also. But they refuse to pursue even as an ideal the illusion of a justice independent from the group administering it. They admit frankly that their law cannot be "absolutely" just. Its justice is avowedly a subjective justice based upon the communal interest. From the point of view of the individuals, of course, this means that the inevitably unequal importance to the community of its various members will put some into a more favorable legal position than others. We, considering the individuals as basic units, feel that this negates equality before law. Fascists, however, are unable to separate law from communal function—from their purely communal point of view the legal discrimination against a worthless community member is a necessary corrective to make for real equality before law instead of for an individualistically distorted one.

There is no better illustration of this difference in outlook than the aftermath of the German Reichstag fire trial. In Germany the fact that Communists—avowed enemies of the state—could be acquitted of treason (which, after all, is nothing but applied enmity to the state!) solely because they were not found guilty of specific acts charged in the indictment, called forth such a storm of popular indignation that this condition had to be rectified at once by creating the "People's Court" as a tribunal for the defense of the state not hamstrung by such individualistic technicalities. It has been charged that the protests against the Reichstag fire verdict were manufactured by the Nazis. This is perfectly true, but does it mean anything? If by "Nazis" is meant the National Socialist Party—it was its essential function to express and stir the reactions which leadership proclaimed to be those of the collective unit. Furthermore, if it was not clear at that time that one cannot draw a line between "German" and "Nazi" viewpoints, it should be clear now; and, as if to prove that, the People's Court was then and is now accepted throughout Germany as something entirely normal and definitely in line with a desirable administration of justice. There were voices against its severity—to about the same extent that Americans will protest against their courts and law whenever a crooked financier or a big shot racketeer slips through some kind of legal loop-hole. In both cases the prevailing system is criticized for abuses, but nevertheless felt, by a vast majority of the people in either country, to stand for justice as they want it handled.

Our other objection to the Fascist view is that it destroys the "certainty" which we consider the main characteristic of "good" law: that the individual, at any time, can know exactly where he stands.[6] That argument does not impress the Fascist either. First, he cannot value the legal security of the single individual highly enough to let it take precedence, on principle, over the security of the state. Second—and this is the important point—since the individual is an "integral" part of the community, he is *presumed to know,* to feel, to participate in the collective will. The *individual Fascist is not supposed to have a different will from that of the community.* For *that* reason every deviation, whether covered by a legal text or not, can be held against him. This is the final and most consistent conclusion from the "organic conception of the state"—and it is the basis of the Fascists' entire "lawlessness." We feel they are putting the individual at the mercy of an arbitrary despotism. And they feel they are freeing the group from individualist disruption. In their view, *our* law—static, bound to the past, apt to lag behind changes in popular sentiment—would arbitrarily impede the flow of collective consciousness. They will deny indignantly that justice might better be served by democratic law. To men who do believe in their essential molecularity, the "dynamic" Fascist law is as "just"— that is, as expressive of their personal feelings about right and wrong—as our "certain" law is to us. Again, law or no law, the basic issue is purely a choice in values between the state and the individuals composing it.

[6] Which, by the way, is a rather weak point to be made by Anglo-Americans, whose Common Law has so often been assailed on the very grounds of its comparative uncertainty!

Only after such a complete re-adjustment of terminology as we have now outlined in this chapter, is it possible really to consider the crucial question of Fascist
government: *how much* of the "lawless despotism," of
the undesirable features familiar from recent German
and Italian history, *is inherent in Fascism*—and how
much is only accidental, or determined by not generally
Fascist but specifically national traits of those countries?
(What makes the question crucial, of course, is that the
answer to it also implies how much truth can *possibly*
be attributed to the emphatic disavowals by Fascist
propaganda in non-Fascist countries—"here it would be
different," etc.) We know that in any Fascism two elements must be accepted as a priori: the unit and its
authority. That the Fascist individual is, and is nothing
but, an integrated part of a given collective body, to be
thought of neither as an independent entity nor as part
of any different group within or outside of that body;
and that the will of the unit is determined and pronounced by a given source and in no other way—*these
are given facts* which, in Fascist eyes, need no justification and are not open to questioning. And before em-
barking on any dialectic or analytical crusades *we must
realize that there is no point in questioning these facts*—
that they represent irrational preconceptions, beyond
proof or argument. In our mind the communal relationship stands for one thing, in the Fascist mind for another; both conceptions are group-psychological axioms
unsusceptible of effective rationalization. But if we accept the Fascist concept as basis of our investigation, and

try to interpret problems of the day in Fascist terms instead of in the democratic terms to which we are accustomed, those axioms will not only reveal the marks that distinguish a Fascist community—they will yield principles from which no Fascist community can depart.

The collectivist conception and application of law is the first such generality. It may not be expressly proclaimed, it may even be officially denied (although a Fascist government, authoritative on principle, is unlikely to pretend to be controlled by individualist norms). But in a really Fascist state—that is to say, in a state based on a genuine, not a forced or imaginary subordination of individual to group interests—the Fascist concept of law is bound to break through any camouflage. To whatever rules the system may promise to defer, a member of a Fascist community must always expect the communal spirit, will, and interest, in the form proclaimed by the a priori authority, to take precedence over any fixed standard. This, as has been pointed out before, does not affect the equal applicability of the law, as Fascism conceives it, to every single citizen. In fact, the citizen who is a real Fascist will not even notice any "outside" influence upon the law—his personality will be so integrated into the collective consciousness, that no law will fit the latter without also expressing his own wishes and ideas. Only individuals who are not thus mentally gleichgeschaltet—cells who refuse to do their part—will have no "objective" law to protect them in their non-conformity. The state will not maintain for them a legal haven in which Fascist purposes, conceptions, ideology and Weltanschauung do not prevail.

In legal routine, as has been shown by German and Italian experience, there will be little change. Where formerly a lawyer tried to convince a judge that his client's prayer ought to be granted for reasons of law, he will now try to convince him that it ought to be granted because of national interest, or Fascist principles, as the case may be. Chances in litigation will remain as predictable as the turn of a roulette wheel—just as was the case under democracy. As a whole, the mills of the law will grind in pretty much the same fashion—except where the fundamental issue plays a part: where individual interests are really pitted against collective interests. Even in such cases the difference in practice will not always be one of eventual outcome. If a democratic community wants to infringe upon individual privileges, and wants to do it badly enough, it does not lack ways to achieve its objective. Nor, if it is a real majority objective, is that something to find fault with even according to the strictest individualist doctrine. What distinguishes the Fascist method, is the purpose and intent of the procedure. Democratic communities wishing to enforce their will against obstructing individual rights, can be compelled to establish—in objective tests specifically designed to prevent the instruments from usurping original power—their intentions as the product of orderly process by majority rule. Fascist authority, on the other hand, proclaims its will—and obstructing rights are *conceptually* removed. It does not matter whether they are claimed by majorities, minorities, or single individuals. If, in any yet-to-be-created Fascist state, the leadership should make a practice of submitting to court decisions as does a democratic government, even that would not mean a recognition of inherent rights of the individuals (theirs because they are conceived as the group's masters). It could only be a governmental bounty, freely retractable. Reduced to simplest terms, it is the practical effect of the Fascist legal outlook upon the average individual, that *in no conceivable Fascist structure can a citizen ever* COUNT *on any of his personal interests to carry weight against communal purpose.* It is the *formal* security of the democratic legal order which Fascists will never know, because with them, law—the rule under which government works—is not, as in democratic doctrine, a means of holding the state to its function of serving the people; *Fascist law is a means of regulating the people's function of serving the state.*

In considering the need for terminological adjustment, we have already found indications of how this reorientation will affect the various possible points of issue between state and citizens. The structural principle of democracy is individual freedom. It is to be preserved for the people, unless its surrender should be necessary for the specific purposes for which they entered into the communal association. Under Fascism, we have seen that individual freedom is conceptually qualified by addition of the words "within the state," and we have also seen what "liberty within the state" means. Thus, with regard to all kinds of "personal rights," questions about the possibility of variations of Fascist practice can unhesitatingly be answered in the negative. In *any* Fascist state, all "civil liberties"—such as freedom of speech, of the press, of peaceful assembly, the right to strike, to be tried by a jury, to be secure from unreasonable searches and seizures—*can* hold good only "within the state," that is to say, as long as they are found in accord with the authoritatively proclaimed collective interest. (This would apply to the humane Fascist states heralded by Lawrence Dennis and Oswald Mosley as well as to Germany and Italy.) And what goes for big rights, goes equally for little rights: a Fascist government might uphold acts which are apparently most un-Fascist if they happen to be in line with its own immediate intentions,[7] but no right will ever be so inalienable nor so insignificant that it will not be summarily withdrawn if Fascist leadership should deem its exercise potentially detrimental.[8] As a rule, the amount of leeway granted

[7] For example: it will surprise many readers to find the *right to strike* included amongst the conceivable instances of "liberty within the state"—it being the general impression that abolition, once and for all, of this particular right of labor is of the essence of Fascism. It may be interesting to note, therefore, that in 1925— *after* the establishment of the totalitarian state!—Mussolini's Workers' Syndicates called a strike in the metal industry, for which a most earnest distinction from ordinary strikes was claimed by the Fascist Grand Council, namely, that it had been called for "definite objectives." The sole objective, of course, was to whip an obstreperous industry into line at a time when Italy was not, as yet, so "fascized" as to make Big Business kow-tow to any hint from the Palazzo Venezia.

[8] It is at this point that the Fascists will argue that democracy, in actual practice, also often suspends fundamental liberties. The difference, as pointed out in our first chapter, is not that the Fas-

by the state to individual choice and initiative will vary in proportion to the security and prosperity of a Fascist country. National stress and peril will always require a stricter discipline than prevailing normalcy. But what rights, at one time or other, the state will extend or curtail, can never be told in advance—because that depends not on conditions only, but on personalities as well. An activity quite harmless in the average man (or in the opinion of one Fascist leader) might become a major threat if taken up by particular individuals (or in the realm of another Fascist leader). It is safe to say that as a consequence of the very structure of a Fascist state *no activity whatever can be considered wholly immune from governmental interference.* The zone of regimentation covers the most intimate fields—a person may be prevented from whistling in his own bathtub if he should happen to whistle the wrong tune. The elimination of the entire "private sphere," the collectivization of life, through and through, as a matter of principle, makes the existence of anything, which a man might *do under any circumstances,* dogmatically impossible.

In one sphere the effects of Fascist rule gave rise to much wonder and dissension: *freedom of religion.* The wonder was due to the fact—apparent at an early stage —that the Fascists have an innate sympathy for the anti-materialist and anti-individualist tendencies to be found in every religious movement. The Nazis, for instance,

cist protestations of emergency are always hypocritical (although they often are, of course) but that Fascism has *built a system* on methods which democracy, on principle, strives to avoid.

have always been inclined to consider themselves defenders of the faith, and are quite indignant at the failure of the Christian churches to be properly grateful for
their help against the "common enemy": Bolshevik athe-
ism. On paper, furthermore, all our present Fascist governments approve strongly of rendering unto God the
things which are God's, as long as people render unto
Caesar the things that are Caesar's. In Italy, where the
régime got along with the Church, as well as in Germany, where it did not, the official attitude has always
been that restrictive policies were aimed only at ecclesiastical interference in secular affairs, and by no means
at religious freedom as such.

However, a somewhat closer inspection of the issues
involved will reveal that this attitude, which may be quite
sincere, is nevertheless not quite realistic. One can ignore the sporadic outbursts of German neo-paganism.
Its importance is generally overestimated because of its
relative strength among Hitler's personal praetorian
guard; it is tolerated, paradoxically, in the name of the
very freedom which its spread is said to endanger; and,
at any rate, it only wants to set up a new religion of its
own, and has been up to now comparatively tolerant of
other creeds. What matters is that the above-quoted
official Fascist attitude is illogical and contradictory in
itself. For as soon as Man's relation to his Creator over-
steps the bounds of individual piety to become the common faith of a group, it invades the Fascist state's monopoly on collective consciousness. The Fascists dis-
avow, quite honestly, every intention of coming between

an individual—or even a number of individuals—and
the Deity. On the strength of that, they claim to uphold
religious freedom. But religion is more than the fear of
God on the part of unrelated individuals: it is a common
bond between men of the same faith. And this common
bond cannot but prove an ever-disturbing influence in
the Fascist state. Fascism does not object to the *allegiance*
which an individual gives to any Divine Being he
may choose. Fascism does believe in the freedom of men
to worship Jesus Christ, Mohammed, or Huitzilopochtli.
What it objects to, is that religious communities, by
creating in their members a sense of solidarity as worshipers of a common God, destroy the exclusiveness of
their sense of solidarity as citizens of a common state.
To prevent—entirely without anti-religious malice—this
infraction of fundamentals of the secular community,
Fascism will always have to be suspicious not only of
political, educational or charitable activities on the part
of any creed, but also of its every attempt to build
among its adherents the common consciousness which *is*
religion. There are only two ways to make a religious
community really fit into the Fascist scheme: either as a
state church (which was the aim of the National Socialist policies responsible for today's famous disputes) or
as a monopolistic or all but monopolistic denomination
(like Roman Catholicism in Italy). A church of either
kind could conform to basic Fascist concepts. But no
other one can possibly avoid implying an anathema to
Fascism: the existence of a self-conscious collective body
neither coinciding with the Fascist state nor developed

within its framework. Every other church, or sect, or private religious group, will always constitute a threat, not to trifling political objectives, but to the most vital concern of Fascism—the unity of the nation. Thus, a Fascist state's professed religious tolerance will always have to be subject to qualifications—the more stringent in that they are not arbitrary but dogmatically essential. The sincerity of official protestations of respect for it need not be questioned—but, as a matter of policy, logic seems to place religious worship under Fascism on the same level with all other human activity: free insofar as it coincides with the state.

Fascism makes freedom, in our sense of absolute liberty of individual action, disappear as a conception. It substitutes for it a collective freedom, with the citizen free to fulfill his functions, to pursue the path cut out for him by a superior will. What this principle of communal organization—which the Fascists call "liberty within the state"—would connote in practice to the individualist mind, is expressed by a perfectly good word in our democratic vocabulary: "conscription." From the point of view of the single human being, that word describes the essence of a kind of relationship where men are drafted into the service of the state when- and wherever common interests should need promotion. Conscription as a principle of social organization is the individualist translation of "liberty within the state."

As a state measure, conscription has a definitely collectivist character. It is no accident that the field we think of primarily in connection with the term, is the military

one—of necessity dominated by collectivist notions. An
army is a concept inevitably absorbing the individuals
who make it up; it is the very prototype of collectivism
—one organization which, as such, *cannot* be construed
in individualist terms. And an army's idea of what it is
fighting *for*, is also likely to be the abstract concept of
its nation rather than the majority-ruled sum of the
non-combatant citizens. And yet, in no major democratic
country has even military conscription been accepted
wholly and with all its psychological implications. Britain and America have stood by voluntary enlistment,
except in war-time. In France conscription was introduced in the fighting days of the First Republic, and has
since been abolished repeatedly, only to be re-established again and again under pressure of international
affairs. Today it is accepted by the average Frenchman
as a most unwelcome necessity; as a surrender of rights
by the individual for his own good, forced by adverse
circumstances, and not without lodging a most emphatic
protest on principle. In none of the three democracies
did compulsory military service ever occur to the population as a natural expression of their being members
of the state—as not a duty but a sacred *right* of citizenship.

For Fascism, however, to employ universal conscription for the maintenance of its armed forces was a
matter of course. Nothing short of that could have satisfied either its basic psychology or its structural logic.
This is so, quite irrespective of the method's actual military value—which, in fact, is very questionable. In the

opinion of most experts, future belligerents will do best
to rely on (a) air, motorized or other technical corps
which are necessarily restricted in numbers, and (b) on
comparatively small and therefore highly mobile units
of picked and specially trained men. From this point of
view, mass armies as used in the World War could at
best be cannon fodder—at worst, however, they could
seriously impede the mobility which is now considered
essential. For example, when Hitler came to power, he
inherited not a conscript army, like Mussolini, but the
Reichswehr of the German Republic, generally regarded
as a superbly effective fighting force, and but for its
lack of modern arms as a match for any Western or
Central European army. It seems to be agreed among
today's leading military theorists that an increase of
this nucleus of one hundred thousand men, to about half
a million professional soldiers with adequate equipment,
would have made a force incomparably superior, from
a purely military point of view, to the present German
army of one million three hundred thousand two-year
conscripts—which has to be constantly trained all over
again and which, after discharge, cannot possibly remain in the physical and technical trim required of
first-class modern soldiers. And yet Hitler, advised by
what is believed to be the professionally ablest General
Staff in the world, took the very first opportunity to
place Germany's armed forces on a basis of short-term
compulsory military service. His decision cannot have
been due to considerations of national independence,
because a large professional army would have been as

much a flouting of the Versailles Treaty, and as unmistakable an assertion of Germany's regained Wehrhoheit, as the conscript one. There was no conceivable reason for Hitler's choice except the Fascist principle of communal organization: the "liberty-within-the-state" idea that the collective military freedom should be shared by every member of the community.[9]

Of course it is common knowledge that the German people have always had a sentimental weakness for conscription. They loved it under the Emperors and they missed it under the Republic. But to attribute Hitler's act to this nation-wide sentiment would be to mistake just another symptom for the cause—as though one attributed that sentimental weakness itself to the justification so frequently put forward by German parents, that "it does the boys such a lot of good." Certainly it does, from their point of view—but argument, popular feeling, and governmental policy all express and substantiate the same thing: the consciousness of the "organic relationship," the existing mentality on which the whole Fascist system is founded. Economic advantages, too—visions of unemployment statistics improving rap-

[9] The effacement of our notion that the function of an army is the defense of "the folks back home," became most obvious in the new German Defense Act's failure to set even an age limit to liability to military conscription! This omission—hailed by Nazi spokesmen for the quite correct reason that it "would have appeared unbearable to the individualistic thought of the past"— shows more clearly than anything else the difference between the concept of sovereign individuals taking upon themselves a clearly defined obligation, and that of "parts in essence" being, in the nature of things, at the disposal of the whole.

idly with the absorption of entire classes—are something which must have pleased the German government enormously. And, by the way, Hitler's more recent decision to extend the service period from one to two years— motivated by a very unreal Russian threat—may well, in fact, have been caused by a simple aversion to letting the number of jobless swell again at an economically critical moment. But that was an administrative measure, not a fundamental change like the restoration of the service as such. As far as the latter is concerned, no economic consideration could have made Hitler exchange a highly effective military establishment for a possibly less effective one, if the change had not also been urgently required as a matter of National Socialist principle: because of the dogmatic need to put in place of the professional army—instrument to defend the civilian population—the "nation in arms," the militarized community whose every single individual stands ready for what may be required from him in preservation of the higher unit.

Even more than in the military realm—where, after all, conscription had been more or less familiar—the reversal of principle came to light in fields where freedom of individual action had always been proclaimed as fundamentally indispensable to the progress of civilization: labor, chiefly, and the arts and sciences.

As far as labor is concerned, the Marxist idea of Fascism as a capitalist anti-labor plot has unfortunately created a tremendous confusion, which for years now has made any rational discussion of the entire complex of questions well-nigh impossible. To get anything like a clear view, it is necessary to distinguish strictly between three entirely separate aspects of Fascism's relation to labor: first, the Fascist attitude toward labor as an economic factor; second, the Fascist attitude toward labor as a political element; third, the Fascist attitude toward labor as an object of administration. The first and second problems we have considered in the preceding chapter, in connection with the principles of a Fascist economy. We have seen how Fascism tries to fit labor into a comprehensive scheme of national economic organization. Seeking to determine the actual economic effects of this process upon labor's interests we have come to the conclusion that as a matter of actual result, under present conditions, Fascism will probably depress real wages; that as a matter of economic structure every Fascist state will insist on labor's thorough organization and on its representative equality with industry; and that as a matter of economic outlook Fascism is neither pro- nor anti-labor, but that its economic policies, variable to the extent of possibly imperiling the system's capitalist base, will always be determined solely by national interests—which method, of course, puts a heavy premium upon the ability of any group to tie its private economic interest to the national welfare. The second problem—the Fascist attitude toward labor's political representation—we have found to be a most controversial subject and full of surprises; nevertheless we did reach the conclusion that politically no less than economically the theory of an anti-labor bias *as a social principle* of Fascism appeared untenable on the premises of this investigation.[10] What we did find is that Fascism—in comparison with democracy—works to *enhance labor's importance in the social scheme,* and to *minimize the economic importance of the rewards* of labor. Keeping this in mind, we shall realize the point of what otherwise can hardly fail to lead to the gravest misconceptions: the National Socialist *conscription of labor.*

Fascist Germany and, to a lesser degree, Italy have always prided themselves on their establishment of the citizen's "right to work." In democratic countries this phrase is a somewhat shop-worn political slogan. In Italy, too, its significance was always largely academic. Industrial unemployment there was negligible even during the depression, and agricultural unemployment traditionally took care of itself. The economic crisis in Italy hit rural and non-industrial urban proletarian masses in a way to which, for centuries, they had been thoroughly accustomed. The acute problem was not to give work to men whom overdeveloped industry in a slump had cast adrift, but to nurse an incomplete industrialization along through a time of failing business.

---

[10] These premises, it may be well to recall at this point, we did not choose at random. They follow inevitably from the decision to accept as genuine, regardless of its unfamiliarity, the psychology on which the two known instances of Fascism have managed to thrive—a psychology reported and confirmed by most of our competent and disinterested observers, the course of which was again and again borne out by events, while all predictions based upon attempts to fit Fascism to our own psychology have been signal failures.

Since so many unemployed had never worked steadily anyway, there was no urgent need to provide more jobs than were readily available. Just as in the military field, therefore, the question of principle can only be investigated in Germany, where circumstances favored action —an action which, once it was taken at all, had to assume specifically Fascist forms.

Re-employment, the most important practical campaign promise of the National Socialists, remained a main concern of their régime. From the start, they worked through expansion and intensification of the existing, Bruening-created "voluntary labor service." While up to 1933 it had been something like the American CCC, under Hitler this institution—at first without a change in form and spirit, but merely by extension of its applicability—quickly became similar to our PWA, CWA, WPA: a public works organization available for state-wide and local projects, and big enough to absorb a really substantial portion of the unemployed. Abroad even this original labor service was often assailed as "forced labor." Actually, its sole coercive element—dropping men who would not take a labor service job, from the relief rolls—is an essential feature of any public works program, democratic as well as Fascist. It is an elementary rule that, once a community decides to handle its unemployment problem by means of public works instead of with a dole, the individual jobless can no longer choose the dole. As a matter of cold fact, the individualist resistance to "forced labor"—which made sense at times when work was plentiful and labor worth more than it could possibly be "forced" to accept—today in most cases simply tends to uphold the individual right to starve. Coming from Communists, whose entire political doctrine is based upon the conscription of individual labor for communal needs, the denunciation of coercive methods seems to be nothing short of hypocritical. Raised by liberal trade unionists, it is honest but silly; no state can possibly afford, in the long run, to apply to relief work standards of normal employment. The suspicion that the Nazis aimed at ousting men from well-paid jobs in order to force them to work for a trifle in labor camps, can be said today to be largely discounted. All reports agree that the labor corps were recruited exclusively from the ranks of the previously unemployed. And this seems substantiated by the fact elaborated on in our previous chapter, that the Hitler government used the strongest possible measures to prevent discharges of even the smallest number of workers. Whatever element of force was present in the labor service of 1933, really appears to be misleading. In its initial form this institution, like any democratic public works set-up, was nothing but the equivalent of a dole—a governmental method of taking care of the unemployed.

Soon, however, this method proved unsatisfactory to National Socialist ideology. Official acknowledgment of a duty of the state to look after its economically disabled citizens would inevitably undermine the self-sacrificial spirit of the people and would tend to make the state again a plaything of economic pressure groups like the old democracy. Of course, as a matter of actual policy, the German Fascist government recognized the necessity not only of feeding the unemployed, but of giving them a sense of security. The only thing to be avoided was the belief of the people that a governmental pledge of help was a basis of individual *rights* against the state. It was as a way out of this dilemma that Hitler developed the idea of turning the Recht auf Arbeit into an Arbeitspflicht, *to fulfill the promise of a right by establishing a "duty to work."* Neither the original program of the Nazi Party, nor even its campaign propaganda contained any reference to this novel feature. It grew out of two acute needs, one practical, the other dogmatic. It was the logical solution of the extremely puzzling question of how to promise work, in a way that would set people's minds at rest, without letting them derive a claim from the promise. Viewed in this way, the plan is a stroke of genius. It is no less so because it appears now as the obvious way to handle the problem of large-scale unemployment relief in a truly Fascist manner. Hitler simply applied "liberty within the state" to the work, the right to which he had promised to establish. The people would get work—but not in the liberalist way of the state satisfying individual claims. They would get work as communal function, work as a general duty to the state to be performed by all individual citizens. Thus evolved the German "labor duty," the first example, in a capitalist economy, of an open and consistent application of the conscriptionist principle in a non-military field.

To use this *compulsory labor service*—no longer affecting only the unemployed, but all members of the community—as a preparatory course for the National Socialist conscript army, was a rather obvious next step. It had the additional advantages of getting the new recruits of every class into good physical condition before they joined the colors, and of bringing youths of all social strata into an even more direct and intimate contact than the army provided. These were agreeable by-products—quite in line with Fascist ideas—and nothing more. A clear indication of that was the extension of Arbeitspflicht to girls, which is not yet generally enforced but has been announced and will no doubt be an accomplished fact before long. There the physical and social considerations could play no very important part, since the actual work to be got out of the girls is hardly considerable and, if anything, at odds with the Nazi principle of retiring women from active wage-earning. The reasons for the establishment of this feminine auxiliary of the labor service were purely practical and dogmatic: it provided an easy method of dealing with female unemployment (although so far little use has been made of it for that purpose) and it re-affirmed the principle that every member of the community is liable to be called into its service according to his capacity. Men for work and fighting, women for work only—their conscription for breeding purposes has been talked about but not yet approached in earnest. Unemployment was the circumstance which set the machinery in motion—Fascist doctrine produced the results.[11]

In other fields, in German and Italian practice, principles of conscription replaced principles of freedom without being incorporated in specific institutions. The Fascist press, for example, is not simply gagged like the papers of the eighteenth and nineteenth century police state, which could print what they pleased if the censor passed it. Nor is it state-monopolistic like the press of Communist Russia, which is owned, managed, and edited by the government itself. The Fascist press, in the last analysis, is a conscript press—made up of private newspapers whose function is not to disseminate information but to serve the community; "free within the state," they are essentially nothing but *individual mouthpieces of the communal will and purpose*. The same is true of radio and of the movies—the other two main factors active in the building of contemporary public opinion. To art and literature the rule is less strictly applied, since, for the present, their effect upon the common welfare is not equally significant. Writers and artists are not yet drafted—they are merely made "draftable." Though the state does not, as yet, directly call

[11] That Fascist Italy did not take up the labor service idea does not argue that it is not deeply rooted in Fascist ideology. As, under democracy, specific liberties will only become practical if the people want them, so Fascism will only practice conscription if the state wants it—in other words, if state interests promise to be served thereby. Conscription—our word for "liberty within the state"—expresses the trend of Fascist social organization, not an inflexible rule for Fascist practice in each or any particular field of human activity.

upon their services, their ancient freedom has been definitely enclosed within the collective consciousness—the principle has been repeatedly enunciated that their output is no more to reflect their individual state of mind or emotion but that of the communal body.

Application of this very principle created a strangely far-reaching stir in the world of *science*. Again, while the Italians had been content with the co-ordination required in actual practice, the dogmatic thoroughness of the Germans made them follow up the issue to a conclusion which aroused a heated antagonism: the elimination of "scientific objectivity." And herein lies a tale about the individualist mind. For even the most convinced theoretical democrat, shades of the past had always made it difficult to condemn, as prohibitive to greatness, the influence exerted by rulers or ruling classes upon arts and letters. Those fields, under pressure of historical experience, had been recognized as subjective—and the taste of the times as the only possible standard. In the realm of science, however, "objective truth" had more and more become one of the dearest fetishes of mankind; and belief in the possibility of its pursuit remained unshattered even when our own materialist philosophers declared all knowledge contingent upon individual sense-experience—and so, inevitably, subjective. From Descartes to Einstein, science itself has moved steadily toward the negation of the absolute—and almost in proportion popular sentiment has insisted on an absolute science. So strongly did we feel ourselves as basic and decisive units, "created equal," that we had no hesitation in calling "objective" our subjectivity as individuals. Now, on the basis of our own philosophy that nothing can be "absolutely objective," collectivism, eminently consistent, refused to accept the subjectivity of the individual as decisive, and insisted on substituting the subjectivity of *its* basic unit, the state. Whereupon liberals indignantly protested against the abandonment of an objectivity which, as a philosophic concept, they had never admitted! That Fascism must demand a state-centered science in place of our individual-centered one, is so obvious that it is hard to believe that anybody should have been really surprised by it. Scientific *methods* have nothing to do with this; their sole criterion is success, in either case. Fascists make airplanes with the help of physics and fertilizer with the help of chemistry just as we do. The point of view changes only the *goal of science*—which, of course, to some extent determines its means. While the purpose of our science is the discovery of individual truth, Fascist science aims at a collective one. Neither science, philosophically, can be objective—both are free; only ours is free from the point of view of the human being who is encouraged to search for the truth as he sees it, while Fascist science is free "within the state" and the single scientist, accordingly, is only free to search for the truth as the state sees it. The principle which, when the German doctrinaires announced it, called forth such an uproar in the scientific world, is nothing but the principle which guides Fascist practice in any field: that a Fascist individual can take no action save as part of the whole, and none that would not at any time be available for the communal purpose.

In conclusion, the outlook for the individual in a Fascist state can be summarized as follows:

1. His personal freedom of action, as understood and practiced by democracy, will disappear as a conception. What, in any field, he may be allowed or able to do by himself, he can do only because it suits the state, and only insofar as it suits the state.

2. He will participate in the state's collective freedom —that is to say, he will be drafted for all activities which, in the opinion of the state's authority, will be of advantage to the communal body.

3. The rule according to which he will be treated by the state—and the only such rule, any pronouncement from whatever source notwithstanding—is the state's authoritatively proclaimed will; and the only standard by which men or their activities will be measured is the state's authoritatively proclaimed interest. While "equality before the law" as such will be fully maintained, a decisive shift will occur in the structure of the law itself: its basis is no more the democratic axiom of the essential equality of all citizens, but the a priori existence of the Fascist community to which its members stand in relations of varying importance.

Beyond that, all the excesses and iniquities commonly attributed to the Fascist system of government are unessential. They can be traced either to given circumstances or peculiarities of administration, or to specific national characteristics of a people, which Fascism may emphasize without being in any way responsible for them. All such features, even those apparent in every known instance of Fascist rule, can be said to be avoidable. We may call them highly probable and even inevitable under certain conditions, but we weaken our own case by insisting that they will be present in any conceivable Fascist state or movement. It is entirely possible that somewhere Fascism may appear totally free from those particular faults; it is even possible that the existing Fascist nations may yet rid themselves of the one or the other. Shall we be forced then to consider them as no longer Fascist? If a totalitarian state should succeed in maintaining such rigid discipline as to exclude completely all Party graft or administrative brutality or minority persecution—should we have to hail it as an example of the kind of rule we approve of? In the opinion of the writer, the most serious mistake to be made in defense of democracy is the failure to distinguish clearly between traits that are essentially Fascist, and traits which, while often found under Fascism, are by no means necessary parts of the Fascist picture.

The first of such traits are those inherent not in Fascism but in a particular Fascist nation. Generally it can be said that Fascism will exaggerate nearly every distinctive quality of a people (except, of course, qualities inconsistent with Fascism as such). Germans, for example, have always been known to be thorough, dogmatic, and lacking in a sense of humor. And what were the main characteristics of the Nazi state? An orgy of

efficiency and organization, a terrifying dogmatization
of life, and the cheerful but completely humorless spirit
of the population. In Italy, the identical system of government was adopted by a naïve, uncomplicated and
eminently practical people. And it excelled in an emphasis on simple principles, in theoretical short-cuts expressing contempt for dogmatic consistency, and in a
marked preference for getting things done the easiest
way, whether "correct" or not. Inevitably, this Fascist
accentuation of national characteristics will affect unpleasant traits as well as pleasant or indifferent ones.
Thus many national faults were noticed only after a
totalitarian régime had made them prominent—and
were credited to the new system, while their roots, in
reality, were embedded in the respective popular psychology long before anybody ever thought of Fascism.

The outstanding example of such a development is
the case of Hitler and the Jews. Since 1933, anti-Semitism has often been described as a Fascist characteristic
—which is an altogether erroneous idea. In a religious
sense, Fascism is anti-Semitic just as much as it is anti-
Catholic or anti-Protestant—that is to say, it opposes the
tendency of the Jewish faith as well as of any other to
establish a separate group consciousness within the nation. In a racial sense, Fascism is anti-Semitic, if—and
only if—its basic collective concept happens to be not
purely nationally but racially determined; as is the case
with National Socialism which, unlike Italian Fascism,
does not embrace all citizens of Fascist mentality but

embraces Germans regardless of citizenship, provided only that they are of "Aryan" stock.[12]

The point is that the Nazi race bias is not, as has been suggested, an invention for publicity's sake. It is the normal emphasis which any German Fascism would have to place upon the rationalization of an *inherently German national characteristic*. Germans have been racial anti-Semites since time immemorial. Never, in German countries, was hatred of the Jews an affair of religion, as it was in France, or in medieval Spain or Italy. In all those countries baptism, in popular consciousness, eradicated the difference between Jew and Gentile after two generations at the most. In Germany it had no effect whatever, even before the Third Reich began snooping for non-Aryan grandmothers. Jews themselves, even the most completely assimilated ones, never found in German countries a completely natural feeling of solidarity with their fellow-countrymen; there was always a sense of "being different," which needed only a few favorable circumstances to develop into a deep mutual distrust.

This is not a phenomenon limited by German boundary lines. It is rampant in Austria, in the German-speaking parts of Czechoslovakia and Roumania, and in the

[12] A point may be made here which seems all too little realized as yet: it is quite useless to argue anthropologically that there is no such thing as an Aryan—because, as we have seen before, Fascist units are entities a priori. They are no more in need of scientific soundness than the famous maxim with which a Jew-baiting nineteenth century mayor of Vienna defended his non-Aryan associations: "*I* decide who is a Jew!"

formerly German-dominated Baltic countries. It did not spread in the Scandinavian countries because there were never any Jews to speak of there. Its development was arrested in Holland by the historical coincidence that after the expulsion of the Jews from Spain a previously practically Jew-less country deliberately invited a large influx of Jews, in an expectation of material gain which was richly rewarded. Even in Anglo-Saxon countries anti-Semitism has a racial tinge—nothing to be compared with the Germans' ever-consciousness of a decisive gap, but still an unmistakable bit of the "foreign body" notion. The most convincing example, however, is Switzerland—the German half of which is, and always has been, alive with a violent racial anti-Semitism, while French and Italian Swiss may accuse the Jews of having murdered Christ or of being usurers, but are otherwise not conscious of any important difference.

In Italy proper, such a difference was never felt. It may be due to the similarity of Jewish and Italian features and complexions (although in other cases that has not prevented racial strife, as between Jew and Arab). At any rate, Italian Jews may have been exposed to religious, economic, even to a historically contingent social animosity—but never to a racial one. Fascism, when it came to power, had neither need nor reason to conjure up something which had not been there before. On the contrary, it would have been an extremely dangerous precedent to demonstrate the fact that a gap *could* be made artificially into the dogmatically indivisible whole of the Fascist nation. Therefore, for twelve years, Italy gave an exhibition of a totalitarian state without anti-Semitism; the roster of Jews important in the Mussolinian hierarchy is impressive and has often been read by others. At the time of this writing, a scare has been thrown into the public by the official Party organ, Regime Fascista, which published a call to Italian Jews for loyalty, in tones which could well be interpreted as indicating a swing toward anti-Semitism. In the opinion of the writer, this suspicion is unfounded. It seems improbable that Mussolini—who has never yet rejected any nominal Italian willing to come into the Fascist fold, not even the war-subjected Tyrolese and Istrians— would start such a thing now, even as a gesture to bind his new anti-Bolshevist alliance with the Nazis. It is more probable that, aware of the strong leanings of Jews all over the world toward either Liberalism or Socialism, both of which he abhors, he became suddenly suspicious of the sincerity of the professed Fascism of his own Italian Jews. It is most probable, however, that the call for loyalty was entirely sincere, that it was occasioned by the imminence of a close understanding with Germany—a country which, for obvious reasons, is anathema to all Jews—and was meant to remind them, in this special situation of conflicting allegiances, that they are required to be Fascists, and nothing but Fascists, and that it would mean failure in their professed loyalty as Fascists if they permitted any feeling whatever *as Jews* to come to the fore. It is very natural that Italian Jews were not overly enthusiastic at the prospect of having to devote their affection and fidelity to the friendship with a nation that lost no chance to humiliate their name and persecute its Jewish citizens—and accordingly it is very natural for Regime Fascista to remind them sharply that their Fascist duty is not to make policies but to carry them out, and particularly, not to let another group feeling (treason in itself!) interfere with their performance of this duty. Again, as so often in Fascism, no explanation jibes so well with facts as the literal one.

In general, it seems to be reasonably well established by now that a Fascist régime will feature anti-Semitism only if anti-Semitism is also a pre-Fascist characteristic of the respective nation. If so, Fascism will quite probably exaggerate this characteristic into monstrous forms. Otherwise, however, it will be content with enforcing against Jews as against all others the totalitarian concept—which, of course, means the breaking up of the self-conscious community which Jews, under the influence of historical pressure, have formed and preserved in every part of the world for nineteen centuries.

The second type of allegedly essential but really accidental Fascist traits are those which Fascism practices but disclaims—the kind of thing which Fascists, when confronted with documentary evidence, blame upon "revolutionary excesses" or administrative negligence, while hotly denying that it has anything to do with the system. And strangely enough, in most cases it has nothing to do with the system—although, of course, it was always the Fascist revolution which provided the opportunity for the trouble to develop.

The principal example of such an unpleasant trait is the development of Party favoritism: Fascism by means of the Party structure re-admitting personal privilege by the back door after having fired it with aplomb through the front door. That after a Fascist revolution government positions of major or minor importance will go mostly to trusted members of the Party, is obvious— and not even in democratic eyes really reprehensible. In a newly-created Fascist state, however, the Party, unless invested with a great deal of power, could never fulfill its most essential functions, in fields which government is technically unable to control. There are so many occasions where only the single Party can really effectuate the superiority of the totalitarian state—all the cases where it has been said accusingly of German and Italian Fascists (and Russian Communists) that "qua Party they do it, and qua government they do nothing against it." To be sure, such powers are not extended, like aristocratic prerogative, as privilege to be enjoyed free of charge, but as authority conferred for specific purposes. As we have seen before in discussing the Party as an institution, its dogmatic function is not to rule but to serve.[13] Its purpose is the perpetuation of the disciplined energy and the self-abnegating idealism

[13] Against this might be cited Hitler's words, in reference to the Party, "the state does not command us; we command the state!" However, it is quite clear that by state—in accord with common German usage—Hitler meant not the national concept but the governmental machinery; he simply wanted to express the obvious fact that administration is no more above the spiritual trend of Fascism than anything else.

on which Fascism is based—not the exaltation over others apt to follow upon the picking of political plums. It is meant to personify the virtues of the Fascist state, not its authority. Yet, as long as in *any* sense the Party constitutes a personification of the superior organism, it is virtually unavoidable that as "essence of the state" it will largely participate in the state's power and glory. And unlike the state, the Party is not an abstraction but a group of men.

That the hatred, on which most of these men have fed for years and years, may run amuck in their new position; that non-membership in the Party may reduce a majority of the people to the mute fatalism of the slave who knows that there is no redress for his grievances; that the advantages of membership may in spite of purgings and supervision bring into the Party just the low-class opportunist type it should be free of—these are extremes which a very wise administration ought to be able to avoid. But not to feel themselves as victors would be wholly unnatural for men so carefully inoculated with the virus of fighting—and a victor obviously requires a vanquished. Thus arises—at least in the early stages after a Fascist seizure of power—a differentiation between the Fascist and the not-so-Fascist members of the community, which no amount of Party discipline could possibly check. And the law, natural arbiter of citizens, expressly disavows individual objectivity. It recognizes man only in his connection with the state— and, therefore, with the movement that has conquered the state. Justice—from the point of view of the single

individual—is no more blind. It is very definitely see-
ing, and in probing for the communal interest it looks
at very definite things—such as that currently fashion-
able mark of distinction, a man's shirt. Irrespective of
justice taking sides, the political upheaval itself will
inevitably offer dozens of practical opportunities for a
partisan of victory to express his superiority over the
partisans of defeat—in importance, in material influence, and in cash.[14]

And still, the example of Italy has shown beyond
question that, for instance, the more complete "fasciza-
tion" of a people sometimes makes this new class differentiation decrease in volume. It seems to be a disease
that may disappear with the cause—which cause is not
Fascism but on the contrary incomplete Fascism, the
continued existence of differences of political opinion
within a people. Russia, after nineteen years of the
strictest Party rule in history, now feels Communistic
enough to restore equality before the law in the individualist sense. Even Germany, where Fascism is young
and still rather unsettled, has already shown a distinct
trend away from clothing the Party with extra-legal
sanctity. It can hardly be doubted any more that the discrimination in favor of Party members which we object
to *can* be largely eliminated. There is as little doubt that
very seldom, in a Fascist state, *will* it be eliminated;
certainly not until quite some time after the establish-

[14] Which gave rise to an often-heard complaint among Fascist
lawyers, that "half the people don't dare go to court any more,
and the other half don't need to!"

ment of Fascist rule—and, human nature being what it is, probably not even then. But that is beside the point. What concerns us is that (regardless of present experience and future probability) *misuse of Party power is not such an essential trait of Fascism that its occurrence in a political system would warrant our diagnosing it as Fascist.*

Neither would such a diagnosis be warranted by the pièce de résistance of anti-Fascist propaganda: Fascist brutality. We know that both in Germany and in Italy the political revolution was accompanied by administrative excesses unequaled in any modern civilized country. From the castor-oil therapy invented by Mussolini's lieutenants to the beatings within an inch of the victim's life, which for some time were a regular feature in Hitler's concentration camps, arbitrary seizures and bodily maltreatment of prisoners characterized the known instances of Fascist rule. We also know, of course, that in this respect Italian experience was as child's play compared to the German one. We need only think of the outcry at the murder of Matteotti, a Socialist deputy who had publicly attacked the government, and then at the vast quiet which attended the authorized or unauthorized executions of several hundreds of former German political figures; or the fact that according to anti-Fascist computations the Italian Tribunal for the Defense of the State sentenced seven persons to death between 1927 and 1932—which number, during 1933 and 1934, approximately equaled the monthly mortality of a medium-sized German concentration camp. But although this indicates that the measure of Fascist cruelty will largely depend on the measure of anti-Fascist resistance, there are certain things which make *some* of it appear highly probable in any case: first the fact that, in a movement which officially glorifies power by force, a good deal of praise will always fall upon plain ruthlessness; second, that such a movement will always and inevitably attract the bullies in a population—the men whose tastes for browbeating other people could find no satisfaction in the legalistic frame of democracy.

The story of German Fascism may make this clear. The core of the early National Socialist movement consisted of young men whose first contact with adult life had been war, who had stepped right out of school into an army fighting throughout in enemy country, mostly among culturally inferior "natives"—in Russia, in the Balkans, and particularly after the end of the World War proper with the various German bands of partisans in the Baltic countries, in Poland and Upper Silesia. They returned to an almost hostile Fatherland, were forcibly demilitarized, their ideals ridiculed by a wartired majority, their soldierly pride—the only one they possessed—humiliated by others who were more adept at the required re-orientation to a life in peace. And all that time those youngsters had the definite feeling— and the future proved them right!—that *they*, and not the mad scramble for money or bread and butter, represented the real German spirit. When they won out after fourteen years of struggle, their accumulated hate and contempt for the "perverters of the German soul" could hardly help exploding in violence. But what made this tendency, understandable in the original "Old Fighters," into a shocking tide were the thousands of others who had joined up not to save the nation but for the fun of fighting, or for gain or revenge. They constituted a majority to whom possession of complete power over former enemies only meant a chance to "show them."

Yet even in Germany there can be no doubt that violence has for some time considerably abated. Arrests are now made in an orderly fashion; the concentration camps have been cleared of the more outrageous sadists and begin to resemble American prison farms; even the Jews (although the drive toward their elimination from German life goes on with undiminished fervor) are practically secure from what the Nazis euphemistically termed "individual actions." Only to a limited extent are these developments due to the fact that all excesses are strongly discouraged from above. Chiefly responsible for them is the love of order and discipline which *is* inherent in the German national character: after the first outbursts had passed, Germans preferred an orderly procedure to the individual satisfaction of their grudges. In Italy, the Fascist movement had been less repressed, and was therefore less violent; when the seizure of power was accomplished after a struggle too short to have fomented real bitterness, it was comparatively easy for Mussolini to curb the dash of his followers and to replace their castor-oil raids with normal, quiet and efficient processes. There have been few complaints about administrative violence in Italy since 1924, and the chances are that in a relatively short time there will be none at all from Germany. And the point is that this would *not* mean an essential change; it would simply mean that an external, unwelcome, and fundamentally insignificant feature had been successfully eliminated.

Anti-Fascists would do well to realize that all signs point to a future in which, from the point of view of outraged humanity, German Nazis will provide much less material for atrocity stories than, for example, democratic Americans—the inventors of lynching and the third degree. The peaceful serenity which greeted visitors to the 1936 German Olympics is of the utmost significance—for although this time we may still be able to discount the impression as manufactured, if repeated once or twice, it will stick. And in the case of Germany it will be repeated—because *atrocities are not inherent in Fascism; Fascism only exaggerates inherent national characteristics.* A rather shocking inference from this contention is that a potential American Fascism would be infinitely more vicious and unpleasant than any European one. Here the violence would be not the overflow of emotions repressed for years but a quite normal part of our Fascist administrative scheme. After all, we have managed to make lynchings, "hanging parties" at public executions, police brutality on a scale unequaled in other countries, into more or less regular parts of our democracy. We have developed a definite popular sentiment in favor of official sadism—as exemplified by our most successful type of gangster, leatherneck, and cowboy movies, the kind which glorifies the fist of authority smashing onto the civilian chin, and which it is no use denouncing as "un-American" because it is as American as ice cream soda. In this country—and that part of Sinclair Lewis's picture, frightening as it is, is terribly true—Fascist cruelty would not abate! If we ever get an American Fascism, authority will not be in the hands of the excitable but fundamentally light-hearted Italians, or of the stiff but methodical Germans. Here national discipline would be administered by the two-fisted, gun-toting, tarring-and-feathering brand, by a blend of the tough cop, the tough gangster, the tough cow puncher, and every other kind of tough—who would proclaim as No. 1 national virtue the ability to "take it," and who would consider it their prime duty to check up daily on the people's progress in that direction. Brutality, we have said before, is not necessarily a Fascist trait. Political unanimity, or rigid discipline, *can* hold it in check. In this country, however, one can only hope for the sake of the average citizen that no Fascism shall ever be put to that test.

CHAPTER SIX

INTERNATIONAL RELATIONS

The Position of War in the Fascist Scheme—and the Concept of "Honorable Peace"

FOR POKER PLAYERS, RECENT INTERNATIONAL HISTORY has been amusing to watch. Whenever one of today's "aggressive" nations made a bold move frowned at by the others, the whole world talked about "calling the bluff." In one case the poker terminology was even adopted in the highest circles of diplomacy itself—when a prominent official of a great European power told the press, "This time we have a royal straight flush and we know we can't lose." Every time, however, it turned out that the supposedly bluffing nations meant every word they said—while the determination not to let them get away with it dissolved into thin air. It was not due to inability to back up the talk, either. In the Anglo-Italian and Franco-German controversies, the aggressive party was definitely the weaker one. They were really clear-cut examples of a bluff that was no bluff. The real bluffers were the players threatening to "call."

Two inferences presented themselves. First, it became apparent that the Fascists could not be relied upon to play the diplomatic game according to Hoyle. Second, the realization that they were not bluffing—that they did not retreat when faced with actual resistance but were perfectly willing to fight things out—seemed to disclose an otherwise extinct eagerness for the international poker player's alternative to the "drop": the showdown. Between nations, a showdown means only one thing: war. The Fascists' willingness to accept war as a consequence of their acts is the decisive feature of their foreign policy. And the failure of other nations to recognize this attitude is what was chiefly responsible for the repeated fiasco of *their* foreign policies. Only by a clear understanding of the role of war in the Fascist scheme—and of the difference between the Fascist and the non-Fascist feeling toward war—can Fascist international reactions be made comprehensible, and perhaps even to some extent predictable.

War, moreover, is the cardinal point of whatever theory of foreign policy the Fascists may be said to hold themselves. In general, the position taken by the powers concerned toward the use of armed force is the universal basis of *all* international relations. No problem can be solved, no alignment tested without, in the last analysis, involving this question. Particularly, however, this must be true of nations which have put such a tremendous *internal* emphasis on war as have Italy and Germany. It is one of their unalterable tenets that war is inevitable, necessary, and a supremely ennobling experience for a healthy and virile nation. Consequently, as a matter of principle, they have reduced all other international activities to insignificance—as necessarily inconsistent, impossible to subject to rules, never more than auxiliary means either preparing for war or exploiting its outcome. Again and again such views have been expressed by Fascist leaders and impressed upon Fascist followers and potential leaders. That these men, when called upon to make actual decisions, would forget their ideas—and adopt instead the non-Fascist thesis of war as essentially evil and of diplomacy as chiefly a means to avoid it—was a pious hope with little chance of realization. From the point of view of Fascism's own psychology as well as from that of the watching world the obvious starting point for an analysis of Fascist international policy is an examination of its stand on the ultima ratio regum—and of the circumstances which determine it.

Wars, we have so often been told of late, do not happen—they are made. Accordingly, it has now become the vogue among historians to search not for "causes" but for "motives" behind any given war. Today the motives discovered in this fashion are usually of an economic nature. This is due not so much to the modern "economic interpretation of history" as to the fact that the course of democracy's recent evolution has done away with almost every other known casus belli. We do not fight any more, nowadays, because our monarch's daughter has been jilted by the neighboring prince, or because our religious beliefs differ from those held in the next country, or just because we dislike its inhabitants. Wars today are fought either to prevent or to avenge actual injuries or to protect or acquire territory; both of which types of aims lend themselves easily to an economic interpretation. So, at present, many people have developed a veritable inability to believe that war may be waged for other than economic reasons—and from there, of course, it was but a step to the conviction that *all* wars, stripped of pretense, are engineered by financial powers behind political thrones.

While in many instances this may be entirely true, to hold it generally applicable is one of the most dangerously misleading ideas of our time. What are usually cited in support of this narrow variety of economic interpretation are the historic conflicts of this country: the Revolutionary War—a merchant and planter rebellion against economic discrimination by the mother country; the war with Spain—an effort to protect our sugar interests in Cuba; the World War—an effort to protect our loans to the Allies. Or the wars in later British history: the Boer War—a diamond and gold mine grab; the Chinese Wars—protection of the Indian opium trade; and the World War—like the Napoleonic Wars more than a century before—protection of Britain's mercantile empire from continental competition. Even supposing, for the moment, that in those cases the logic of the economic interpreters were unimpeachable, the looseness of their generalization is a scientific outrage. Again it is blithely assumed that what is true of us and of the English will be true of the rest of the world—completely overlooking the fact that Britain and the United States are not only alike in their national mentality but are the only consistent exponents of a quite peculiar form of nineteenth century "commercial democracy." The strict economic interpretation is not even applicable to other types of nineteenth century democracy, as is clearly demonstrated by France—not a merchant state, but essentially a democratic nation, at least since 1830. We need but cast a glance at the comparatively recent reign of Napoleon III—who, having exchanged his title of President for that of Emperor under the slogan "L'Empire c'est la Paix," succeeded, within the following twenty years, in plunging his country into five different wars, none of which could by any stretch of the imagination be said to have been caused by economic motives. Even in fights in which others had a decided economic stake (as the British for instance had in the Crimea expedition) the "Second Empire" managed to participate just for the fun of it, without either claiming or expecting material remuneration—and the people of France were with it to a man. It seems reasonably certain that there must have been active some moving spirit other than a desire for tangible advantages—whether lust for glory, or for revenge, or for fighting as such. However, the most convincing argument against the theory that wars can invariably be traced to economic "interests," springs not from past but from present experience. Today we see Europe poised for a war which, it is expected, will be unleashed by Germany recapturing Danzig from the League or Memel from Lithuania, or

effecting Anschluss with Austria [1]—all of which undertakings, even if successful, are bound to prove material
liabilities rather than assets to the Third Reich. We saw
Italy risk destruction in a war with Britain for the sake
of seizing Ethiopia—which most practical economists,
including those of Italy, consider a gamble that will
never return an interest and hardly the capital invested.
We saw the Japanese army revolt to enforce an active
policy of conquest in the Far East—and then heard
from the best-informed observers that the groups it was
rebelling against are the country's economic experts and
financial leaders, who apparently want to avoid war and
think it wiser and more profitable to pursue Japan's indicated expansionist aims by peaceful penetration.
Without twisting facts, all attempts to explain adequately these very acute problems of the present in
purely economic terms have been obvious failures.[2]
Neither has it been possible to trace the underlying psychology to chauvinist propaganda. It may be that propaganda can anaesthetize fear—but a conspicuous feature
of the official propagandistic treatment of war under
Fascism has always been a direct emphasis on the fact

[1] Since this was written, the distinction of being the foremost
powder-keg has gone to Spain—where Fascist intervention is economically at least as unreasonable as in the cases listed above.

[2] Of course, this contrast between the applicability of the
method to American and British policies and its incompatibility
with the policies of other nations only confirms what has here
been contended from the beginning: that we cannot simply apply
our mental processes to problems of others and expect practically
tenable results. During our investigation of the Fascist state structure we saw how basic political conceptions, like "freedom" or

that for the individual, at least, any modern war would be very unpleasant. If we want to get at what is really beneath the overwhelming mental readiness for war in Fascist countries, we must start out on an entirely different track.

Public opinions on war have changed profoundly throughout the world as a result of the conflagration of 1914-18. Before that time, to a great many if not most individuals, male or female, war as such possessed definite attractions. It was a source of personal danger, but hardly more so than the pursuits of foxhunting or automobile racing. It was not only held in traditional esteem as the supreme calling of a man and the final testing ground of his virtues, but it actually did provide thrills and excitement not to be had otherwise. Since the fourteenth century, the increasing use and range of artillery has lessened the sporting chance of participants, but in all pre-twentieth-century wars the physical prowess, the fighting skill, the mental agility and resourcefulness of the individual were still factors of at least equal impor-

"responsibility," acquire meanings quaint and unusual to us when applied on Fascist premises. How much more is this bound to be the case in international relations—i.e., relations not between individuals, who *might* be thought to be mentally alike the world over, but between national communities, whose psychological dissimilarity even the most doctrinaire political scientist will admit more readily than that of single human beings. It is the premise of this investigation that an undistorted view of *any* Fascist problem can be secured only by considering it in terms of Fascist ideology—but even if this meant taking unnecessary trouble in every other instance, it would still be the only possible approach to the Fascist scheme of foreign affairs.

tance with pure chance. In past centuries war was an opportunity for a man to *do* things, to get rid of his pent-up energies, to win, in risking his life, not only glory but also a very real satisfaction of his fighting instincts. In those times, therefore, not only did the profession of the warrior attract the most vital as well as the most brutal part of a people, but to every "real man" the actual experience of war as such was definitely alluring.

The World War has put an end to that. Our grandfathers may tell about their Civil War adventures with proud and fond remembrance. But most of our 1917-18 doughboys, when the subject comes up, will either shut up tight or say frankly that their memory of pure horror outweighs almost everything else. Now this is clearly not because the last war was bloodier than others. It did not really increase the danger to combatants. Men cannot lose more than their lives at any time, and the wounded and maimed surely do not suffer today the way they did when medical science was less advanced. While total casualties have mounted to staggering figures, the casualty percentage of today is much lower than it used to be in ancient times when it was no rare occurrence for an army to be butchered to the last man. Yet in those days few men would dream of seeking honor and achievement elsewhere than on the battlefield; returning, they would boast pleasantly of their bloody accomplishments and send their sons out onto the same path. The progress of civilization can have little to do with the change—for the fighting instincts of the race have not diminished, as witness the enthusiasm for the manly art which increased in proportion with the vanishing opportunities for other kinds of fighting. Neither could it be due to fear of ordinary danger. A man should certainly have been more afraid of war when he had to expect to be tortured or mutilated as prisoner, or to be thrown into a subterranean dungeon instead of being carefully attended to in a sanitary outdoor prisoners' camp—or when he knew that the slightest wound would probably cost him the use of his limbs, or cause permanent disfigurement and, in any case, long and unmitigated agony instead of aseptic treatment by capable physicians and Red Cross nurses. Other things caused the reversal of attitude: The mechanization of warfare—the utter helplessness of the trenchdweller in the face of artillery and aerial bombardment and gas and other devices of homicidal engineering. Its collectivization—the complete insignificance of the fighting individual, his permutation into a pawn, or rather an atom of a pawn, to be moved around and sacrificed for "strategic objects" by the real actors who stayed far from danger in sheltered and comfortable surroundings. The extremities of suffering and privation without any of the gratification of individual combative action. The change of war from a pastime for men into a game of numbers for master minds in GHQs. The replacement of the soldierly virtues of strength and courage with mute patience and nerveless stolidity. The end of the notion of war as a romantic activity, and its terrifying appearance as an irresistible and uncontrollable runaway force of destruction—a Frankenstein monster set to devour its creators. For these reasons, while in the past nine out of ten men who had been to war secretly treasured the experience, nine out of ten who saw front line service in 1914-18 dread and detest war.

This is true of individuals throughout the world—Germans and Italians no less than French and Americans (and probably even of Russians and Japanese, although in these cases the different Asiatic mentality might produce other reactions). Consequently, it can be said with assurance that since 1918 all major democracies have a sincere desire for peace. By definition, the democratic state is instituted for the purpose of serving the interests of its individual members, and under normal conditions (unless influenced by extraordinary pressure from inside or outside) cannot but reflect a distaste for war prevalent among its citizens. With respect to the United States, France, Britain, the British Dominions and most of the smaller European countries, therefore, it is perfectly safe to reason that they are not likely to start war, because the majority of their people are against it. Also, that the best way to counteract possible war-propaganda of interested groups would be to strengthen the anti-war-position of the men making up the majorities—by constantly keeping before their mind's eye the horrors to which, in war, they would be subjected. The scheme is pretty sure to work in any country with an individualist state structure. Where our pacifists make their big mistake is the question of whether it will work in truly collectivist communities.

In other words, whether a trend to war will be checked by emphasizing its horrors to men who are *really* free from the subconscious notion that the state is there *for them*—to individuals who really visualize themselves as destined only to advance the superhuman collective unit. The answer, briefly, is "no." What is more, the familiar kind of pacifism *cannot* work there—neither pacifist propaganda, nor pacifist logic, nor the whole pacifist approach. This is sad—but fooling ourselves will not make it any less so.

Most individual Fascists (or Soviet Communists, for that matter) do not *like* war at all. What they really dislike, of course—quite in accord with the premise of militant pacifism—is not the concept of war but its unpleasant aspects as applied to themselves. Few humans would be virtuous enough to hate war if they could be guaranteed (a) freedom from any danger, hardship, or responsibility, and (b) that they would be on the winning side. With this dislike of war, or really rather of the risks of war, the Fascist combines a deep personal, and carefully nursed communal conviction that war is inevitable. Personally he knows that he and the millions of other particles of the "higher organism" cannot do anything about international affairs, and that when the call comes they must go. This, to him, is not the consequence of an oppressive dictatorship. Since his is a collectivist mentality, he feels that it cannot be otherwise. Communally, he and the millions of others are told day after day that sometime the call is bound to come, that in warning them beforehand the state is really just protecting their own interests. So what would any man do who was very much afraid of a conflict from which he could see no escape? He would try to make himself as strong, as invulnerable, as likely to come out on top as possible. Which is exactly what the Fascist governments are doing; and which is why even those of their people who might be inclined to look askance at other points of their program will heartily endorse the armament part —and why in all Fascist countries the pacifist emphasis on the horrors of modern warfare only serves to add to the zeal of preparing for it. No Fascist propaganda office has ever attempted to minimize the frightful aspects of war. On the contrary, they have played them up as much as possible, so that every individual might appreciate and join in the collective effort to guard against all weapons an enemy might employ. The war-mindedness of a Fascist population is nothing like the ignorant braggadocio of a "man without fear." It is the grim and dead-serious attitude of a man who knows what he has to face, does not like it at all, but is conscious of having done his best to prepare himself, and determined, once it must be, to come through with flying colors.

To Fascist individuals the facts are plain and the consequences patent and inescapable: it is their own personal paramount interest to have their community as strong as possible. Whenever it becomes weak some stronger unit will attack it, they will have to fight in its defense and will be at the wrong end of the gun. The question of what they are fighting for, or whether it is reasonable for them to fight, does not enter into consideration at all. Fascist soldiers do not fight "for" something; they fight as parts of the collective unit. The state fights, for its existence or for any material or immaterial advantage, and its members share in whatever it is fighting for—but *their* fighting is not that of individuals for a common goal but simply an expression of their nature as parts of the community. To them, the duty of fighting is an incident of community life just like the duty of working. They may not like to work— but they know that, unless they do, the community could not go on. The same reasoning applies to their taking up arms; and in neither case would they dream of holding the right of the state to make them do their part dependent on the goal of their activities—because their subordination of personal to common interests is real and instinctive. And as long as they stick to this mental attitude, no peace propaganda is going to change their position on war. There can be only one possible way to change it: to upset their basic concept of their own relation to their community. Which, if it can be done at all, seems to be a task for psychiatry rather than for an Anti-War League.

The notion of the inevitability of war is the real keystone of the entire Fascist treatment of foreign affairs. It follows logically from the premise of a national collectivism. In the Fascist scheme, the world—a limited area —is populated not by men grouped into nations but by a number of dogmatically indivisible collective bodies. Among these bodies only one law can prevail—the rule of the strong. In the community of the individuals, order is maintained not by the abstract compact of the law itself but by the communal power enforcing it. In the community of nations no such communal power exists. If attempted, it could hardly ever be effective, because it would either have to rely upon the strong nations for enforcement, or it would have to be independently stronger than any possible international combine. The latter course the presently powerful nations would be very unlikely to permit, while under the former the international order would simply be another hegemony of big units. Also, since even the most carefully devised "balance of power" is too delicate a structure to last forever, the time would always come again when every man would have to look out for himself. Furthermore, it is inconceivable to the Fascist that a strong unit, for any length of time, should deliberately deprive itself of things it could have—whether territory or natural resources or industrial facilities or additional consumers or taxpayers or soldiers or purely enhanced prestige— just for the sake of not inflicting harm upon a weaker unit. Although peace may well constitute an advantage in itself, Fascist realism does not permit the probability to be obscured that a large expected gain will generally outweigh the disadvantage of a little war in the eyes of the country that means to win it. And as a collectivist nation—not being, like the democratic state, a kind of association for the protection of the interests of the incorporated individuals—cannot imagine that the other would not fight back, it can only conclude that international conflict is an unavoidable occurrence.

This, of course, does not mean that it is not considered avoidable at any particular moment. While the Fascists refuse to see in war an abnormal state of affairs, they do not go so far as to consider it *the* normal state of affairs. They rather view it as a natural process to restore lost balances, to adapt the face of the earth to changes that have taken place during periods of peaceful development. According to their reasoning, the practicable way to avoid those spontaneous balancing processes is not to conclude treaties or arrange for arbitration or otherwise to set up fictions of an international legal order that can never really mean anything without sufficient power to back it—but to prevent the inequalities that upset the balance. In other words, to have all potential enemies become so strong that everyone will be afraid to attack anyone else. This is the essence of the constantly repeated preachings of Germany's Nazi diplomacy. They sound twisted and hypocritical to us— and it shall not be said here that there are no ulterior motives behind the peace theories of Messrs. Hitler and Von Ribbentrop. They themselves would be the last to deny them. But the point is that what they say is also the honest and unselfish opinion of all Fascists. Moreover, it is the only logical one for groups that are not only under no restraining influence from their members but do not even recognize their members' individual interests. Again our democratic unwillingness to believe in the sincerity of other than our own ways of thinking obstructs our view of a logical connection of first-rate importance. Whenever in recent years the Germans protested they were re-arming to the level of their neighbors only because they thought this was a better guarantee for European peace, we—the democratic observers—struck various attitudes of sardonic disbelief. No matter how often we had heard the argument, we could never quite see how one could honestly contend that arming might prevent war. Whereas the slightest attempt to consider the Nazi point in the light of Nazi philosophy would let us realize the sincerity of this attitude: thinking in terms of collectivist and irresponsible a priori communities, *they simply cannot conceive of any other check upon a prospective aggressor than fear of his intended victim.*

This is the reason for the dislike invariably shown by Fascists toward all schemes of "collective security"— even in small countries which could only profit by it: a conviction of their inevitable futility based upon an inability to believe that a state could voluntarily subordinate its interests to those of other communities. Because of this attitude the Fascists can conceive of any state as entering wholeheartedly only into such international commitments as it would deem to be to its own advantage. The maintenance of peace alone they have been trained to consider as not necessarily an advantage. Accordingly, they will look upon any collective security plan as merely a structure of alliances [3]—as regards

---

[3] Obviously, skeptics will point out that this is the only realistic view of collective security for us no less than for the Fascists. But the fact remains that it was certainly not the view of Woodrow Wilson in 1918, or even of the British League of Nations Union in its "Peace Ballot" of 1934—that democrats feel that collective security today has degenerated from what it should be, while Fascists are unable even to imagine it in any other form.

their own country as well as any other party to it. The
Germans, for instance, thought of the League of Nations
as just such a structure—which is why they were so
stubbornly insistent on the contention that it was directed
against *them*. Abroad this contention was usually construed as an admission that they wanted to do what the
League had been designed to prevent—upset the status
quo, attack small nations, suppress minorities, etc. In
reality, although they might well have harbored such
intentions, their conclusion of the anti-German character
of the League was reached in a much simpler way: they
knew it was not an alliance in their favor—and therefore, since no big power would have assumed its extensive obligations for unselfish reasons, it could only be
an alliance in their disfavor. The same attitude controlled the Italian relationship with Geneva. Before the
African crisis this was not apparent because—the then
dominant League forces being Italy's old World War
allies—Mussolini found it possible to play the League
game just as he would have played the game of an
Anglo-Franco-Italian hegemony over Europe. Yet even
in those days he showed a marked preference for less
ambiguous schemes—such as his pet brainchild, the
Four-Power-Pact. Since then, however, the Italians have
displayed a sincere indignation at the League's attempt
to check their conquest of Ethiopia, and an inability to
comprehend any other motive for Britain's leadership
therein than Britain's material advantage, which allows
only one conclusion: that in their minds the League was
never what its democratic sponsors intended it to be—an

instrument to create a rule of law in international affairs
—but simply an instrument to pursue the policies of the
leading League powers. Since they were one of these,
they firmly believed in Geneva's availability as a means
of enforcing their own needs and interests—as witness
their naïve accompaniment of the opening hostilities in
Africa with a plea to the League that Ethiopia be expelled as a member of that organization and declared
unworthy of the privileges of a sovereign state. After
this childlike confidence had been betrayed, Italian rav-
ings against Geneva did not express the resentment of
the exposed villain. Theirs was the furious bewilderment of a businessman who devotes time and effort to
the promotion of a scheme from which he expects to
profit—only to find out that he has been aiding a philan-
thropic institution. He feels gypped—and so did the
Italians.

Neither would it be possible to exclude such misunderstandings if the French and English should succeed in enticing Germany back into the fold of collective security. Hitler's personal bluntness, which has so
often been unfavorably compared with Mussolini's
"statesmanlike" adherence to accepted diplomatic for-
mulas, might spare him the extreme embarrassment of
the Italian—who, after all, got into his recent troubles
only through the ambition to manage his international
relations according to a set of rules essentially at variance with the philosophy of his own state structure. But
even if such major catastrophes could be avoided, it
should be clear by now that making Fascist countries

join a League does not imply their adoption of a League
mentality—not even if they join with the best intentions
in the world. The plain truth is that it is senseless to
draft Fascist nations into schemes of international order
democratically maintained by mutual responsibilities—
and to hope for their co-operation in the genuine spirit
of the thing. It is senseless not because they would be
unwilling to co-operate—that, at any rate, might be
worth trying—but because they are *unable* to. Because
their minds work in a way that makes acceptance of the
idea of collective security without reservations impossible. We all know the venerable figure of the stout believer in capitalism who will readily admit the injustice
of the unequal distribution of wealth and the desirability
of Communism as an ideal—but will always insist in
the end that "the industrious and the able would soon
again have more than the lazy and stupid" and that
Communism is all right in theory but "against human
nature" in practice. Collective security puts the Fascist
into exactly the same predicament. To his mind it is the
counterpart of "individual liberty"—a beautiful dream
which unfortunately cannot become practical as long as
the several national units retain their individuality, because it is incompatible with the nature of nations. Of
course, the Fascist employs here the same technique of
generalizing his own attitude which we have condemned
in his critics. But he has some justification, because it is
clear that a scheme of collective action which is really
incompatible with the nature of even one essential participant can be of no use to the others. Whether collec-

tive security can be achieved without the Fascists, is a different question. Their participation, however, may let such a set-up work in the nature of a comprehensive alliance—surely, when all is said, not the worst practical way to preserve peace for a time!—but never as what it is supposed to be. A Fascist nation as a factor of collective security is a contradiction in terms—because the goal of safety in peace for all, as well as the method of voluntary surrender of individual national interests, are both diametrically opposed to basic concepts of the Fascist dogma.

Two poles delimit the possibilities of Fascist international policy: war, and an *egocentric* collaboration for peace. Beyond the latter no Fascist government will be able to go—which excludes not only the peace-at-any-price policies advocated by democratic pacifists but even a genuinely unselfish co-operation—because it would be a betrayal of the national egotism which the self-sacrifice of its members imposes as sacred duty upon every collectivist community. That this egotism is of the essence of Fascism, is as apparent logically as psychologically. The logical way to deduce it will appeal, and be useful, to those willing to believe that the collectivism of a Fascist people is not just a kind of readiness to submit to regimentation but a sincere and profound attitude—an inbred and ingrained feeling of every individual that he does not count, that, whatever his personal fate, the really important part of his existence is his share in the life of the collective body. The rather obvious psychological argument—which should be particularly compelling for the materialists inclined to doubt the spontaneity of Fascist self-abnegation—concludes that men who have had to subordinate their own most vital interests to those of their community, can hardly be expected then to subordinate voluntarily *its* interests either to those of other communities or to any moral purpose materially at variance with its interests. Be it war or peace—a Fascist state can never pursue any policy for its own sake. The same consideration, whether of dogmatic reasoning or of political psychology, dominates its every choice: its only paramount interest *must* be the one to which its members surrendered their individual interests—the collective self-centered interest of the Fascist community. If a peace effort will coincide with that interest, so much the better. But to relinquish it for the sake of preserving peace in general, or for any other unselfish reason unrelated to the advantage of the Fascist community, would lay its entire structure open to question. The selfishness of Fascist nations is not a flaw in their character but an inescapable necessity.

Immediately, the aims of Fascist policy are influenced by this logical compulsion: they have to correspond to the collectivist character of the whole system. But equally affected, and with much more far-reaching consequences, are the means and methods with which these aims are pursued. With a great show of indignation, the Germans and Italians have often been denounced as international law-breakers. They have been accused of "undermining the foundations of world peace," of "putting their selfish interests before their international obligations," and of breaking their word whenever they thought it to their advantage. Before going into that it should be made quite clear that if the outraged attitude of the non-Fascist spokesmen meant that they had *really* been taken unawares, it would show up an atrophy of their mental faculties which no old-school diplomat could ever have lived down. That world peace as a paramount aim has again and again been expressly and officially disavowed in Italy as well as in Germany, is a matter of common knowledge. There was no need whatever for interpretative exertions. Whether the genuinely surprised international moralists had taken these disclaimers to mean the contrary of their plain language— or however else they arrived at opinions justifying astonishment when their peace edifice began to topple—will probably remain a diplomatic secret forever. Selfishness in foreign politics also is not only a logical feature of Fascism but a psychological necessity. No practical politician could be so ignorant of popular reactions as to contend that a country, after exacting from its citizens such sacrifices to the national interest as the Fascists demanded, could then make this same national interest subject to "international duties." Accordingly, we can safely say that there must be more than such simple misconceptions behind the universal denunciation of the Fascist methods. Its real essence affects something very dear to the democratic heart. It is the charge that the Fascists "dishonored their signature": that they specifically violated freely made *contracts*.

In civil life, a contract is a set of legal obligations

originating with the individuals who voluntarily assume them. This "individual-made law," of course, is the perfect legal expression of individualism—and it is no wonder that the extremists of that persuasion even sought to define the law in its entirety not as an emanation of group power but as a kind of fictitious collective contract held to have been entered into by whichever individuals were subject to it. In any event, the emphasis of the individualists fell inevitably upon the idea that the individual *could make law by himself*—from which followed that the contractual promise, which he said should bind him, would actually place him under a valid obligation whether there happened to be a judicial structure to make it practically enforceable or not. When, therefore, our modern individualist states attempted to "legalize" their relations without any such structure with powers of enforcement, it was only to be expected that they would turn to the theory of the "law by signature." Today, we are so used to this conception that we cannot see how one could possibly do without it. Yet not so many centuries ago, when religion still was a dominant influence in individual and social life, no international compact could have claimed any validity unless solemnly confirmed with sacred oaths—and it was generally understood, at the time, that a party was bound not because he had *made* a promise but because, in doing so, he had invoked the Divine Presence as witness that what he promised to do would be pleasing to Him. One might also think of the fact that even today the Anglo-American common law rule refuses to acknowledge a promise as binding unless it is accompanied by a legally sufficient consideration—in other words unless there is some ground to invest a promise or a "signature" with the force of law, *besides* the expressed and confirmed intention of the party that it should have this force. It seems obvious that there are ways of thinking about the origin of obligations different from the one upon which we have based our notion of the sanctity of international agreements. None of these ways, of course, contends that a binding promise should not be kept—but they prove that, from various points of view, other elements than a signed, sealed and delivered agreement might have to go *into the making of a binding promise.*

That the collectivists would require such an element —and what that element would be—should not have been difficult to foretell. The analogy to the aforementioned medieval requirement of the implied assent of God, as the sole holder of the power to bind and loose, is really too close to be missed. To the collectivist, the state is the sole source of law. What private contracts have of binding force, they have only because the state has generally granted it to them. Likewise, agreements entered into internationally on behalf of the state itself derive their force of law from the state; not, however, as we would be inclined to say, in its capacity as party to the agreements but in its capacity as state consenting to accept them as of legal nature. Furthermore, Fascist law as such—whether directly ordained by the state or legalized by it after initiation by individuals—is essentially nothing but a means to serve the ends of the state. As soon as any type of law, prescriptive or contractual, clashes with the collective interest, it automatically ceases to be law. It is law *only because* it serves the purpose of the state—and therefore *only insofar* as it serves the purpose of the state. "The collective will is the soul of the law"—when the law no more expresses this will, it becomes lifeless, a mere set of technicalities, a "scrap of paper." To the Fascist mind two things are necessary to create an obligation: a legal cause—legislative prescription or contractual promise—and the fact that its fulfillment is not to the disadvantage of the community. Whenever a conflict arises between a national promise and a national need, there is no more reason for the promise to be binding and it must give way to the higher purpose—nothing short of practical impossibility can be allowed to stand in the way of the collective interest.

That these ideas must apply to international obligations no less than to any other kind, is to the Fascist unquestionable. Neither the law of nations nor the treaties on which it is based are essentially distinguishable from the totality of legal precepts emanating from the Fascist state. They cannot represent a "higher law"—because to the Fascist there *is* no valid law outside of the law of the "superior organism." And no law can be divorced from its sole intent and purpose—the furtherance of the collective interest—no matter whether it bears the contractual signature of the state or the seal of its command. Again the theory, logically developed, confirms only what psychological considerations would have shown anyway. It is quite natural that a democratic people, restricting the state internally to a rule of law designed for the protection of the individuals, might have no objections to restricting it externally to a rule of law designed for the protection of all nations. But it is equally natural that the Fascists, who have made the good of their community paramount over all their own personal rights, should also insist on its taking precedence over any rights of other communities. Again the simple reasoning that the Fascists cannot be expected to treat foreign nations better than themselves, proves that their observance of international rights—whether created over their own signature or not—will always depend on whether that observance will serve or harm their national community.

This necessity not only bars the theoretical recognition of any kind of obligation independent of the collective interest, but makes it impossible for the Fascists, as a matter of principle, to submit unreservedly to any outside judgment designed to pass on their fulfillment of such obligations. The manifold schemes—the attempts to bind them somehow, from World Court and League Forum to simple arbitration treaties—are all the same to them: instrumentalities of an outside law presuming to supersede the only one they can recognize, the "eternal right to live" of their community. It is a matter of record that the World Court proceedings over the intended Austro-German customs union provided one of the most effective National Socialist arguments before Hitler's advent to power: that Chancellor Bruening had "sold out" his country by submitting its vital interests to an outside tribunal. And during the whole Ethiopian controversy the placard most frequently seen on the streets of Italy proclaimed, "We, and we only, are to judge our interests." The Italians would have felt much less resentment if the English had come out against the occupation of Abyssinia on grounds of Empire interests, however forcefully. Resistance against his actions is something the Fascist understands and expects, because the realism of his views is not obstructed by having always to profess peace as an ultimate goal. He is perfectly aware of the fact that every satisfaction of his needs in this crowded world of ours must necessarily hurt someone else. In his opinion such a conflict must be fought out, if the weaker side will not give in peacefully, until the strong unit has what its strength entitles it to demand and the endangered balance is thus restored. That is something which no Fascist would resent or even expect to be otherwise. What he cannot but resent is the attempt to drag him before a quasi-judicial forum like a criminal, to give to what he thinks is a plain conflict of interests the appearance of a trial for wrongdoing, under a law which in these implications he cannot recognize. What he can never acquiesce in is to have to answer for his needs to a pseudo-"court" of meddling outsiders; to have his *established right*—for nothing else is the vital interest of his community—submitted to a paper jurisprudence dealing in lifeless technicalities, to have necessities to his collective existence jeopardized by "scraps of paper."

Of course, we must not assume this generalized doctrine about the identification of international law and national advantage to be a hard and fast rule. Such a conclusion would be clearly at variance with known facts: That the Fascist states have actively collaborated in many schemes of international co-operation, that they not only made promises but kept most of them faithfully, that they very carefully refrained from the repudiation of international law in general that might have been expected to ensue from their instinctive rejection of its basic validity. To avoid this possible misconception we have only to recall that in its pursuit of the national interest Fascism is always guided by considerations of efficiency. It considers its purpose to be the achievement of results, not the sticking to principles. That the Fascists place the interest of their country over any divergent obligations, does not mean that they have to adopt a bull-in-the-china-shop attitude toward all traditional international institutions as long as those interests are not directly and vitally affected. Obviously, in the great majority of cases, the Fascist national interest will best be served by utilizing the co-operative machinery at hand. The advantages to be derived from such use will even offset many an instance where the machinery might work against some minor Fascist interest. There can be no doubt that this adherence to customary methods is entirely selfish—but as long as no major points are involved international co-operation will produce the same results, whether rendered with the loftiest idealism of a democracy or with the Fascist mental reservation of vital national interests. When no such interests are imperiled, when the subject matter at stake is not of sufficient moment to the Fascist community to warrant relinquishment of the benefits that can be drawn from international collaboration, then their scheme of foreign policy—however different basically —will produce a practical course that from the outside looks completely like that of any democratic nation. Still, the existing difference in principle had to find some kind of expression. Some phrase was needed to define this scheme resulting from a utilization of general international machinery with the mental reservation of national interest. The Fascists found a beautiful word for it: "Honorable Peace." For once a slogan was not eagerly sought for but created by dire necessity. Peace is the avowed objective of all present-day international co-operation. The Fascists wanted a part in the latter— and realized they could not get it unless they declared their willingness to accept the former as its basis. To declare for peace without reservations would not do; first, because it would have been indefensible internally; second, because the Fascists honestly did not want to enter an international scheme under false pretenses. To make their co-operation openly dependent upon their national interest also seemed inadvisable. So they evolved a qualification of their own and introduced into diplomatic practice the conception of "national honor."

That this, like so many other terms, has a different meaning in the Fascist vocabulary than in plain English soon became apparent. Honor previously had been something intangible, which was mentioned in speeches and editorials but not in diplomatic correspondence. Its conception was not essentially different from traditional Old World ideas about individual honor. It had been understood as an immaterial value, an objective standard clearly independent of and often in direct contrast with material interest. Unscrupulous pursuit of advantage had been considered a blot on the honor of a country. It was just when circumstances offered *no* material incentive that a nation's honor was relied upon to make it act; the things that touched its honor were the very things that had no material significance. It did not take the Fascists long to show that they understood national honor differently. Insults which would have brought most democracies up in arms, they swallowed without batting an eye. The Germans heard their governmental policies literally described as "brigandage and gangsterism" by responsible statesmen of the same British Empire they had been wooing since Hitler came to power. They saw the wreath which their official representative placed upon the London Cenotaph flung into the Thames without even an official apology—and they took it. They embarked upon a policy of friendship with Poland—the only European power which, besides having carved deeply into pre-war German territory, practiced and continued to practice actual and cruel suppression of German minorities. Thrice now, since Hitler's ascendancy, a total about-face has taken place in his relations to Mussolini—and what the government-controlled press of either country wrote about the other in the time between the Dollfuss murder and Italy's clash with the League, would have been sufficient to blast a dozen alliances of democratic nations. Yet their national honor did not prevent the two from being on the friendliest of terms again when circumstances made it seem profitable. Clearly, Fascist honor, like Fascist responsibility or Fascist freedom, is something other than honor as we know it.

The Fascist concept we encounter in two cases: as an excuse for not assuming international obligations, and as an excuse for not carrying them out. In the first instance the Fascists say they cannot make commitments which would oblige them to act in a way incompatible with their national honor, and in the second they say they must obey its dictates even if other moral or contractual duties should stand in the way. Never, on the other hand, in our experience with Fascist political practice has national honor been found to interfere with Fascist *advantage*. No policy that appeared materially beneficial, has yet been impeded even by the *identical* points of honor that had proved insurmountable obstacles to the assumption or discharge of international obligations. Every example from recent history—the Anglo-German Naval Agreement, the German attitude toward the Polish and Italian minority policies, the Italian attitude toward the League as an international instrument during and after the Ethiopian conflict— tends to make it clearer that Fascist honor works hand in glove with general Fascist policy—that it will always be compatible with the things the Fascists want to do anyway, and generally incompatible with things they want to avoid. The more we scrutinize the workings of the honor concept in Fascist foreign policy the more obvious it becomes that the national honor with which the Fascists qualify their international obligations, is nothing but a synonym for the vital national interest by which we have qualified them before. *In the last analysis, Fascist honor is Fascist advantage.*

This is a statement of fact and in no way meant as a slur. It is the normal, logical and inevitable result of the collectivist mentality. Again religion offers the most convincing analogy: the Crusaders killed and pillaged, the Inquisition burned and tortured, the Societas Iesu schemed and intrigued and prevaricated—all ad majorem Dei gloriam, although God's honor obviously did not require it. Men whose lives were dedicated to the Deity quite naturally came to believe that He was to be honored not only by following His precepts but by spreading, strengthening, unifying the faith in Him— and that the means employed for the purpose were a matter of secondary importance. Likewise men whose every effort (in a "religious conception of life") is dedicated to the community will develop a tendency to honor it by tireless and fanatic pursuit of its advantage. The objective standard, which honor among nations had acquired in a mentality devoted to the supremacy of the individual, was bound to get lost in a mentality which saw the nation not as a thing for a purpose but as the sole purpose of life in itself. Like the glory of God, the honor of a Fascist country is not an objective valuation but at once a quality inherent in its existence and a task for the individuals composing it. The nation can never dishonor itself—only the individuals can dishonor it by failing in their duty to serve its interests.

This, therefore, is where the vicious circle closes: while every restriction the Fascists are willing to place on the pursuit of their national interest is expressly or implicitly qualified by their national honor, this honor in turn requires the relentless pursuit of their national interest. Their foreign policy stands for "honorable peace": for peace as long as the national interest can be served that way, and for war if that is no longer possible. And this policy is altered neither by their promises of co-operation nor by the strings attached to them; it means exactly nothing if they promise a co-operation which they qualify by their national honor which in turn signifies only their national advantage. It all comes back to where it would have been in the first place, to the absolute and unrestricted dominance of their authoritatively determined national interest. What this interest requires (not at any fleeting moment, of course, but from the long view) will be done, whether it is most expressly forsworn or not. Should it be practically impossible for the present, it will be worked for and prepared and approached with the dogged determination which only a group that is wholly one in purpose can maintain for any length of time. Its achievement will always be sought the easiest way—if possible, for nothing, otherwise for the smallest exchange; if possible, in peace, otherwise with the least hostilities. The range of practical policies to be employed is unlimited, absolutely unlimited—there is nothing that cannot and will not be done if the vital purpose cannot otherwise be achieved. "They can't do that" was a favorite phrase of German democrats which they were forced to eliminate from their vocabulary in 1933, and which sooner or later non-Fascist nations will have to eliminate from theirs. They can do everything, if they should think it necessary to achieve their purpose. Only the purpose itself is as rigidly fixed as if it had been born with every single community member. No legal, no moral, no religious consideration can vary it. Fascist authority determines it, and once so determined its pursuit becomes the unswerving course of individuals and community alike —subject to no other rule than to exert only a minimum of effort.

Concerning the supreme effort—war—one thing can be said with assurance: no Fascist state will ever wage war without reason. It follows logically from their way of considering war as an unpleasant but normal and potentially quite useful means of national policy rather than as a national disaster. War to them is something like castor oil; of course, they are for peace—who in the world would dream of making war—unless a paramount need inexorably required it? This is probably the only ray of solace in the dreary specter our pacifists will find when they snap out of their roseate dreams: there will be no Fascist wars to avenge personal insults, like the Franco-Prussian War of 1870, or for "saving a poor and oppressed people" like the Spanish-American War (if we forget Mr. Hearst's sugar for a moment), or for "making the world safe" for anything whatsoever. When the Fascists go to war, they know why. Their reasons may seem insignificant to others— as when, for instance, the Germans were grimly prepared to fight, if need be, over the re-militarization of the Rhineland—but they are always of vital importance to the Fascist community. They will fight with absolute certainty if their régime should ever be in danger from internal unrest—though this possibility, of their having to wage war as an escape from trouble at home, is very much overestimated in non-Fascist public opinion. They will most probably fight for an eventual outlet for the population surplus which—in another vicious circle— they are deliberately creating in order to increase their manpower. And in any event it seems impossible, in the long run, that the process of balancing their ever-increasing strength with the relative weakening of the other powers can be wound up in peace.

Their strength is not just a matter of armaments— although, of course, their belief in the inevitability of war makes their preparations for it much more comprehensive, more consistent, and better planned than those of other countries. As a consequence of their concentration of communal energies they are continually growing stronger in every field. In the realm of economics, they weld and co-ordinate all forces and resources into a condition which, while very different from the democratic concept of prosperity, is the last word in economic preparedness and in the utilization of a capitalist economy for international aggrandizement. Their population policy makes their armies grow bigger. Their official application of practical eugenics makes them grow healthier and sturdier. They grow even in cultural strength—which means not an objective cultural level but a controlled and dirigible cultural tension. Today many people are still inclined to pooh-pooh the possibility that the Fascist countries may soon become stronger than all the other Western powers combined. Those skeptics had better recall what Germany, armed well enough but without any of the comprehensive and scientifically planned all-around preparation of the Nazi régime, did from 1914 to 1918. But, furthermore, we must realize that the Fascist nations will win future wars not because they are prosperous, or financially or culturally superior to their opponents. They will win because every fraction of their military, political, economic and cultural energies is prepared and available for, and adaptable to, the needs and purposes of the fighting community.

This process—in which every activity is constantly and increasingly made to serve the communal interest, and every new force in any field is immediately drawn into the collectivist net-work—makes for what we call the "ever-increasing strength" of the Fascist nations. It presents the last—and worst—of the vicious circles; for *it can only hold them permanently in the position of "have-nots."* Even if they keep acquiring new territories, resources and markets, their proportionally increasing strength will keep upsetting the balance—and forcing them into new demands. Here, finally, we encounter the ultimate distinction between the rules governing Fascist and non-Fascist foreign policy. Nobody would deny that democracies, internationally, are also largely guided by pure self-interest (although it will seldom be displayed as naïvely—or barefacedly—as by Fascist nations). But because democracy is individualistic, its egotism will never exceed a point where the people, the sovereign individuals, feel that they have enough—that it would not be worth their while to risk their lives and present fortunes for further enrichment. The Fascist state's national egotism, on the other hand, is completely divorced from the interests and preferences of its citizens—*and the growth of a Fascist nation, therefore, knows no saturation point. Its every expansion, whether justified or not, serves to increase its strength—and every increase in its strength, in turn, calls for new fields to conquer.*

No doubt, the Fascists' belief in the inevitability of war is well-founded. The only question is how long prospective victims will oblige them by postponing the necessity for it until the Fascists have really become invincible—either because of a mere distaste for war, or because they fail to realize that the more a Fascist country gets the more *it is bound* to desire. At any rate, though at first a peace-desiring world may surrender what the Fascists want, without a fight, sooner or later they will meet with resistance—if not before, then when, at long last, they come face to face with another Fascist power. At some point a threatened country will get tired of yielding—eventually, as they have all along expected,

the Fascists will have to fight for their objectives. But
they will never fight for nothing. And they will never
be "drawn" into a war. If they get into one, it will be
of their own free will and choosing. Since war is nothing to them but the sharpest implement in their tool-box,
they will never lose control over its use, and they will
never permit themselves to confuse it with the purpose it
is intended to serve.

It is very difficult not to lose sight of this realistic
sobriety and efficiency which guides the policies of those
same Fascist nations whose patriotic frenzy seems to
belie every thought of rationalism. Yet this is one of the
superficial contradictions that are intrinsically Fascist.
Just *because* Fascist patriotism is not a phenomenon
apparent only in moments of common danger or other
exaltation, it allows for the coolest possible deliberation
on the part of its leaders as to when and where and how
to put it to use. Just because the nationalism of a Fascist
people is always alive, it is also always under control
—it is ever available but never unmanageable. Moreover, it is keyed to its master's voice—to that it will respond immediately while indifferent to all others. This
has been the despair of the unfortunates who have to
deal with Fascists internationally: that they cannot get
at a Fascist people in the same way as at a non-Fascist
one. A democracy can be approached through its individuals. If one can scare them sufficiently they may keep
their state from a war. By threatening them with a sufficiently harmful boycott one may get them to change its
policies. To try these tactics with a Fascist nation is like

hitting a wall. They may be frightened but their collective determination remains unshaken. This must be fully understood to appreciate the cruel irony in Hitler's recent suggestion to the French to "hold a plebiscite on war and peace in both our countries." Of course, the vote would have been for peace on either side; but in France it would have expressed the will of the people and would have gone far to bind the state for times to come, while in Germany it would have represented the will of the nation, laid down by Hitler—and, by Hitler, freely changeable.

The reality of this mutual interpenetration of the Fascist communal will and the millions of individual wills is what the non-Fascists seem completely unable even to grant. As far as the internal affairs of Fascism are concerned, this resulted only in a rather sad accumulation of erroneous conceptions—in international politics it became practical. For years now the non-Fascist powers have based their policies on hypotheses such as "the people (of the Fascist countries) won't stand for it," or, when some moral, or economic, or other pressure "makes itself felt (to the individuals), they (the states) will have to desist," or simply the Fascist governments are "bluffing." The outcome, at the time of writing, has been that there is now not a single major international aim of a Fascist nation which is not at least far on the way to realization. If the non-Fascists do not change their stand, the further outcome will be that the Fascists will continue to pursue a policy of following up increases in inner strength with "balancing" expansion—through peace and war, *and for the duration of their existence as Fascist nations.* They will not be deterred by temporary set-backs—whether they retract themselves or are beaten in a test of strength. They *cannot* change their fundamental attitude in international affairs as long as they remain what they are. To change it, it will be necessary either to end their Fascism or to end their national existence. The prospects for the first alternative we shall discuss in the following chapter. The practicability of the second has been discussed in every chancellery in Europe—after the time to act had passed.

CHAPTER SEVEN

HAS DEMOCRACY FAILED?

Causes and Development of Fascism in Fascist Countries

TIME AND AGAIN, IN FASCIST THEORY AND PROPAGANDA, we find the assertion that the democratic system of government has failed. Besides being used as an argument for the conversion of other countries, it is also advanced by all Fascists as the main reason for their success at home. Which is of great interest to us at the present stage of this investigation, when, having deduced what abstract Fascism means to its adherents, we come to the analysis, in concrete instances, of the conditions and effects of its practical application. Our logical first step is an inquiry into the reasons for the reaction of Germans and Italians, converts to Fascism who were at least outwardly democratic before. If their own explanation is to be believed, they went Fascist only because the other system did not work. That we cannot simply dismiss that explanation as dishonest without further looking into it, will seem reasonable to anyone who has so far been able to go along with the point of view of this study. From that point of view it is clear that the Fas-

cists—even though we resent their presuming to tell us
what is wrong with *us*—ought to know best what helped
them succeed. We may receive their opinion with the
skepticism merited by any statement in their own cause,
but it certainly deserves our close and careful attention.

To avoid unnecessary misunderstanding: what does it
mean to say a system of government "has failed"? Evidently it must have failed in something it was expected
to do. But what was expected from democracy? Our
"working definition" of a democratic system of government laid down two requirements. First, the system must
be based on individualism—that is, the state must be
conceived not as a unit a priori but as an association of
individuals formed for the definite purpose of securing
the greatest good for the greatest number—which en-
tails all the dogmatic features of the individuals' superiority over their community: praeter-legal rights, protection against the state, etc. Second, the measures by which
this general purpose is to be served must be decided on
by majority vote, of the people or their elected representatives. Thus the raison d'être of the community is to
benefit the individuals; and how to do that in practice,
is to be determined *not objectively but subjectively*—the
democratic state must do, not what *is* good for the people, but *what they think* is good for them. A wisely constituted democratic set-up, of course, will not let this
determination of the communal will depend on mass
imagination running riot. It will provide for veto powers and judicial review—checks upon the passing fancies of popular majorities, to be exercised by men fit to

use a more objective judgment. But once these possibilities within the system are exhausted, no agency of the state, however competent, will be justified in interfering with the popular mandate; executives whose veto is overridden, or judges without pertinent jurisdiction, cannot within the scope of democratic principles prevent a course of action even if they are positive, and rightly so, that it invites disaster. It follows that a legitimately arrived-at communal action of a democracy, no matter how unfortunate it may eventually turn out to be, *can never fail to achieve its dogmatic objective:* what the people, at the time, thought would be good for them. If they were wrong, the error of judgment on their part cannot be blamed upon the system. This—that democracy itself must not be held responsible for its material failures—is really the strongest rational argument that has yet been made in its favor. That majorities will reach objectively sounder conclusions than selected minorities, is an uncertain guess at best. But one thing is sure—if, under a democratic system, the people do not always get the best results, at least they have no reason to kick.

According to its own premises, an ill-fated democracy is no failing one. And, in fact, while empires and kingdoms have been overthrown when things went wrong and for dictatorships it has become almost a rule that they cannot survive defeat, history has rarely seen a democratic system upset because of external or economic misadventures. If, therefore, the groundwork for Fascism is a "failure of democracy," this must mean something else than a failure to be materially successful. And what other kind of "failure" is possible, will become very clear as soon as we manage to forget our ingrained notion that a state *is* nothing but an instrument for the achievement of material benefits. For to people who are free from that prejudice, who seriously believe that the state is a unit a priori and an end in itself, an attempt to effectuate a democratic system must seem doomed to fall for the simple reason that *it would constitute an inversion of the natural relationship between individual and community.* It cannot work —not because it would not benefit the individuals but because it would put them in a position contrary to their natural and instinctive feeling. It would be resented *not because it was functioning badly but because it was functioning at all.* The Fascists reject the democratic coat not because it does not keep warm but because it does not fit. Once we are able to assume, for the sake of argument, that people *can* think along the lines of what we have heretofore termed collectivism, it becomes strikingly apparent how unrealistic, how unsatisfactory, how unworkable in every sense of the word a democratic set-up must appear to them. It contradicts their whole manner of political thinking. It requires them to act in a way which to them does not make sense. It puts them into a relation to their community which they feel is topsy-turvy. No wonder that to people with this mentality a few years of such a system must seem a manifest "failure." Democracy, for them, cannot set up a workable state structure because, as Mussolini said, "the state has changed in the consciousness and the will of the people."

Whether, and how far, the breakdown of existing democratic systems can actually be traced to their conflict with national mentalities of this sort, we can only find out from the rise of Fascism in the countries which adopted it. What was responsible for this rise has been speculated about by every commentator—particularly in the case of Germany. To analyze the causes of Fascism in Italy beyond the personal influence of Mussolini,[1] the experts have been noticeably reluctant—presumably because it was rather hard there to detect any obvious circumstances which were not equally prevalent in a dozen other countries without having produced any such spectacular results. There has even appeared a marked willingness to admit that the Italian people, economically backward and politically uneducated, were not democratically inclined anyway, and that, perhaps, Fascism did spring from their unfavorable reaction to something for which they were not ripe. As our interpretation does not substantially differ from this, we can defer stating our reasons for it until after we have discussed the prevailing theories of the causes of German Fascism.

---

[1] Mussolini's background, his intellectual development from the Socialist blacksmith's son into the Duce of Fascism, the influence which the teachings of others—mainly Sorel and Pareto—had upon him, all this has been investigated ad nauseam. The Italian national mind, on the other hand—the mentality which Mussolini in turn could mold into the spiritual entity of Fascism—was paid no more attention than a sculptor's lifeless clay.

Germany's successful experiment in democracy for years made liberals all over the world wax enthusiastic —in fact, until Hitler so sadly disillusioned them. In Germany one could not talk of economic backwardness and lack of political knowledge—and, fortunately for our embarrassed pundits, an abundance of unusual conditions made it easy to pick some that seemed more or less likely to have led to a Fascist upheaval. What has been most frequently mentioned in this connection, is the economic breakdown between 1930 and 1933, and the unyielding attitude of the victorious powers against the Reich (once they had not been farsighted or consistent enough to dismember it at the opportune moment). That both these elements were among the most emphasized points of National Socialist propaganda, particularly effective in the last "big push" which gave Hitler his overwhelming parliamentary majority over any of the other German parties, is a matter of record. That they played an important part in the historic development leading up to the "national revolution," cannot be denied. But it cannot be denied, either, that the hapless court camarilla of Von Papen and colleagues had its share in shaping the actual course of events; yet nobody has ever credited Von Papen with the rise of Hitler. As a matter of principle, it should be evident to every believer in democracy, that a movement with sufficient impetus to swell in five years from nothing to thirty per cent of the electorate—being opposed, then, not by a majority party or coalition but by an incongruous conglomerate of disagreeing, inefficient, weak, split politi-

cal groups—neither could, not *should,* when it continued
to grow, have been kept out of power by governmental
resistance. Again the individualist nature of democracy
asserts itself—its own basic idea enjoins the system
from interfering with the formation of the popular will,
even of a will that would oblige it to commit suicide.
Hitler's battle, for all practical purposes, was won in
1930. After that it was a wrangling, not over whether or
not to assume power, but how to assume it. What established National Socialism, or something like it, as the
political future of Germany, was the period from
1924-25—the apparent collapse of the movement after
the abortive Putsch in Munich—to 1930—its triumphant entry into the Reichstag with one hundred and
twenty deputies, topped only by the trade-union-
supported Social Democrats whom it promptly proceeded to surpass at the following general election.

The inescapable conclusion is that the Third Reich
was a product of neither economic distress nor Allied
mistreatment. When the nightmare of inflation had
passed, Germany enjoyed more than five years of universal prosperity—unsound in its foundations, it is true,
but at the time the people could not know that. Later, of
course, depression and the rise of unemployment made
magnificent sales points for Nazi propaganda—but the
substance of the movement, the force which in any event
would have been sufficient to sway the fate of the nation,
came into being at a time when few were suffering from
hunger. Neither was Allied stubbornness more respon-

sible for its growth than as a concomitant cause.[2] The Reparations, which Dr. Schacht now holds to blame for non-payment of German debts, were paid out of borrowed monies and did not immediately weigh upon the German masses. In the years following evacuation of the Ruhr, Dr. Stresemann achieved equality of international influence for Germany in practice, if not in theory. But the *results* obtained by the various republican governments were hardly ever targets of Nazi criticism (with the possible exception of the very acquiescence in the Polish frontier settlement, which later was to mark the first feat of Nazi diplomacy!). What was criticized, were *methods:* recognition of the League of Nations authority, submission to World Court judgments, acknowledgment of the binding force of "extorted" signatures even if conflicting with national interests—in one word, Erfüllungspolitik, "Policy of Fulfilment." It had nothing to do with either economic or

[2] Naturally, a more conciliatory post-War policy on the part of the Allied governments might have altered the international attitude of the National Socialist movement. But it would hardly have prevented its emergence. Hitler, in that case, would not—as he actually did—have come to power firmly convinced that force was the only way in which to receive justice; and, consequently, he would probably not have grown into the permanent war-cloud of 1934 et seq. If satisfied that the international set-up was sufficiently elastic for German interests, Hitler—true to Fascist principles of efficiency—would have been sincerely for peace; not, as today, in words only. He might even have become a second Mussolini and a mainstay of a temporary status quo in Europe—about the role which the British, with their usual hindsight, are now trying to coax him into. But the point is: whatever its foreign policies might have been for the present, some kind of German Fascism would have emerged in any case.

international realities. Undoubtedly the movement was helped along by the effects of depression and the troubles of foreign policy, but what gave birth to it was neither economic nor international disadvantage. It was a dissatisfaction purely internal and exclusively political.

The one fundamental fact is that throughout the fourteen years of the Republic the German people were politically uncomfortable. Their feelings may well be compared to the dissatisfaction of an essentially democratic population with an existing absolute monarchy, however benevolent and materially beneficial. What irks them also is not that the monarchic set-up does not work but that it does. They resent a quite intangible infringement of their freedom—in other words, their having to live under a system that does not conform to their basic inclinations, even if it accords them every other advantage. With the Germans from 1918 to Hitler, it was never a question of whether the democracy, as democracy, was functioning well or badly. Anglo-Americans have often ascribed the difficulties of the Republic to its failure to adopt a two-party system as practiced in England and in the United States. But, aside from the practical impossibility of creating such a system other than by historical tradition, the many-party system had worked well in pre-War Germany and in most of the other continental democracies without producing a monstrosity of thirty-eight parliamentary factions. Moreover, what actually brought about the downfall of German parliamentarianism was not the splitting up of big parties but on the contrary the gobbling up of the smaller parties by the huge extremist groups. The Republic flourished through the years when there were from seven to ten different parties with political vitality, but it collapsed when between the Nazi-dominated Right and the half-Socialist, half-Communist Left stood nothing but emasculated relics of parties without a viewpoint and without a following among the people. Technically, the framers of the Weimar Constitution had done a good job. The German basic law made remarkably effective provision for the representation of divergent interests and for the presentation of issues to a real majority decision; it was adaptable to changing circumstances, gave sufficient leeway to the executive to prevent the recurring deadlocks that proved such a nuisance in France, and was generally recognized as a model instrument for the effectuation of democratic principles under twentieth century conditions. What made it ineffective was not its structure but the lack of response. Much has been made of the truism that a democratic system could not have been expected to work properly with the essentially anti-democratic personnel which the Republic retained from times before the War. What is completely overlooked is the fact that this retention was nothing but the democratically inevitable acknowledgment of the fact that the majority of the people—even in the parties which supported the Republic—*were*, consciously or subconsciously, anti-democratic. The people preferred the old officialdom to continue in office—not, as was generally thought abroad, only because they were proud of their civil service, but because they considered it a kind of insurance against the democratic experiment, a device guaranteeing the maintenance of standards which the new system might tend to overthrow. What the German people wanted in 1918 was not a new order but a state of things that would eliminate the monarchy (then untenable because it had lost the War) and leave everything else as far as humanly possible as it had been until 1914. The result was that strange phenomenon—the anti-democratic democracy. It was caused by the fact that the German masses, whose task it would have been to fill the new form with substance, did not realize that the monarchic idea had been the very thing that held the pseudo-democratic structure of pre-War Germany together. With the removal of the Imperial crown the old set-up lost its meaning—and the Germans were neither prepared nor willing to accept an entirely new system with all its implications. This insoluble contradiction between the real desires of the people and the means they chose to pursue them was at the bottom of all the troubles of the Weimar Republic.

It was a typical case of the "failure of democracy" apt to create Fascism: what bothered the people were not shortcomings or excesses of their democratic set-up but the thing itself. The average German never had the Englishman's or American's pride in partaking in the government of his country, or the Frenchman's desire to assert his liberty. He only felt uneasy at having a responsibility thrust upon him which he thought belonged properly to someone else. The German never progressed to a feeling of gratification at being able to tell the politicians what to do—he always had a suspicion that by making him vote they were really dodging their responsibility. What puzzled him was the *principle* of popular sovereignty on which any system of representative government rests. The spiritual coherence of a community which is conceptually devoted to the satisfaction of divergent material desires was something he was unable to comprehend. That a state could exist in unity while committed to serve the interests of the various individuals or groups composing it—could, in fact, exist through and on the basis of this interrelation of interests—was beyond his understanding. And it must be admitted that, from a strictly logical point of view, the combination of "liberty and union" *is* something of a paradox; but the true democrat has no qualms in accepting it as possible in practice *because he knows* it is possible—because he lives it daily. To the Germans it was nothing but a dead sophism, meaningless on the face of it. Throughout their experience with democratic government they had a feeling of "coming apart"—of losing, not, as yet, their regional or political unity, but its spiritual foundation. Though there was never even an expressed fear, much less a real danger, of the Republic jeopardizing German unity, there was a constant impalpable and indescribable uneasiness about it—a subconscious worry about how a state without the centripetal effect of the monarchy could stay "one and inseparable," while relying for the determination of its communal will upon political parties violently opposing each other and for the very theory of its existence on the satisfaction of the divergent interests of individual groups. Democracy, in their unexpressed opinion, could not but destroy the unison of purpose which they felt to be the prerequisite to any unity. It was the longing for a basic purpose, common to all and transcending every individual interest, which democracy by virtue of its conception could not satisfy—and which threw them straight into the arms of Hitler.

It was as the result of this longing that they developed the state of mind that proved incompatible with democratic government. The vague dread—which, however, went to the very roots of the democratic idea—put a terrific pressure upon their weakest spot, for German national unity was not a given and natural state of affairs, real since time out of mind, but a relatively new, long-desired, hard-won and accordingly prized possession. Even to the present generation, which had inherited it, the Reich, as set up by Bismarck, represented a dream come true—or rather not *quite* true yet. Whoever is familiar with nineteenth century European history, will find in this the answer to an otherwise rather baffling question: why the German and the Italian nations, essentially so different, should both have hit upon the identical solution to their national problems. What determined their choice is also the one important common feature in German and Italian political development: the desperate quest for national unity, achieved in long-drawn and bitter fighting against heavy odds and apparently unsurmountable obstacles. In both cases this

urge was instrumental in giving to the conception of the
nation a supernatural stature. In both cases Fascism
completed what the prophets of the early nineteenth
century began—Mussolini made the vision of Mazzini
come true no less than Hitler the vision of Fichte and
the men of 1848. That most of the forerunners thought
in democratic terms makes no difference; their attitude
was one of revolt against the political and spiritual en-
slavement of their people which had grown out of
eighteenth century absolutism, and it was only too natural to impregnate the collective freedom for which they
fought with the ideas of individual freedom with which
the French Revolution had colored every fight against
the absolutist tradition. At that time, democracy was a
revolutionary notion that almost inevitably slipped into
any insurgent movement. All over Europe youth dreamt
of freedom and democracy—only in Germany and Italy
the freedom they envisioned was collective rather than
individual, and what spurred them on, what they longed
for, what they fought for, was not "liberté, égalité,
fraternité," but "La Italia Unita" and "Deutschland
Über Alles." France and England had been centralized
national units since the decline of feudalism. There
absolutism had done the job of unification; and the most
obvious ideal to inspire the revolt against it was the
freedom of the individuals who were a nation anyway.
In Germany and Italy absolutism had kept them from
becoming a nation—so when its hour struck the right for
which it was overthrown was not the right to be free
men, but the right to be a free people. This, a national

urge private to Germans and Italians, equally deep and of equally long standing as the national urges that made the Western democracies, is the psychological root of Fascism. It produced the *mental attitude* of the people, which, on the *factual* basis of modern capitalistic development, found in Fascism its most adequate expression.

Out of the longing for unity in a people, out of the rebellious trend against forces of time and tradition that tended to keep them apart, grew the deification of the national unit, the sublimation of all individual consciousness into the superhuman collective being, which we have termed collectivism. It is hard for us to conceive how, even with time and circumstances working in its favor, this mentality can really become as natural as our "normal" individualist way of thinking. We can never quite get over the instinctive reaction that, after all, Herr Stein and Signor Rocca *are* individuals like Mr. Stone, and how in the world can they feel differently about it than Mr. Stone does? Again it may help to look somewhat further afield. In the Far East, ancestral worship has exalted the conception of the family far above anything we could possibly understand. In the early days of European feudalism, the retainer did not question the precedence of his feudal duty over his personal interests—and it took the double force of feudal deterioration and of national intervention to break down this ingrained consciousness. The priest of the medieval Church did not dream of setting his own good above the good of the ecclesiastic community—not because he had sworn an oath to that effect, and not even because the

Ecclesia stood in the place of the Almighty (that was dogmatically very much disputed), but because in his mind his individuality had been sublimated into the collective organism. We may be tempted to discount these instances from past ages and Oriental nations as proving nothing for the Western mind of today. But at this very moment our literary experts are acclaiming André Malraux, the French novelist whose entire work consists in the glorification of a political collective spirit prevailing to the extent of effecting a complete interchangeability of individuals. Jointly with the historic cases of true collective consciousness, our willingness to accept it for the present as a subject of fiction may make it easier for us to believe that the development of the Fascist mentality is not just a fake. Its genesis is really much less astonishing than, for example, the rise of feudal collectivism from unknown sources, unaided by distinct religious or political movements, to the domination of at least two centuries of European culture. The Fascist spirit is nothing but the natural outgrowth of a popular desire, intensified by resistance, and articulated by the vociferous pronouncements of a political doctrine set upon its gratification.

Of course, this mentality is not of equal strength throughout a people. Presumably there were many feudal retainers who felt they had a right to look after their own good as well as after that of their lord. There were predatory clerics in the Middle Ages, and there were probably Japanese even before the intrusion of Western influences who doubted the essential precedence of the family spirit over their individual interests and wishes. In the case of modern political collectivism this is bound to be much more so, because its growth is comparatively recent, and all the people except the very young ones have been exposed to other and contrary teachings and influences. Particularly among the Germans, whose high cultural and intellectual average encouraged the development of cosmopolitan ideas, such a large sector of the population had absorbed the democratic way of thinking, that no one but the Nazis even dared to call them apostates, constituting an unrepresentative and "spiritually alien" foreign body. It does require a great mental effort on our part to admit that the line of thought, for instance, of Thomas Mann is not typically German. Yet the author of *Buddenbrooks*—as German a book as was ever written—and most of the other exponents of what our idealists still insist on calling the "best German tradition," are German in everything but their conception of Germany. Their dreams of the future never centered on Germany but on Europe and the world. Much as it may disgust us, the Nazi description of the position of these men in German cultural life is absolutely correct: they represent a thin layer of internationalized intellectuals, with huge literary or artistic reputations and with no emotional connection whatever with the mass of their countrymen. For the "fourteen years of disgrace," as the Nazis like to call the republican era, this so-called cultural élite of Germany thought to exert an influence upon the German national consciousness— and in 1933 found out that while they were looking forward the mentality they thought they were leading had been marching in another direction. Even before 1848, the movement for German liberty had been a matter of *individual* freedom for a small élite group, which the superior forces of reaction quickly scattered into exile—Heinrich Heine, Ludwig Börne, Carl Schurz are examples—while the masses of the people were interested only in collective freedom and, after Bismarck brought them together into one community, had no further desires. The Weimar Republic, too, was a matter of genuine democracy for a comparatively small group. For the overwhelming majority it was the best available refuge after the collapse, a bread-and-butter affair which in the long run could not satisfy their spiritual needs— democracy "failed."

In Italy the development of the collectivist mentality was somewhat different. First of all, the inhabitants of the peninsula had been exposed, since the breakdown of the Roman Empire, to infinitely more numerous and more varied influences than the Germans. Fifth century Italy, a mixture of Roman, Greek and Oriental cultural notions, was overrun by the conquering Germanic tribes who set up Germanic kingdoms from the Alps to Sicily, with a considerable part remaining under the rule of the Byzantine Empire. Then, as part of the German "Holy Roman Empire," it was a place of continual and all-pervading quarrels—between Papal and Imperial authority, Germans and Italians, different factions of Germans and Italians. Under the guise of a revival of antiquity, the Renaissance gave birth to a new Italy—

spiritually centering in a classicized Catholicism and
secularly in the town-states which so strongly resembled
the "poleis" of ancient Greece. The fifteenth and six-
teenth centuries saw the flower, the seventeenth and
eighteenth the decadence of this development. So the
people of Italy had just about lost every vital relationship to the various state structures constituting their
political set-up, when the French Revolution postulated
the abolition of those outdated remnants of another age
and the Napoleonic conquest proved that it could be
done. And when after 1814 the old order returned, the
seed had been sown and went up in the Risorgimento.
Outward success was achieved when by the grace of
Napoleon III the House of Savoy ascended a newly
created Italian throne. Actually it turned out that the
new Italy was nothing but all the previous petty prince-
doms rolled into one. Hardly born, it was already as
decrepit as any of the other century-old relics in the
Mediterranean area. It was a state without substance,
without vigor, and without a purpose. Worse than that,
it was a state without any spiritual connection whatever
with its individual citizens. Its monarchy was without a
tradition and without much hold on popular imagination. Its public life was a playground for a decadent
nobility and a pitiable assortment of professional statesmen (a potentially much more noxious species than mere
professional politicians). The bulk of the people managed to exist—starvation being no real menace because
of the country's bountiful nature, the few material needs
of its inhabitants, and the prevalence and comparative

honorability of stealing—but were little better than pic-
turesque "natives" who multiplied like rabbits and disposed of their surplus offspring by emigration to the
United States. The contact between Italy, as a state, and
her people—in the perpetuation of which much more
than in mere external unification the Risorgimento had
seen its paramount goal—was less alive in the early
part of the twentieth century than in the early nineteenth.[3]

Then the War came and *forced* them together. They
were frightful soldiers. In spite of vastly superior numbers they could not hold their own narrow front and
had constantly to signal for help to Allied headquarters.
But, for the first time since 1870, it was impressed upon
every one of them that he was one of a kind. By French-
men and Englishmen this was so taken for granted that
they had long developed a philosophy of individualism
as an antidote. With Germans, in a short half-century,
the idea had grown into the most powerful agent of
their entire being. To the men from the peninsula it was
like the resurrection of a half-buried instinct, and doubly
stirring. It made it quite impossible for them to go back
to their former life as utterly unrelated individuals
within a communal frame with which they had no spiritual connection. They had been one in war, how could
they not be one in peace? "The state changed in the

[3] Recognition of this, in the upper social and intellectual strata,
was the mainspring behind the pre-War Nationalist Movement,
which fostered the Austrian Irredenta, did most to get Italy into
the War, and was later officially acknowledged as precursor of
Fascism.

consciousness and the will of the people." They leaped
at every chance to keep their collectivity alive—which
explains, among other things, the astounding spread of
Communism in a largely unindustrialized country with
a politically ignorant population at the end of a victorious war. The "liberal" governments of post-War Italy
missed their cue completely. They dabbled at economic
remedies when what was needed was recognition of a
nascent political mentality. They played regulation politics when what was needed was a spiritual renovation
of the state. So the people turned to the extremist groups
which were all based upon some collective concept. "The
people" is here not synonymous with the electorate. In
a country where voting since its inception had been a
rather meaningless act because of the lack of *any* living
relationship between community and individual, the
votes naturally stayed in the channels into which un-
political considerations—the influence of the priest, the
landlord, the employer, or the buyer of votes—had traditionally guided them before. But it was clear in 1920
that there were many more participants in the Communist factory raids than Communist voters—and it was
even more obvious that the Fascist activities, the seizures
of municipal administrations, the "town-regiment" of
the early Fascist "Rases," must have had the emotional
assent of a huge number of Italians who never voted a
Fascist ticket. Even after the March on Rome, when
Mussolini became the head of an ordinary coalition government, the parliamentary resistance of his opponents
was paralyzed from the start by their feeling that the

people at large, even in their own party ranks, did not really want their system but the unsystematic collectivism of the enemy. So when the Communist competition was disposed of, it was a simple question of either forgetting the experience of the War and going back to the spiritually empty past, or going forward into an uncertain, undefined and undefinable future in which only one thing would be sure: they would be integral and inseparable parts of a whole again, as in the days of Gorizia and Vittorio Veneto. Their emotional choice was inevitable—and for that reason the expression of their formal decision came to be of no importance.

In Italy, as in Germany, the new mentality was not a completed fact throughout the nation, when Fascism came to power. The sources of non-conformity, however, were different. Hitler, supported by an overwhelming and deep-rooted mass sentiment which had been articulate for over a century, had to contend with an intellectual minority of world-wide fame and influence. Mussolini found no significant opposition from such a source.[4] His real work began when he set out to make the urge toward "nationship," which the Risorgimento had created and the World War resurrected, conscious and general. What he had to overcome was the natural indolence of a three-hundred-year-old tradition of political insensibility. Since the Renaissance had begun to

[4] Some of Italy's greatest minds—Benedetto Croce, Guglielmo Ferrero—went into exile and were properly pitied abroad; but there was nothing like the rallying of international civilization to its maltreated offspring, which took place at the suppression of German intellectualism.

decay, the Italian population had been nothing but "people." To make them over into "*a* people" was bound to prove a Herculean task even though the instinct had already been awakened. Thus, although the slogan "A noi!"—"To us!"—met with a response of boundless enthusiasm in the most advanced as well as in the most backward groups of the population, it *was* necessary for the Fascists to plaster the country with it in a way that never fails to give the visiting foreigner a touch of nausea. Where Hitler had to fight the effects of an intellectual overdevelopment that, had transcended the bounds of the national feeling, Mussolini was confronted with the fact that, for lack of such development, the bulk of the people were not yet even awake to that feeling. What stirred the Italian masses was a tremendous restlessness which only the Fascist vanguard managed to connect with the collectivist tradition. German Fascism after its seizure of the state had to provide a form for an existing spirit. Italian Fascism had to cast a latent and slumbering spirit into a mold which itself was only just being formed under the impact of practical necessities—and according to a largely instinctive notion of what the finished spirit eventually would require.

Thus, while German democracy failed because it was unable to express an existing national mentality, Italian democracy failed because in the fifty years of its formal existence it had not been able to create a national mentality. In one case there was a popular conception of the communal relationship with which democracy was incompatible, and in the other there was no such popular conception whatsoever—only a powerful but vague sub-conscious urge toward it—and Fascism offered an idea while democracy did not. The unforgivable sin com-mitted by Italian democracy—and expiated by its death —was to have left a people with the vitality of the Italians without a rallying point for the very collective instincts to which it owed its birth. After having been created by the desire of the Italian people to become a unit, the Italian version of democracy let them slide right back into the same disjointed and integrally un-related communal set-up from which they had sought to escape. Instead of attempting to base a democratic national feeling on the achieved national unity, it set up democratic institutions and, since "all men were created equal," trusted to nature to make them work. It was the most striking example of a "failure of democ-racy" imaginable. Its guiding spirits had provided a theoretically very sound system, and had made it per-form its material functions remarkably well for several decades. They had forgotten only one little thing: that a democratic form might need a democratic substance, that a democratic structure might be meaningless with-out a democratic spirit in the people who were to live under it. Whether an attempt in that direction might have worked, is another question—the Italians of the later nineteenth century were still such political raw material that they *might* have been convertible into good individualist democrats even after the collectivizing trend of the Risorgimento. But the leaders of Italian democracy during that period did not even try. The only thing that can be said in their favor is that they really were not very much surprised when the thing collapsed in 1922.

This also answers the Italian side of the often-asked question—vital for the outlook of democracy in general —why the rise of Fascism has not been prevented, or at least impeded, by popular concern for the "liberties of Man" which democracy had made safe for its individual citizens. As far as the Italians' civil rights are concerned the answer is very simple: they did not know them. They *had* them, to a large extent even enjoyed them not only in theory but in practice—but about eighty per cent of the people did not know what it was all about. The Italians were not even in the position of the politically disfranchised and economically enslaved pre-War Russians—their situation was much more like that of happy South Sea islanders who get suffrage and civil liberties from their white colonial administration. They exist, nature providing for their little wants, religion and secret societies filling their spiritual life, in a child-like way without quite understanding the import of those new toys handed to them by the grown-ups. As the Soviets realized when they found it necessary to exercise the proletarian dictatorship not only against the subdued capitalist class but against the entire population of Russia: civil liberties *presuppose* a democratic conception of the communal relationship, they cannot create it. Americans were fortunate enough to receive this conception with their English heritage, and could build upon it. The English had to fight for centuries, not only for their rights but for the philosophy on which they claimed them. The French— though a large proportion of even the lower classes had absorbed the teachings of the eighteenth century forerunners of Liberalism—had to go through the Terror of the Revolution, the dictatorship of the Empire, *and* the contrasting experiences of the Bourbon Restoration and the Royaume Bourgeois, before the new-born love of liberty, which in 1789 had sufficed to blast a one-thousand-year-old kingdom out of existence, became sufficiently clear and general to assert itself in any practical contingency. The Italians had been a people without any live communal consciousness for generations, had suddenly awakened to a violent collective urge, and in reply to that had been presented with a complete set of modern democratic fixtures. They had not specifically wanted them in the first place, and after they had got them they had no very good idea what to do with them. They went on considering communal affairs a hobby of the selected few, and living a happy and primitive life as before. That they, when roused to a recollection of their slumbering collective consciousness, did not weigh it against the threatening loss of liberties they had never quite known how to use, could really not surprise anyone halfway familiar with the workings of what in Italy passed for "democracy."

In Germany, however, the argument could seem to carry a great deal of weight. There many civil liberties had not only existed for a long time in a thoroughly conscious acceptance by the entire population, but they had even antedated not only the young democracy but

its cause, the nineteenth century movement for unification. Equality before the law had been an accomplishment of eighteenth century Prussian benevolent absolutism, before a united Germany had even stirred the
imagination of the Teutonic poets. Freedom of speech
and freedom of the press had been first theoretically
championed before the French Revolution, and vocifer-
ously demanded after the Napoleonic danger had been
averted. Later, while the "police state" of the early
nineteenth century drew the fire of all German patriots,
the granting of constitutions with elaborate enumera-
tions of rights reserved to the subjects became a favorite
pastime of the smaller German monarchs. In the Bismarckian Reich the powers of the state were large and
virtually unhampered, but the strict formality and legality of the way they were exercised generally gave the
impression of a basically individualist character of the
communal relationship. The Republic, of course, emphasized this character; its constitution contained ten
sections exclusively devoted to an enumeration of the
rights upon which the state should not be allowed to
infringe—provided, however, that by emergency decree
the executive branch of the government could suspend
every one of them, indefinitely and without any possibility of review. In itself, of course, such a provision is
not necessarily undemocratic. But the interesting point
was that while continuous attacks by virtually all parties
were made upon the emergency power of the executive
to *make laws*—to determine the national will—its au-

thority to suspend fundamental rights has never even
been questioned!

The basis of democracy—the sovereignty of the individuals—never really touched a chord in the German
soul. Its most significant practical expressions—the right
of the sovereign individual to make his own law (freedom of contract), his right to have the law applied to
him only by his peers (trial by jury), his right to criticize his servant, the state, and its government (freedom
of speech and of the press), his ability to enforce the
precedence of his individual privileges over the communal interest (judicial review)—never inspired anything in the Germans except the very thing they were
not meant to call forth: acceptance as manifestations
of state benevolence. After the Weimar Constitution had
established trial by jury, a law passed by a parliamentary surprise majority all but abolished it again—the
people did not even take notice. That the state could
protect its interest against transgressions of the individuals in any way it saw fit—was that not elementary? If
the individual was subordinated to governmental action
against his interests—what of it? Was he not part of
the state? The state giveth, the state taketh away—what
was to prevent it? Even today the "nullum crimen sine
poena" policy of the National Socialist government
caused only some anxiety that individual Nazi officials
might use it for the gratification of personal grudges—
but resentment at the submersion of individual rights?
Not a bit. From the earliest periods of their history—
when the collectivism of the Germanic tribes developed

into that of the feudal organization and then into that of
petty absolutism which was hated not because it was
absolutism but because it was petty, not because it enslaved the individuals but because it split the national
community—the Germans have never really stopped to
think and feel collectively. There has never—with one
notable exception—been an individual right which actually stirred them deeply.

The exception—as notable today as it was five hundred years ago—is freedom of religion. England and
France had their religious conflicts; but their actual civil
uprisings, from Cade's Rebellion to the Paris Commune
in 1871, took place to win freedom for the individual
to serve *his* interests and not those of his monarch, government, or governing class. Even in the Puritan and
Huguenot Wars the material and political interests at
stake all but outweighed the religious issue. Civil wars
in Germany were always fought for the privilege of
serving God according to the dictates of conscience.
Even the "Peasants' War" in the fifteenth century—
bloody vengeance of the serfs and villeins bled to starvation—from the outset sought to connect itself with contemporary religious movements; rebuffed by Luther,
they finally ended up in an alliance with the Anabaptists.
It is a striking illustration of this, that the only real
resistance with which the National Socialist efforts at
Gleichschaltung have met, occurred in the field of religion. Any other co-ordination individual Germans may
personally dislike but will never feel to be fundamentally wrong; it springs from a source which they ac-

knowledge even if it hurts. Their collective relation to the Deity is different. It is the only field where, in the course of the centuries, their national collectivism has been largely supplanted with something still stronger. It is the only field where the axiomatic supremacy of the state over everything else is challenged in the consciousness of the people. While for every German it is "Deutschland Über Alles," quite a few make an exception for God Almighty.

That the religious issue is a German and not a Fascist phenomenon is shown by its conspicuous absence in Italy. Co-ordination went equally far in both countries, and the Catholic Church that is getting along so well with Mussolini is the same whose representatives stir up so much trouble for Hitler. But for the Italians, since the days of Savonarola, religion had been a wholly unproblematic routine part of their daily lives, while for a large percentage of the German people it was a deep and vital influence and problem up into the present. How vital—as always in such matters—became apparent only when it was interfered with. And so, while in Italy the Azione Cattolica could work out a modus vivendi with the Fascists quickly and easily, German churches have now been jammed for years with worshipers seeking refuge for their troubled souls. Let nobody indulge himself in the hope that here is a seed of *political* rebellion.[5] Few of the worried Catholics and Protestants have

[5] It *might* have been one in Southern Bavaria, where the old specifically Bavarian royalism was long alive and intelligently tied up with the Catholic question. Even there, however, the younger

any objections whatsoever to Hitler, or National Socialism, or any feature of the régime except to what they
consider its interference with their duty to God. None
of them would ever align himself with any of the essential enemies of the régime—such as the despised Communists. They are as German as any Nazi and as collectivist as any Nazi. In fact, if allowed to do their
religious duty as they see it, they would in all probability be the most model Nazis of them all.

The real core of the question is that what is here
resisted is not the infringement of a right but an interference with the performance of a duty. What the ob-
jectors want is not freedom to think or to do—they want
freedom to serve. They resent not their extermination
as sovereign individuals but the encroachment upon
their status as servants of the Lord. Their stand is not a
reassertion of individualism but a defense of another
collectivism, the conception of which they have inherited
from past generations as being not of this world. They
do not refuse to submerge themselves individually—they
only have trouble in producing for submersion a part
of their individuality which is already submerged elsewhere. Viewed as a whole and in its historic connection,
the religious controversy is the strongest possible proof
of the spontaneity and originality and nativeness of German Fascism. That it took this, their oldest and deepest

generation seems glad to exchange its Bavarian restiveness for
German collectivity, and Hitler's masterstroke of selecting Munich
for the "Capital of the National Socialist Movement" (as opposed
to Berlin as Capital of the Reich) is liable to do away with whatever vestiges of Bavarianism are still extant.

and most ingrained of feelings, to stir the people to a show of resistance, is just as telling an argument for the system's basic suitability as that the Italians grew restive only when after thirteen years of Fascism Mussolini sent them out to be emasculated by ferocious Africans.

To recapitulate our construction of the psychological developments leading up to the evolution of Fascism:

At the end of the eighteenth century the people of Germany and Italy had lost all touch with their respective political systems. The essence of both was an atomized absolutism—the two countries were split up into countless absolute monarchies of varying size. In Germany the national connection was reduced to a completely ineffective formal domination of the Emperor (the Holy Roman Empire was not formally dissolved until 1806); in Italy it had never come into being. The mental attitude of the people was in Germany an obedient acceptance of absolutist rule which had grown out of feudal collectivism; in Italy it was a complete indolence, an extinction of *any* communal feeling, that followed the decay of the exaggerated individualism of the Renaissance.

Under the double influence of the philosophy of enlightenment and the impact of the French Revolution, there developed in both Germany and Italy a movement of revolt against the historical set-up. But in contrast to the direction which it took in France, the main trend of the German and Italian rebellion was not anti-absolutistic and democratic, but anti-*petty*-absolutistic and nationalistic. Their driving force turned out to be not (as that behind the French Revolution or the American Constitution) the desire of the individuals to escape from the fetters of a community which could so easily fall into the hands of a tyrant, but their desire to escape from the separating fetters of hundreds of little tyrants into one national community. Consequently, from denying the rights of intra-national groupings to impair the unity of the nation, the state of mind created by these movements quite naturally arrived at a conceptual subordination of individuals and groups of individuals to the community—which came to be viewed as an organism of a higher order.

The rule of reaction after the Napoleonic Wars tended in Italy as well as in Germany to spread and deepen this collectivist mentality. However, while in Germany it fell upon an already extant collectivist inclination, in Italy it had to overcome a vacuum, a complete lack of any communal sense. So when the political unification was achieved and an outwardly similar type of pseudo-democratic constitutional monarchy adopted in both countries, the Germans managed to work out a thoroughly practicable benevolent absolutism on a collectivist basis under the guise of democratic institutions. In Italy, on the other hand, where the unfinished collectivist basis was still in the stage of a popular desire, the new state appeared to the people as just another spiritually empty set-up like the one they had cast off. The pre-War German Empire was popular and commanded loyalty. The Italian constitutional system depended for its existence solely on the lack of political interest in the vast majority of the people.

Developments after 1914 were entirely different in the two countries. In Italy the War, having forcefully resurrected the slumbering collective consciousness of the people, ended victoriously and left the population in a state of violent group excitement, of unleashed collective energies, and with the "soulless" democracy unable to cope with it. The result was the fall of the democracy at the hands of the movement that promised to fulfill the old and newly-remembered dream of an Italy united not only in area but in spirit and purpose. In Germany the War was lost, the Bismarckian set-up of benevolent absolutism became untenable, and an attempt was made to erect on the ruins a genuinely democratic structure, without, however, changing the old basis of political feeling. After several years of this the people found out, slowly, that the democratic system somehow did not suit them. They did not recognize clearly that the system presupposed an individualist conception of the state which they did not have and were not willing to adopt—but they felt that something was wrong with it. And so when Adolf Hitler proposed a system which appealed to them emotionally, and whose basic premises they found congenial, it was only natural that they decided to discard democracy and try that.

In both cases Fascism grew out of inherent desires of the people, constituted their revolt against a spiritually unsuitable and therefore unpopular system, and led to an overwhelming feeling of gratification at having ex-

changed it for something better. Again we need not concentrate upon Italy—where Fascist unanimity is hardly
questioned even by the most pronouncedly anti-Fascist
writers; in Italy the democratic set-up was a pushover.
In Germany, however, it was intellectually well fortified,
built upon the outwardly democratic semblance of a
popular and well-remembered pre-War system, and sus-
tained by a powerful political machine. So its overthrow
was to be effected only after severe political fighting,
and after a long and gradual rise to a commanding
position of the group which consolidated the anti-democratic tendencies. In both countries the movement won
out on the strength of its emotional appeal. Mussolini,
before seizing power, made few material promises, and
Hitler's many promises swelled his army of street-
battling rowdies but had little to do with the decisive
swing, of Germans everywhere and from all walks of
life, to his following. Of course they expected him to
perform miracles. But here cause and effect were reversed: they followed him not because they wanted the
things he held out to them but because they wanted him
as their leader—and that they expected miracles was
just the consequence of their belief in him. So when,
as Chancellor, he said in deadly earnest, "I have never
promised you any material reward," there was no storm
of indignation but an ecstatic avowal of their readiness
to follow him on the path of glory and sacrifice.

And this is the crucial point—which it is impossible
to *prove*, which can only be confirmed by the opinions
of men who went there to find out what was actually

going on and for no other reason—since he *is* in power, they *are* satisfied! If there were no noticeable grumbling in Germany today, one might attribute that to Dr. Goebbels' propaganda or to General Goering's concentration camps. But there is grumbling—only it is different, essentially different from the criticism that was leveled at the old democracy. In those days the people were well off and blamed the Republic for their little unpleasantnesses. Today they are pinched, and complain of being pinched, but they have no fault to find with the new Germany. They criticize individual Nazis, even "the Nazis," but the word "the system," which had such devastating effects in Hitler's campaign, is erased from their vocabulary. Throughout the people, the feeling of today, conscious or instinctive, is that at last the set-up under which they live is "right."

It shall certainly not be said here that Fascism is objectively *good* for the people of the nations who adopted it. All that is contended is that it is inherently *right* for those people. There is no doubt that a great many, possibly a majority, of Germans and Italians would be materially better off under democratic régimes, and possibly even—although this is open to grave doubts —individually happier. But unfortunately mankind is not given to discarding inherent traits or beliefs for happiness or advantage, however well rationalized. The best example is just those Jews to whom the Nazi race furor gave such an ill-fated prominence. For almost twenty centuries now, most Jews would have been better off and—in the opinion of the non-Jews—happier if they had adopted the religions prevalent in the countries in which they lived. And yet, in this—according to popular opinion—so practically-minded race, the inherited attitude toward the supernatural proved strong enough to preserve their religion intact in the face of every sensible reflection. Should the considerations of material advantage which, in this case, were unable to destroy the cohesion of a religious community scattered throughout the world and subjected to every torture and indignity, be capable of dissolving the bonds of national communities strengthened by every means at the disposal of virtually omnipotent states? Of course, as long as we stick to our notion that a national community *is* nothing but an instrument to guarantee our supply of bread and butter, the comparison will seem preposterous. But once we realize that this premise is not an axiom but just our special, private, and particular way of looking at communal matters—once we realize the essential similarity of basic conceptions in religion and communal mentality —we may well ask why the criterion of success should be more applicable to the "true" system of government, than it has ever been to the "true" faith.

Whether the conversion of a people from a collectivist to an individualist mentality is at all possible, by other means than material argument, is debatable. Mussolini himself recognized at least the possibility of spontaneous change—he even based his whole state structure upon a "new" popular conception of the community reversing nineteenth century Liberalism. German scientists categorically deny the possibility of an "unnatural" conversion. The weight of scientific authority seems inclined to doubt the existence of fixed psychic "racial characteristics," as assumed by the Germans. Psychiatry, moreover, contends that the mentality of every single individual can be influenced to the extent of complete inversion, and there does not seem to be a reason to deny to groups what we concede to individuals. Far be it from us to assert here that these authorities are wrong. What shall be contended—and what no ethnologist, however orthodox, will deny—is that group predispositions, though not racially fixed, are developed by tradition and environment, and that, so developed, they are apt to prove exceedingly difficult to dislodge. Once a group has acquired a characteristic attitude towards a problem, an extremely potent force of inertia works against any changes. This does not mean that such attitudes *cannot* be changed. It means only that to change them requires the application of an influence stronger than the inertia which tends to keep them as they are. There can be no doubt that a primitive people will be more easily swayed in this respect than a highly developed one; nor that a situation like that of Russia in 1917—the aftermath of a complete collapse of a whole political, social and economic order—is particularly auspicious for such a change. It is even conceivable that a collectivist government, to which the people have been carefully conditioned to defer, might itself effect a change in their way of thinking of it—and re-condition them to consider themselves its masters. If the Soviet Union, at present, should actually, and successfully, undertake the introduction of an individualist democracy,[6] it would prove the possibility of such a planned reversal. But most emphatically it must be maintained, that in order to reverse the basic attitude of a people its government must do more than say it isn't so. Even the most powerful dictatorship would not be able to effect such a change by proclamation. Yet that is what the men of the Weimar Republic attempted—with what deplorable lack of success is a matter of history.

A democratic community is kept democratic in spirit by the fact that its superiors, the individuals or groupings of individuals, use organization and propaganda in instinctive perpetuation of the individualist set-up. A collectivist people is kept collectivist by the fact that its superior, the community, uses organization and propaganda to perpetuate *its* superiority in their relationship. Should it be possible to create either one of these mentalities—which, even if already in existence, need such an amount of care to be kept functioning—by mere declaration? Anyone willing to think the question through must admit that to answer it in the affirmative would require a rather exaggerated optimism. But the worst is yet to come. After logic has shown how slim the chances are of achieving such an alteration by other than catastrophic events or long-drawn-out historic processes of evolution, and after the experience of the German Republic, amongst others, has shown how right this

---

[6] To the writer, however, the new Soviet Constitution seems to combine representative government and civil liberties with a rather scrupulous maintenance of basic collectivism.

logic was—after and in spite of all that, some people will insist that such a change *can* be successfully attempted *not by,* but *against* a collectivist government! In other words, there are those who will seriously contend that by economic pressure or by underground political work it is possible to overcome not only the force of inertia tending to maintain an existing mentality which in Germany, for instance, fourteen years of democratic rule could not shatter—but to overcome this force of inertia *plus* all the official forces of organization and propaganda working for the perpetuation of the respective collectivism!

The same men would laugh at the chances of a German to promote a Fascist dictatorship in the United States with the threat of an anti-American boycott. Yet this is exactly what our anti-Fascists are doing. With some it is clearly a case of "hope springs eternal." But a majority, who in other matters have never yet allowed a crusading urge to obscure their sense of realities, might conceivably be made to see the quixotic character of that undertaking when reminded of their faculties of logical reasoning. We may grant them that Fascism is an abomination. We can agree with them that for us as well as for the people of the Fascist countries themselves it would, according to *our* standards of value, be better if it could be overthrown. We are just as convinced as they are that continuation of the Fascist régimes cannot fail to plunge the world into more and more terrible conflicts. But we must try to open their eyes to the fact that no outside influence short of a destruction of a

Fascist nation as a nation is going to cure it of its Fascism—because it is not, as our moralists so love to call
it, a "ghastly disease spreading over Europe" but the
quite healthy, logical and natural state of affairs for
capitalist communities with a particular popular mentality.

To the often-asked question of "what can be done,"
the only possible answer is "nothing"; moreover, nothing *should* be done—unless, for reasons of our own, we
want to force upon the people in Fascist countries a
system which essentially disagrees with them. Whether
or not it is the duty of the outside world to do something for the expelled or fleeing victims of Fascism, is
another question. So is the problem of whether it is not
the duty of other communities to protect their nationals
from Fascist aggression, and from the attending possibility of eventually falling under Fascist rule—which,
as a matter of practicability, would probably require
them to deal with the Fascist danger in the *only way* it
can be really dealt with: by overpowering the Fascist
states, and ending their national existence. But as far as
concerns our moral penchant for "saving Germany, or
Italy, from the yoke of Fascism," we had better get
down to facts and realize that to the vast majority of
Germans and Italians—as they have been, as they are,
and as they will be barring a cataclysmic upheaval of
their mentality—Fascism is not a yoke. What we could
offer them instead, would be. Our idealists are so strong
for religious freedom and yet cannot see that it is infinitely more vicious to force a man to accept an alien

·communal relationship than to force him to accept an alien creed. The plain truth is that if the people of a country have experienced democracy in all its material aspects, have experimented with it in all directions, and have finally cast it off, we have no business setting up our judgment against their contention that they have tried our system and found it wanting.

CHAPTER EIGHT

CAN DEMOCRACY SURVIVE?

The "Fascist Dangers" in the World of Today

"WE ARE FIGHTING TO SAVE A GREAT AND PRECIOUS form of government for ourselves and for the world." [1] Some time ago, in our country, these words stirred even the most outspoken critics of the man who uttered them. They marked a turning point in the attitude of the chosen guardians of democracy toward its detractors. They discarded the assurance with which, for more than half a century, democratic government had taken itself for granted. They refused to cling to the traditional assumption that the system was its own guarantee. They called attention to the fact that in other countries the people had "yielded their democracy"; and to the possibility that our democratic heritage might not only be worth fighting for—but might again, as in bygone days, need to be fought for. It has always been a familiar gesture of the opposition to cry that democracy is imperiled, but this was the first time that this new, very special, and constantly increasing dread of democratic peoples

[1] President Roosevelt accepting the 1936 Democratic nomination.

255

found recognition from a source in office. That the fight against it was claimed for partisan politics is of small moment compared to the fact that it was claimed at all—that democratic authority itself had faced the issue: Can democracy survive?

Before the World War, the functioning of government of, by, and for the people was frequently encumbered by ignorant and unsympathetic administration—but its theoretical validity was unquestioningly accepted in every civilized country. Today, throughout this same world, democracy is challenged not because of practical shortcomings but as an ideal. Two key nations of Europe have adopted communal structures expressly designed to represent, in theory and practice, the direct antithesis of democracy. In several Old World countries of lesser importance we find a democratic framework with an admixture of Fascist features. In the great Western democracies, political groups under the nom de guerre of Fascist movements are openly advocating dictatorial régimes. Closer to home, South American republics abandon their traditional form of government—the sham democracy—and proudly proclaim themselves Fascist nations. In our own United States, nearly every political faction is called "Fascist" by some one or other, though the targets all anxiously disclaim the charge. Considering all that, the question of whether or not democracy can survive can no longer be called rhetorical. It is an eminently practical issue. It is open to analysis and debate. And, while hardly any tenable results can be expected from the haphazard, wish-fulfilling, fact-twisting way in which the question is usually discussed, the logic employed here may provide a somewhat sounder foundation. We have defined Fascism as a state order *based* upon a collectivist conception of the communal relationship and a prevailing capitalist economy and *maintained* by consistent and efficient application of the principles of hierarchy, authority and discipline. We have considered its logical development in the principal fields of communal action. We have tried to discover the roots of Fascism in the prototypical Fascist countries, by tracing the history of the collectivist mentality that eventually sought and found its adequate expression in Fascism. Thus we have gained a picture of Fascism, which like every product of analysis may be erroneous but is at least consistent within itself and apparently also with the facts as we know them. And now we should be able to inquire with some increased confidence into the alleged or threatening Fascism of the nations of the world.

Of course, within the limits of this book, this can be done only in an extremely cursory fashion. Yet even a short survey, reserving the right to err on all counts, may serve a useful purpose—to indicate the way in which it will be possible, in concrete instances, to investigate the alleged Fascist character of any political phenomenon in accordance with *Fascist* concepts, instead of under rules fixed arbitrarily by every man for himself. The natural point of departure for such a survey is Austria—the one European nation outside of Germany and Italy which officially calls itself Fascist and totalitarian (although recently, since the eclipse of Vice-Chancellor Prince Starhembcrg, the term has become rather rare in Vienna's governmental proclamations). Considering it somewhat more closely, however, we will notice that this self-description is about the only feature of Austro-Fascism not at variance with the German and Italian model. The Austrians did not have one authoritarian leader. They had first two, then three, then again two, one of whom now seems to have reduced the other to insignificance without daring to remove him altogether. They had not one single Party, but each "Leader" had his own semi-military band of followers which served as pressure group and praetorian guard but naturally could not assume any of the really essential organizational and propagandist functions of a genuine Fascist Party. The announced economic "Order of Estates" remained in the realm of speculation.[2] Industry and labor are still virtually unorganized. There is no planned control of youth other than the Catholic Church's ancient control over education; no planned control of social activities; hardly any control of even governmental jobs. The only totalitarian features of this "Fascist state" were the suspension of civil liberties and the confinement of Nazis and Socialists in jails and concentration camps.

The riddle has a simple enough solution: Austria never was a Fascist state in any sense of the word. Just as government is not democratic merely because it says

[2] The recent "election" of "advisory councils" was a gesture which so far seems to be devoid of any functional significance.

it is, the Dollfuss-Starhemberg-Schuschnigg Dictatorship, Inc., did not become a Fascist régime by virtue of
its frequent proclamations. What it lacked was the basis
of Fascism—the collective spirit. The old multi-national
Empire of Austria-Hungary had been held together by
the twin loyalties to an age-old monarchic tradition and
to the unchallenged authority of the Catholic Church.
The new Austria created by the Empire's defeat in 1918
never had a chance to develop a national mind. Its popular mentality was split in three directions: (a) German
nationalism of the kind that across the border culmi-
nated in the Third Reich, dominant in the Austrian
Nazis *and* in the pointedly "Deutsch-Oesterreicher" majority who even now cling to the idea of Anschluss
though disliking almost everything about Hitler; [3] (b)
Austro-Catholicism of the Seipel-Dollfuss-Schuschnigg
type, the governing bloc, strongest in the rural and alpine
sections of the country, with a large dash of Hapsburg-
Legitimism; (c) progressive individualism—democratic
or Socialist—born in the nineteenth century revolt
against Metternich's absolutist régime, resurrected in
1918, since then developed particularly in Vienna by
ten years of successful and beneficial Socialist administration, and even now too strong to be totally ignored.
Austrian politics in the last decade have merely reflected
the constant interplay of these trends. As long as Ger-

[3] Cynics who doubt this should think back to what happened in
the Saar—overwhelmingly Catholic, largely Socialist, economically
predestined for a union with France—in an election which was
supervised not only by a League of Nations administration but
guarded by international military detachments!

many was democratic, the tremendous Austrian majority in favor of Anschluss was quite incongruously made up of members of all three groups. After Hitler's ascendancy, the Left and the Catholics swung around to form a violent anti-Anschluss coalition, which, however, very soon clearly appeared unable to stem the Nazi tide. At that time Chancellor Dollfuss and the Heimwehr began looking for outside help. A Hapsburg restoration, which might have turned the trick, was ruled out by the Little Entente, frightened of irredentism. London and Paris exuded moral support and did nothing. This left only Rome—and Mussolini made his active interest contingent upon the eradication of Austrian Marxism and the establishment of a "stable" authoritarian government, which could be held responsible by Italy for its acts and policies without being able to take refuge behind popular mandates. Dollfuss fulfilled both conditions; and by the grace of Il Duce Austria "went Fascist"—adopting the name of a political system, for the substance of which it possessed not even the most elementary requirements.

In a way, this set-up—we may call it pseudo-Fascism —was typical of the post-war political development of all Southeastern Europe. Austria alone publicly claims to be Fascist, but fundamentally the entire group of little nations in what Western Europeans disdainfully call "Semi-Asia" have the same form of government: dictatorship not based on a developed collectivism, but on the power of national, economic, military, or simply machine-political groups. In some of these countries an old and strong nationalism seems likely to provide a fertile ground for Fascism. But then this collective trend is always either neutralized by other influences—as the ancient nationalism of Hungary is completely dominated by an aristocratic tradition rooted in that agricultural country's economic structure—or, as in pre-War Italy, the collectivism does not penetrate beyond a politically mature "upper class"—which was the case in Poland, where a minority had managed to keep the national consciousness alive through almost two centuries of Russian rule to which the Polish masses were largely indifferent. In Yugoslavia—indefensible conglomerate of three distinct and spiritually quite incompatible nationalities—the contest for the power of government is fought on national lines. In Roumania, where French influence all but succeeded in making democracy work, economic differentiations seem to be decisive. In Greece, General Metaxas is using Fascist and National Socialist platitudes with a vengeance, in order to make his dictatorship palatable to Western public opinion—but, alas, there is no shadow of doubt in anybody's mind that his rule is not the realization of a national urge. It is nothing but the last recourse of the military, whose traditional power has been imperiled for more than twenty years by a Western-influenced progressive trend.[4]

[4] The most interesting evolution seems to be taking place outside of Europe, in Turkey, where in a seemingly quite Fascist manner Mustafa Kemal Atatürk has been striving to prepare the ground for modern democracy! Kemal's rule presents the perfect antithesis to the German "November Republic": the Weimar constitution attempted to establish democracy by decree in a basically

In these countries we have as little Fascism as we have democracy. Theirs are forms of primitive government, adapted to the undeveloped political mentality of the people. They express not a philosophy of government but a composite mixture of elements of historical tradition and of accidental power. Whether or not any of them may eventually blossom into genuine Fascist régimes, it is too early to say. Theoretically, they may well do what Italy did: use the vague collective urges extant in nearly every politically backward psychology, and nurse them—in the absence of a developed individualism—into a genuine, active, conscious and pervasive collectivism. Today, in practice, this requisite of Fascism is not there. However valiantly men like Prince Starhemberg and General Metaxas may insist upon the totalitarian character of their states, however well they may copy German and Italian governmental techniques —they remain not "leaders" but real dictators, in office because they are the most powerful individuals and not because they are individuals considered by a uniform collective consciousness to be vested with the function of leadership. Today, no Fascism is discernible among the Balkan nations. Their rulers have the power, and reasonably favorable psychological conditions, for creating one. But so far none of them has shown much understanding for what is *behind* a Fascist form of gov-

undemocratic nation, which eventually resulted in Hitlerism; the Ghazi seeks first to create, slowly and with all the undemocratic means familiar to his people, the emotional and psychological basis on which alone democracy can function.

ernment—and, though Mussolinian gestures are the trappings of Fascism, they do not make it.

Most of the remaining European nations might be classed as working democracies. This group includes the Scandinavian states and—with certain reservations—the Baltic republics (one of which recently presented the amazing spectacle of a perfectly free plebiscite to decide whether to continue or discontinue authoritative government). It includes Holland and Belgium; the latter has recently acquired a young and vociferous Fascist movement—M. Degrelle's "Rexists"—which is capitalizing on the drawbacks of the Belgian geographical position between France and Germany, and the nation's split into two distinct nationalities, and yet does not seem to present any serious danger unless unduly aided by international complications. The group includes Czechoslovakia and Switzerland, where democracy is still working despite terrific propagandistic pressure from adjoining Fascist countries—and working in Switzerland despite an instinctive racial sympathy of the numerically prevalent German Swiss for Germany proper (stronger now than when German monarchs used to voice their distaste for the Swiss republic) and despite extensive socialization of industry and governmental regulation of business, which would make Fascist regimentation seem like nothing out of the ordinary. But Fascism as a political system—championed by "National Front" organizations with German and Italian backing—found no response; famous for their traditional opposition to centralized authority, the Swiss had no desire to become completely absorbed in a collective concept. The proto-type of a democracy that works, finally, is England—where the Mosley appeal so far has fallen flat for the same reason that the Communist one has: because the people have realized the issues involved, and are there-fore not only willing but able to assert their sincere and inbred individualistic preference for their own system of government.

The other "great Western democracy"—France—for a number of years now has been a democracy, but defi-nitely not a "working" one. In France, representative government threatened to fail, *not*, as had been the case in Italy and Germany, because it did not express popu-lar mentality, but because it *really* was not functioning properly—because the machinery did not make ade-quate provision for the translation of the popular will into governmental policies. France's troubles have al-ways arisen from an extremely narrow interpretation of executive responsibility to the legislature, forcing cabinets to resign over every parliamentary defeat in a minor question. In 1934 and '35 the constitutional crisis nearly came to a head. Since then the formation of the Front Populaire and its victory in the May election of 1936 for the first time in years gave a French govern-ment a sufficiently broad basis on which to work out policies to their conclusion without fear of being jeopard-ized midway by shifts in parliament. Of course, the Blum government is no more immortal than any of its predecessors. While it seems still fairly safe, its over-throw is *possible* at any moment. What will happen then, particularly if the people really begin to get tired of incessant cabinet crises, it is impossible to predict. But one thing should be made clear: even if the Right, led by Colonel de La Rocque's Croix de Feu, should capture the government, theirs would be no Fascist one.

France, since 1789, has not been collectivist. But France, in 1789, was torn apart into two huge factions, still in existence, which a French publicist around the turn of the century aptly termed "la France revolutionaire" and "la France anti-revolutionaire." ("Revolution," even in its social sense, is in France a word without any disreputable connotations—since the nation traces its lineage to the paragon of modern social upheavals.) This perpetual split has always been much deeper than the Right and Left divisions in other countries. It is an irreconcilable conflict in principle—which, in the grandiloquently-inclined French public mind seems to mark political parties and programs directly as being either on the side of the defenders of the Bastille or on the side of its attackers. Until 1933, leadership of the French Right was held by a group around André Tardieu—conservative, economically reactionary, internationally cautious, not one Fascist notion in their minds. A few would-be Fascist extremist groups—the legitimist Camelots du Roi, the chauvinist Jeunesses Patriotes, the anti-Semitic Francistes—formed a French "lunatic fringe" with no more than nuisance value. In 1933, the Croix de Feu, formerly an organization strictly limited to war veterans who had actually been under fire, entered the political arena. They did it not

as a party, but as a "non-political movement," a device
that had been used to advantage by Hitler and Mussolini. De La Rocque also emulated the Fascist leaders in
devoting about two years of his political build-up to the
creation of a "mystique." It was so successful that, when
Rightist Premier Doumergue resigned in 1934 over the
constitutional issue, the Croix de Feu was prepared to
take over. For the next eighteen months, under three
Premiers—the unsympathetic Flandin, the sympathetic
Laval, and the unsympathetic Sarraut—the Croix de
Feu held undisputed leadership of the Right. In 1935
its leader could proclaim that government in France
could function only by tolerance of his organization.
But during all that time it lost its Fascist features one
by one, until, in the famous "national reconciliation" of
December, 1935, it agreed to the dissolution of the private "Leagues"—and, while this brought gains among
the conservative majority, it definitely established the
Croix de Feu as traitors to their extremist ex-fellows. In
February, 1936, the Camelots du Roi forced the issue
by beating up Léon Blum. Sarraut promptly dissolved
them under a law passed by Laval with Croix de Feu
backing. In the ensuing general election, de La Rocque
pretended to take no part—reserving to his movement
the role of "arbiter"—but nevertheless in the public
mind the line was clearly drawn between the declared
Popular Front and the undeclared conservative front
with the Croix de Feu as standard bearer. So when the
Leftist victory became known, the French were quick to
give de La Rocque a new name: "le grand vaincu," the

Great Defeated. In the strike wave of Blum's early days, the Croix de Feu apparently remembered its previous Fascist ambitions, and began to encourage strikes and to set up unions of its own. But when Blum, realizing the danger, dissolved the organization, and all the other Rightist organizations with it, de La Rocque transformed his "movement to save France" into a political party, decided to wait for the "Blum experiment" to fail, and otherwise settled deeper into the calm of respectability. No, Colonel de La Rocque is no Fascist danger.

Neither is the new white hope of French reaction: the rabid, blustering, ex-Communist leader of the Parti Populaire Français, Jacques Doriot. But not for the same reason: Doriot knows what it is all about, his Fascism is conscious and intentional, he is no conservative at heart. The fact that he seems unable to make any noticeable headway supports our conclusion drawn from the story of the Croix de Feu: that in France the division into Right and Left is a genuine one, of vital significance and alive to popular sentiment—a division which fits the political temperament of the French people, who are inclined to expect a maximum of benefits to result from parliamentary battles of opposed groups, and who are not inclined at all to waive material benefits for an abstract immaterial national concept. The Croix de Feu proved that French Fascist groups, in order to become politically important, must turn conservative; Doriot seems likely to furnish the supplementary proof that, if they insist on keeping their Fascist character, they will remain insignificant. Barring war—which once before, over a century ago, brought a one-man government to France out of an individualist revolution—the Fascist prospects there today seem dark indeed.

However, to the south of France, the world seems about to be treated to a truly magnificent test of all theories about political trends—Communism, Fascism, democracy, anarchism, etc. At the time of this writing, a Popular Front government in Spain is fighting a military rebellion, led by a generals' junta, using mostly foreign legionnaires and colonial troops and probably foreign armaments, supported in Spain proper apparently only by the Church and by a small legitimist clique with little strength outside of Navarre—and calling itself Fascist. Of course, we do not know, as yet, whether this Ibero-Fascism is not the same thing as Austro-Fascism—a Fascism induced only by the wishes of an interested foreign power. The chances are that General Franco's Fascism was not born in his own or in any other Spanish mind. But be that as it may, the question testing our entire analysis is this: should the Spanish rebels win, with or without the help of any foreign power, and should they set up a Fascist or at least an outwardly Fascist régime—what, then, becomes of our thesis of Fascism as an expression of an inherent popular mentality? The answer is: if, after a few years, Spanish Fascism *works as Fascism,* then our theory is wrong. The chances of its working seem slim to us.

The historical parallel to twentieth-century Spain has been drawn by many writers on the subject—it is nineteenth-century France. Just like France after 1789 (*not* like Russia after 1917!), Spain seemed engaged in fighting its way toward democracy. A basic individualist trend was strongly evident; the Left centered not around Third International Communism but around First International anarchism, the Right centered not around any Fascist movement but around the traditional pillars of individualist reaction, Church, army, and large land-holdings. Never, not even under Primo de Rivera's post-War military dictatorship, did Fascist notions play any part in Spain. The Spaniard, down to the last boot-black, was proud of being a hidalgo, an independent individual of standing—submersion into an unidentifiable mass of collective humanity did not appeal to him. And it is quite unlikely that General Franco will be able to change that. Whether Spanish individualism is as strong as French individualism—that is, strong enough to come back after four monarchic reversals in a half century—no one can tell. But, however the present civil war may end for the time being—and allowing for the difficulty in overcoming the hatreds engendered by it, which will make the formation of any government by popular agreement impossible for some time to come in any case—today it appears that neither a Communist nor a Fascist victory would find the collectivist mentality they need to function.

Outside of Europe, the Fascist phenomenon has made few appearances.[5] In South and Central America, we

[5] Extremely interesting, but impossible to discuss here at length, is Japan—a country with a strongly collectivist population, and

have recently heard the term—partly in accusations against government, partly (as in the case of Paraguay) in proclamations of government itself. Generally speaking, the political development of our sister republics strongly resembles that of the pseudo-Fascist nations of. Southeastern Europe. They were usually ruled by military dictators, mostly under the guise of democratic institutions in which, however, the people as a whole were completely disinterested. When things became too bad, one gang was turned out and another one turned in. There was little or no communal feeling, except in a small quasi-professional political aristocracy. The Paraguayan Fascist rule proclaimed a few months ago seems very much like a modern adaptation of this traditional form of government—an adaptation to which the sounding title of Fascism was given to make it appear more important in the eyes of the great powers. On the other hand, three years of war in the Chaco might well have aroused, in a little nation, a collectivist feeling strong enough to bear a real Fascism. What is really going on it will be impossible to say for at least a year or two. Elsewhere in Latin America, Brazil and Argentina in the last decade seem to have progressed toward democ-

apparently an individualist and democratically inclined upper class, supported by the modernizing tendencies of the Crown since the middle of the nineteenth century. The semi-divine position of the Emperor and the whole Asiatic psychology make any opinion difficult and of questionable value even if coming from experts on Japanese affairs. Japanese collectivism (impregnated with the worship of the Crown) as well as Japanese capitalism seems to be too different from ours to allow a comparison with the essentially Western Fascism.

racy, while Mexico, under its socialistically-inclined present government, seems about to acquire some sort of communal mentality. Whether it will be democratic-individualistic or soviet-collectivist, we cannot tell—and not only we: the Mexicans do not know themselves.

In the United States the democratic system is based upon a developed and definitely individualist national mentality. Nowhere, not even in England, has the spiritual evolution of a people been so completely dominated by the conception of the state as an association for a purpose. "Americanism" at its best—the spirit of the Puritans, of the Frontier, of the mid-Western Progressives in our time—grew out of the same roots as the worst "rugged individualism" of the Erie pirates in the nineteenth or Samuel Insull in the twentieth century. It has always embodied an uncompromising view of the individuals as masters of the group, and scorn of the idea of their having to defer to a collective concept unrelated to the will and advantage of the human beings constituting the community. The excesses were due only to the fact that, when obeisance to the state was discarded, the necessary regard for equal rights of others —which alone can provide the necessary balance for an "individualist community"—was also discarded. The "rugged" kind of individualism actually reduced the democratic state to the absurdity which Communists and Fascists profess to see in it: an organism whose every cell could walk off by itself. Democracy, refusing to enforce rights of the "whole" against the interests of its members, could avoid this absurdity only by requiring every member to show enough consideration for the interests of his co-members to sustain the cohesion of the group. The Puritans based this duty on the Bible. The pioneers based it on the ideas of human freedom and equality; and so brought order—an order of grubstakes and vigilante committees—into what was potentially the worst chaos in modern history. Rugged individualism simply dropped the requirement altogether. Its theory, in spots, came quite close to the political gospel of the First International—only the economic aspect, the worship of property as long as a man could hold on to it, separated it from straight anarchism. In practice, as has been pointed out earlier in this study, it worked differently: the initially successful individualists took control of the state and operated it as a "double standard community" for their own benefit—as *their* servant and other people's master.

That every individualism without a curb on success should bring forth such tendencies is only natural. It has happened more than once in this country. In Colonial times the Puritans, having asserted their individualism against the absolutist policies of the British Crown, sought to guard against excesses by basing a rigid moral standard on the equality of men before the Almighty. Yet by 1776, an "upper class" had already become so strong that it could force secession from Great Britain, and afterwards write the Constitution of the United States virtually of, by, and for itself. The first half of the nineteenth century was spent in a continuous struggle against this distortion of individualism—the Jacksonian revolt, the spirit and development of the Frontier, eventually the coup de grâce to the Colonial concept of "planter aristocracy" in a Civil War which Lincoln at Gettysburg could assert had been fought, not to liberate the slaves, but to reclaim the government of America for "the people." Soon, however, after the individualism of our democracy had thus been re-established, a new group of front-runners in the devil-take-the-hindmost race for profits reached a commanding position in the community—the place vacated by the landed gentry was filled by a nobility of corporations. The "men who made America" set up a more airtight and intricate control over other people's lives than any old-line collectivism had ever attempted. And again the outraged basic sense of their communal relationship made the people rebel. The insurgence began with Populism, continued in Free Silver, New Democracy, New Freedom, until the bursting bubble of the nineteen-twenties finally exploded the notion that it might be practicable to combine rugged individualism with a democratic order.

Today we have reached a point where not only the present administration but every group in our public life pays at least lip service to the need for restricting the individual's pursuit of happiness to a moderate consideration for the rights and interests of his fellows. In questions of degree, however, we find a disquieting inclination to describe this as a trend toward collectivism. "New Deal Fascism" has become a slogan not only for

the superficial sophistry of political opponents [6] but for
some of our clearest political thinkers.[7] Especially denounced as outposts of collectivism were the numerous
present attempts at *collective economic action*. Some
people nowadays are frightened whenever the word
"collective" is mentioned. Some shield, behind their defense of individualism, a very material personal interest endangered by organization of groups they have to

[6] Who, for example, made a great deal of the likeness between
the corporative set-up and the now defunct NRA. As if even the
identical administrative device could not, if used by different systems, carry a totally different import: every state employs a judicial system, yet in a democracy it serves to protect the citizens
while under Fascism it serves only to protect the state!

[7] They got there by a somewhat roundabout way. Aware of the
collectivist nature common to Fascism and U.S.S.R.-Communism,
and of the large anti-capitalist potentialities inherent in Fascism
in spite of its capitalist base, they—like we—defined Fascism and
Communism as different forms of a single phenomenon. The common denominator, however, they did not see in the subordination
of individual to group interests, but in the aggrandizement of the
economic organization of the state. Believers in the liberal premise
of the individual's pursuit of his own economic interests as the
motivating force of community life, they saw the beginnings of
collectivism at the point where the priority rights of this pursuit
were communally invaded. Though theoretically willing to accept
curbs on economic individualism, they drew a line at the intensification of the state's right and duty to look after the workings of
the economic set-up.

At least as far as Fascism is concerned, this view confuses part
of the picture with the whole. The aggrandizement of the economic organization of the state is no more than on a par with the
aggrandizement of its *entire* organization—whether economic, political, military, cultural or administrative. In all these fields Fascism, by virtue of its "organic conception of the state," logically
requires an emphasis on communal organization unknown to
democracy—and economic organization *may* be the one most emphatically collectivized but by no means must be.

deal with. But, aside from those unscientific types of individualists, large numbers of people do sincerely believe that economic co-operation is a step toward group supremacy and a collectivization of the democratic state. What they do not see is the fact that the very conception of this democratic state itself—as a group made up of individuals seeking to gain from association—refutes their argument. There is no essential difference between the democratic community and those organizations within it which are designed to further the material interests of their members. If labor unions and consumer co-operatives work for collectivism, democracy itself does, too. Again the defenders of individualism come close to the anarchist argument: that the concepts of individualism and of community life are incompatible. But our political individualists surely do not want to go that far. They are only frightened by the outward resemblance between various means of democratic group co-operation and certain materializations of Fascist or Communist group control. To them it does not matter that nothing in the ideology of economic organization serves to exalt the collective abstract over the interests of the individuals. They are content to reason that once the people get used to corporative practices, a change in spirit might either pass unnoticed or be willingly accepted—an argument so superficial that with respect to known and established institutions, like the courts, or the police, it could never even have gained consideration. Drawn solely from outer aspects of a political mechanism, it disregards all the things that *make* a political device: its drive, its intent, its inherent purpose.

To view with alarm the trend toward economic control and planning—as apparent in Progressivism, in the New Deal, and (relatively speaking) even in the 1936 Republican platform—as a "trend toward collectivism" does not make sense. It is individualism pure and simple—individualism fighting its perversion. All the restrictions that we hear so often decried as "governmental collectivism" are nothing but protection of majority interests from minority privileges—so as to make the state really serve the people instead of special groups. A worker is forbidden to work for more than certain hours or for less than certain wages not because of a national interest but so that his fellow workers shall not suffer from his sub-standard competition. A businessman is prevented from running his shop as he pleases insofar as his employees need protection from sweatshops, his customers from excessive prices, or his competitors from being driven out of business. A financier is subjected to control of his operations so that he may not take the unsuspecting public for a bigger "ride" than is customary and inevitable in financial dealings. Even where the government goes into business itself—the pet abomination of our self-styled defenders of individualism—it does so with the avowed intention to *serve* as "yardstick," that is, to protect those dependent on the particular business from unwarranted exploitation. One would be at a loss to find there an exaltation of a collective concept (other than the democratic one of the majority of the individuals). All our hotly contested party platforms of today are equally individualistic; their differences are solely differences of degree and of interpretation—throughout our political life, the supremacy of the individual rules exclusively. *At no point is any individual right interfered with for other reasons than the protection of other individual rights.* No measure taken or advocated in this country would tend to establish for the United States, dissociated from the various groups of the American people, a claim on any services or sacrifices on the part of individual citizens *because it is the state.* But *collectivism is* the subjection of the interests of the people *as such* to the "higher interest" of a dogmatically superior communal body. Neither the most radical New Dealer nor even an exponent of the American brand of Socialism could be accused of that; nobody except, on one side, those conservatives who still wish to place the conspicuously collectivist conception of "business" over the wants of the people—and, on the other, Mr. Browder of Kansas, who would do the same with the "proletariat."

As a matter of fact, the lack of response to the Communist appeal, on the part of the American masses, seems to confirm most strongly the individualist sentiment in the people of this country. Only one explanation is possible for the complete failure of Communism to make headway in a period as full of social unrest and urge toward governmental and economic changes as our past few years have been: an overwhelming popular dislike of any form of state organization that would burden the people *as individuals*. All our political development, past and present, illustrates this dislike. No political or demagogic group in this country has ever dared to base its campaigns on a philosophy of individual sacrifice. Our "lunatic fringe" and the most reactionary conservatives—both appeal to the people's desire to *get something from* the state, not to give something to it. All our proponents of regimentation advocate it as something that will materially aid the people—not as an exercise of inherent rights of the community. This is not only because American politics has always been a "gimme" game of votes for promises. It goes deeper. With all the changes which the last few years have wrought in programs and platforms and the emergence of special Leagues and Unions, no politician has yet told the American voter to his face that the state should be his superior—except the Communists who are paying the price in unpopularity. And this popular reaction is what appears to doom the prospects for an "American Fascism"—by which is meant not the Austrian or Paraguayan pseudo-type but the genuine, popular, and well-grounded brand of Italy or Germany. Real Fascism— in our day—seems to have little chance in this country. Whatever circumstances may seem favorable—and some seem favorable indeed—cannot make up for the absence of the only ingredient that is really indispensable: the popular state of mind. Americans might take kindly to every detail of Fascism; but the necessary foundation of the system, the prerequisite to its functioning, the basic condition for its being and remaining alive—the people's readiness to sacrifice their individualities—we seem, as yet, entirely unwilling to accept.

Of our so-called "Fascist movements" the non-political type—Ku Klux Klan, Black Legion, etc.—are based on a primitive but typically American predilection for public cruelty and secret societies (Fascism is never secret!) and upon racial and religious prejudices which *split* the national community instead of uniting it. When the Klan attacked Catholics, it did not attack "political Catholicism" as a menace to the totalitarian state, as the Nazis do—it fought thirty per cent of the national population *as such*. This alone would suffice to set it apart from Fascism. Fascism can exclude half a million Jews from a national community of some sixty million Germans, but it will never set up a barrier that would shut a really substantial percentage of the people off from the national body. The secret society, too, is an American favorite that is decidedly un-Fascist; the entire appeal of Fascism is based on its comprehensiveness, on its being open to every member of the nation, on the confidence that its very bigness of appearance will save it from a closer scrutiny of its details.

Of our political "Fascist menaces" Huey Long's empire in Louisiana was nothing but an exaggerated example of good old rabble-rousing American boss-rule (which has always maintained a strong class, anti-Wall-Street, anti-Big-Business attitude) and entirely without any collectivist ideology. Huey's slogan "Every man a king" stands in marked contrast to the Fascist "Live dangerously!" as well as to the German "Common good before individual good." Huey fought against the "money changers" for the "common people of Louisiana," and managed to do well by himself in the struggle. If he had appeared on the rostrum of even his own private Legislature in Baton Rouge to ask these common people to "sacrifice their individual welfare for the greater glory of the state of Louisiana," he would have been laughed out of the chamber. And his Share-the-Wealth appendage, like Coughlin, or Townsend, or Epic, or Utopia, represented a purely economic appeal to the Have-nots based on the very notion which Fascism scorns more than everything else: that it is the function of the state to take care of the individuals.

The coalition of some such groups into a "Union Party," for the purpose of boosting a widely unknown Congressman into the White House, did not, itself, affect the political nature of the "lunatic fringe." Only recently, beginning with the 1936 Townsend National Convention, did the fringe show signs of changing its color. Its political leaders, Father Coughlin and the Reverend Gerald L. K. Smith,[8] left the materialist path.

---

[8] Who, by the way, in a recent interview for a New York magazine revealed himself not only as a would-be "Leader" of a slightly farcical yet conceivably quite dangerous kind—but as a man with a surprisingly clear grasp of Fascist basic notions. The mere fact that, aware of the quite different attitude of his present following, he placed his success in a much more distant future than his more distributive political brethren, stamps him as today's only United States demagogue with a definite conception of what he is aiming at. Surely Father Coughlin—to say nothing of Dr. Francis H. Townsend, the venerable Elder Statesman of the lunatic fringe —is blissfully ignorant of the theoretical and practical realities of

They put Red-baiting and Jew-baiting upon a charismatic level. They dug up a yearning for redemption with which to support vote-getting intolerance, creating a tie-up between revival meeting and polling place, that may yet conceivably blossom into a "religious conception of life." So far, however, no collectivism has yet become articulate. The movement has not dared to unveil a group concept upon which to base its appeal and to train its energies. There is no denying the fact that today an undetermined number of our population is taking steps that may turn out to be preliminaries to the individual self-abnegation that characterizes a Fascist mentality. But, though this trend should be fully recognized with all its possibly dangerous implications, we can hardly conclude, from a display of some outwardly collectivist traits by a particularly predisposed group, that the people of America are ready to shed their individualist way of thinking and to embrace Fascism.

That a Fascist movement would have no trouble in finding enthusiastic *backers,* is beyond question. Hearst, MacFadden and the Red-baiters in Congress would be

the path he points out; and if the two gentlemen should eventually be damned to play Bishop Prang to Gerald Smith's Berzelius Windrip, it will serve them right. Smith also seems responsible for the first clearly Fascist turn which the Union Party has taken during and after the 1936 Townsend Convention: the quasi-religious, self-sacrificial, self-submerging trends which are so completely at variance with the obvious materialist individualism of the original Townsend-, Coughlin Social Justice-, *and* Long-Smith Share-the-Wealth premises and promises. Whether he will prove equal to the task of making this strange concoction of religious urges and $200-a-month over into an American collectivism, is a matter of conjecture.

glad to sponsor one any time, and the National Association of Manufacturers would probably be as willing to pay for any kind of anti-Communist activities as Thyssen and Kirdorf were in Germany. Of course it seems almost unbelievable that Hearst, for instance, should not remember the fate of Hugenberg. However, indications are that they have learned nothing and forgotten nothing, and that if ever Berzelius Windrip should become a candidate for the presidency of the United States, he could use all local Chambers of Commerce as district headquarters, and draw blank checks upon every Clearing House bank in the City of New York. And yet this country seems to hold no chance for Fascism.

This does not mean that "it can't happen here." It does mean that what Sinclair Lewis describes is no Fascism. Lewis appears to have been well aware of this, or else he would hardly skirt so carefully the question of how the people at large respond to the Windrip régime —beyond relating the effects of individual cruelty to non-conformists and the "peace and quiet" bulletins of foreign correspondents. Through his whole story, up to its climax of armed revolt, runs the implication that the "Corpo State" is *not* in accord with the ideas and real sentiments of the American people of its day. Buzz Windrip is a lunatic fringe demagogue who gets himself elected on promises of a very material kind (not by the emotional appeal that democracy is an invention of the devil!), and who is unscrupulous enough to use the powers of his office and of a well-oiled political machine for the overthrow of the Constitution and the establishment of a personal dictatorship. The people, Lewis permits us to infer, do not quite like it—although, for some time at least, they take it. Whether or not that could happen here, is debatable—in any case it is no Fascism. It is as much Fascism as Cuba, or Venezuela, or Japan of today are democracies—all ostensibly democratic institutions notwithstanding. From a practical point of view it might seem to be of small moment whether the Windrip danger, as long as it is real, is Fascism or not. *It is the theory of this book that it is of vital importance;* that an existing danger will be more easily averted if recognized as what it is—a native phenomenon based on certain definitely American traits—than if we continue to confuse it with imported ideas which we do not understand. Again it cannot be emphasized too strongly that this does not refer to what the defenders of democracy may find it expedient to *say*, when the time comes, but to what they really *think themselves.* As far as that is concerned, however, our habit of dubbing "Fascist" everything we dislike in this country, is a potentially fatal mistake. We are tying our own hands. We are depriving ourselves of our best line of defense if we take Huey Long, William Randolph Hearst, the CCC, J. P. Morgan, Jim Farley, and Adolf Hitler—and fight the resulting hash as Fascism.

Our strongest argument against a threatening American Fascism is not that the Germans or Italians are enslaved, or impoverished, or unhappy; *it is that we are different.* A few years from now it is quite possible that Italian anti-Fascism and even German anti-Nazidom (aside from the Jews who by then will have been absorbed somehow by the rest of the world) will have become as insignificant as the present remnants of Russian anti-Communism. There will be émigré colonies in Paris, New York, and Hollywood, and otherwise all observers—except the never-say-die type which it is safe to ignore—will be compelled to consider the proposition that Fascism, for the people of the nations who adopted it, might have turned out to have been—not a scourge—but a blessing. If, when this realization begins to force itself upon us, a genuine Fascist movement happens to be rising in our midst, we shall ourselves have opened the door to it by refusing to take the view that Fascism might be all right for the Germans and Italians and yet conflict here with an inherent national mentality. And if, at such a time, we are confronted with not a genuine Fascist but a pseudo-Fascist movement whose democratic stupidities we have insisted on calling Fascism, we shall have no defense at all. *To recognize the validity of Fascism for others—and to realize and emphasize and strengthen the distinctions which make it unsuitable for us—is our only chance to offset the proselytizing effect of future Fascist successes abroad.* Simply to deny them is not only erroneous but stupid. As Talleyrand once said: it is worse than an outrage; it is a mistake. It is a mistake that might well suffice to doom what we want (and, with a measure of straight thinking, would easily be able) to defend: American democracy.

American democracy at present is endangered. But it faces a danger very much like that of France—the danger that the system fails to provide for adequate translation of popular wishes into governmental policies. In France this threatens because of an impractical construction of parliamentarianism. Here it threatens because of overextended powers of the judiciary. Our Supreme Court, for some time, has been busy invalidating legislative enactments. That, under our system of government, is its function—it has to see that the legislative or executive branches do not deprive the individuals of the rights which their conception of democracy (whether expressed in a basic law or not) guarantees them. No democrat can say anything against that. In recent months, however, the majority group of the Court has gone further. They were not content with guarding the Constitution as *the people's* idea of democracy. *They substituted,* as the yardstick of their control of legislative and administrative action, *their own idea* of a democratic system. They established types of action which, because the judges thought them undemocratic, were "verboten" to democracy itself—and this, unfortunately, contravenes its very concept. Democracy may make it hard for the people to do certain things—and surely the provisions for amendment of the Constitution of the United States are cumbersome enough—but there can be *nothing* in a democracy which the people cannot do *at all.* Basic law cannot stand in the way—because basic law itself is only a particularly sacred expression of the popular will. The concept of democracy cannot stand in the way—because the concept of democracy is just that: a state serving the people under majority rule.

Even in the extreme case of the electorate of a democracy voting, in the manner constitutionally prescribed for decisive changes, to set up a Communist or Fascist state, the old government could in duty not hold out for the old system—it is emphatically *not* "undemocratic" if a people, by democratic process, forces the democratic state to end itself. A majore ad minus, they must also be able to make it do everything else. *Why* our Supreme Court majority takes its stand is quite beyond the point. It may be credited with the loftiest motives. But its activity could not be more pernicious and more unwarranted if based on an avowed intention to save the respective judges' own money. Their stand is not a stand for individualism against collectivism. It is a stand against the effectuation of individualism—for what cannot be called other than a judicial oligarchy. It is as effective an imperilment of a working democracy as a Communist or Fascist movement. In fact, it is more dangerous because, barring a complete inversion of our national mentality, no collectivist movement would have much of a chance here *at present,* while continuation of the judicial dictatorship might well serve to undermine our individualism by shattering the people's faith in democracy *as a means to get what they want.*

The issue of individualism versus collectivism is: whether a communal organization shall function through the people making the state do what *they* want, or through the state making the people do what *it* wants. But the issue with which today we find ourselves confronted in this country is the very different one of whether or not, in a system *designed* to be individualist, the people *are actually able to make* the state do what they want. This issue does not distinguish democracy from Fascism or any other system—it distinguishes democracy working from democracy not working. A democratic system can "fail" in two ways. It can fail to express a conception of the communal relationship that prevails among the people. This is the case of the formally democratic nations who went Fascist. Or it can fail to function according to its own theory—this is the danger which now faces so many other democracies. Democracy can fail in a country because its people are not democratic at heart. Or it can fail because, while the people are democratic, the governmental set-up really is not—in other words, because the system, in practice, does not effectively provide for the realization of the people's wishes. It makes no difference whether, as in France, this is due to an overemphasis on chance majorities in the legislative body—or, as in this country, to the exaggerated power of a non-responsible judicial branch to impede effectuation of the democratically determined popular will. In both cases democracy is endangered in its functioning because its driving force, the will of the people, cannot be determined and translated into communal policy without unreasonable delay and difficulties. If, in the long run, a democracy is unable to amend such a situation, it has failed—a failure that will result not in the immediate emergence of a new political system but in a stagnation which in the near or distant future may make the old system insufferable.

What, in such a contingency, will eventually pick up the pieces, is a matter of political accident. Seldom, if ever, will it be Fascism—because even a long-enduring deterioration of democracy will hardly suffice to develop a Fascist basic mentality; the impulse will be lacking. Real Fascism—a genuine collectivist movement rising and sweeping an individualist country, a democratic population really turning to the Fascist way of thinking, of conceiving the state as the individuals' master, of embracing personal sacrifice for the glory of a superior unit, the state actually "changing in the consciousness and the will of the people"—stands, in the opinion of this writer, a slight chance indeed. Neither in this country nor in any other of the more important democracies does there seem perceptible today an inclination of the people thus to reverse their inherited attitude toward the communal relationship.

Real Fascism, however, is not the only "Fascist danger" in the world today. Much more imminent is the danger of *pseudo-Fascism*.

This is the case of Buzz Windrip. It is the case of the military dictators of Eastern Europe and South and Central America. It is the case of Austrian "Fascism"— or, perhaps the most accurate example, of the Machado-Batista type of "democracy" in Cuba. It means the erection and maintenance, by persuasion or force, of any kind of authoritative rule *not* in accord with, or even against, a genuine will and inclination of the people. Its chance comes with the disintegration of existing systems —by open collapse, by lack of a developed communal sense, or in the wake of democratic stagnation. In France this has happened in the past century and now looms again as a possibility on the political horizon. According to Sinclair Lewis it may happen here. And it may happen in every country where the people feel deeply that their state should serve *their* interest as *they* see it—and are driven to despair by the governmental machine's refusal to make that hope come true. Such a situation—when the people lose patience with the democratic system as a means of effectuating an individualist conception of their community—is the most auspicious setting for the emergence of a pseudo-Fascist form of government. It makes no difference under what name it appears. It may call itself Fascism; it may call itself democracy and look like Fascism; and it will certainly be called Fascism by its opponents. All that does not make it Fascism—and its enemies are only sapping their own strength if they confuse creations of a desperate and misguided individualism, due for a sorrowful awakening, with real Fascist régimes grown normally out of existing conditions and responding to genuine popular trends. Dialectically, the anti-Fascists weaken their case by laying themselves open to objections which they should never have to answer. But, beyond that, they seriously impair the logic of their own convictions when they put the case of democracy going mad—which they are concerned with—on a plane with developments to which even they may soon be unable to deny a large measure of validity. All "Fascist dangers" may be one and the same in the vernacular of politics—but for the would-be defenders of our system it might prove disastrous to overlook the fact that desperate results of truly "failing" democracies are still *essentially* different from Fascism.

The third, and most imminent Fascist threat (though no threat "of" Fascism) is international aggression. That a modern democratic population should suddenly and without warning adopt a collectivist attitude is improbable, to say the least. That any of our more important democracies should so lose its vital energies as to fall a prey to a pseudo-Fascist dictatorship is also not to be expected as long as circumstances remain half-way normal. But that, under any circumstances, the present Fascist nations will seek to expand, and, failing to succeed in peace, will attempt to expand by force, and, being repulsed once, will try again and again until they either succeed or cease to be Fascist nations—that is a course of events with all the inexorability of a law of nature. Their democratic neighbors are very much in the position of mountain villagers in a flood zone: they can erect a dam, or build a reservoir for the surplus water of the stream, or they can even try to deflect it in another direction. Or they can evacuate their villages. But they cannot hope to persuade the river not to rise in the spring—even if they succeed in getting it to sign an agreement to that effect. There is no mistaking the fact that this "law of nature" puts the anti-Fascist pacifist in a serious quandary. Ordinarily his theory is that (a) the state has no right to disturb the individual's peace (in his opinion it is there for him and cannot make him lay down his life in its defense) and that (b) the individual need not care in the last analysis to which community he owes allegiance as long as it provides him with the benefits which are the purpose of its formation. Where his logic runs afoul of reality is that the Fascist state, if ever it should get him under its jurisdiction, would not bother about fulfilling state obligations according to individualist theory. Once our pacifist becomes a Fascist subject, his personal attitude will cease to matter—he will become an object of Fascist discipline and lose his coveted "individual rights" whether he likes it or not. Of course, he might emigrate before the annexation. But we are not concerned here with what any single individual might do, but with the behavior patterns suitable for masses of people. And so we cannot dodge the realization that democratic victims of Fascist attack are confronted with the choice of either waiving their basic individualist right and taking up arms for their community, or running the risk of exercising that right for the last time.

It is true that today this applies only to the Fascists' neighbors. But in a larger sense it is true for all the democracies of the world—because Fascist power is an avalanche that cannot stop until its motion is halted completely. More and more this logical compulsion is being realized in the democracies of Europe. Few voices have been raised in France, Britain, Belgium, Switzerland in protest against the increased armament expenditures of those countries, and only a past master of political sophistry like David Lloyd George has seen fit to question a British Cabinet member's recent statement that today it was "the duty of those in authority to frighten the people out of their wits." The United States is a country in the fortunate position of being defended by oceans from all but two neighbors, and those two of reliably pacific intentions. Therefore—but *only* therefore!—the pacifist view may be quite correct that even our present moderate scale of armaments is exaggerated and that the D.A.R.'s cries of sorrow over our unpreparedness deserve the same skepticism as many other policies of that redoubtable organization. But as a general rule for the nations of the world the fact will have to be faced that as long as Fascist nations exist democracies have only three alternatives: either to deal with the Fascists now, or to make themselves strong enough to repel them at any time they should choose to strike—or to get ready to submit, at some inevitable moment, to Fascist rule. After all the progress of civilization we were so proud of, this is an extremely saddening truth. And it may be altogether fitting and proper to make our rising generation peace-minded by giving prizes for the best sophomore essays on the elimination of war. But it seems rather unwise also to force those of us who are charged with the responsibility of looking ahead, to close their eyes to the realities of the present—which breed the necessities of the future.

Whether peaceful means—moral suasion, economic pressure, international co-operation by democracies— are adequate to "deal with" the international Fascist danger, depends on facts which are not, as yet, available to the international public. The Ethiopian conflict, which occurred at what was perhaps the last possible moment for the democracies of the world to learn their lesson, seems to have answered the question in the negative; not, by the way, as our League enthusiasts can already be heard to say, because in some nations it disclosed an unwillingness to make "sanctions" effective, but because it indicated very strongly that a Fascist nation, threatened with peaceful pressure, will always be able to convert any conflict into a military one. Geneva failed in the African crisis not because its members were half-hearted in the application of sanctions but because it became obvious that Italy would retaliate with war, for which they were not prepared. The gist of the problem is again nothing but the old "bluff" argument: *peaceful* sanctions can be effective *only* if the punished nation does not dare to fight. If it does so dare—and, as we have tried to show in an earlier chapter, no Fascist nation will attack unless prepared for a showdown—sanctions can still be effective as preparation for military action. But, if the sanctionists recoil from that, the inevitable result is—well, Ethiopia. Economic boycotts mean exactly the same thing. A Fascist nation will bear them as long as it is not vitally affected—and for that time the others might just as well save themselves the trouble and expense, for what is their purpose if not to affect the Fascists vitally? And as soon as the Fascists *do* begin to suffer from the pressure, they will strike to break it—and again its effect will plainly depend on the willingness of the non-Fascist powers to sustain it by force. When all is said, the net result of our reflections is the kindergarten truth that a party willing to apply force will get away with murder until stopped *by some stronger force.* What the Fascists did was simply to build a system of international affairs on this platitude —while the entire "civilized" world was straining its cerebral muscles to find some way around it. At present they are beginning to see that there is no way around it. And this scientific discovery is being paid for with the most serious jeopardy of what took centuries of humane and political development to create—the democratic system of government.

There is no use denying that democracy today is in dire straits. From every angle its continued existence is threatened beyond its power to stay alive on its own. Germany and Italy have shown that a real trend of popular mentality toward collectivism will wipe it out— and, moreover, *should* wipe it out according to its own principles. The little states of Europe and America have shown that, even where there is no developed collectivism, democracy cannot work without a developed individualism. France and this country have come perilously close to showing that internal stagnation, a disability of the system to provide for the realization and enforcement of the popular will under changing circumstances, can lead to its downfall. And lastly, to top it all off, Fascist expansion looms as equally menacing to democracy from outside as Fascist subversion is from within. None of these dangers can be met successfully without conscious acts on the parts of a democratic people, based on a clear view of what is at stake. Fascism, when in danger, is in a position to defend itself. But democracy—instrument of the individuals—has to rely on those individuals for its preservation. Only they can save it, and only by a firm determination to spare no cost that may be necessary—sometimes in actual combat, mostly in self-restriction, in consideration for the rights of others, in voluntarily foregoing the pursuit of individual interests for the sake of enabling the democratic community to continue to function.

When we ask today if democracy can survive, we are afraid that this cost may prove too high for those of us who would have to pay it. We are tempted to infer that they consciously want to sacrifice democracy. The truth is probably only that they cannot see yet how a system that is based on the interest of the individual can at the same time require the individual to restrict himself in the pursuit of this interest. They fail to recognize that individualism implies not so much the material egoism of the individuals as their will to be superior as individuals, their determination to bow to no collective concept but their own majority—whether nation, or élite, or "business"—even *if* it should take care of them better than they could themselves. Democracy was achieved by past generations at the sacrifice of lives and fortunes and of all sorts of protections and conveniences for the sake of being able to set Man up as master of his community. The driving force of its founders was their will to run their state as they pleased, to have the purposes of their humanity take precedence over every fixed consideration of tradition or selection or advantage. In our consciousness democracy has always been more closely identified with personal freedom than with prosperity or quality or "good government"—it has never stood for the most materially beneficial form of government but for the form in which men found embodied a conceptual superiority for which they were willing to forego material benefits. Should it be so strange, then, that the preservation of this form of government will require efforts and sacrifices just as did its establishment? Should it be so inequitable to ask the democratic citizens of today to assume, in defense of democracy, a small part of the inconveniences which their predecessors gladly assumed to create it? Should it be so illogical that to keep alive what we think is the highest form of government does demand a deeper popular allegiance than to maintain other systems—with cruder but more tangible centers of loyalty than just the interest, personality, and freedom of every single individual?

That the existence of a democracy is more delicately conditioned than that of any other system, is a fact—and we may be proud of it. A Fascist nation has hundreds of perpetuating devices to take care of its Fascism as long as it is a nation. But a democracy remains—and should remain!—democratic only as long as the people really want it to. And "really want" means more than to profess allegiance, or swear it, or even to signify it in the processes of representative government. Democracy is not a gift that nations will receive from Heaven in exchange for good behavior. It is the manifestation of a popular will—and to maintain it a people must be ready not only to express but to enforce this will, no less against the insidious threat of communal stagnation than against conquest or collectivism. It is a fatal error to underrate the dynamic requirements of democracy. It is doomed if its trend toward peaceful development causes it to stop moving forward. It is an achievement that daily must be won anew. It will live as long as the people of a country are willing, not only to vote, but to fight that "government of the people, by the people, for the people shall not perish from the Earth."

Notes on the Development of Fascist Organization

(A) POLITICAL:

Throughout the history of Fascism the Italians worked out the original ideas, which the Germans took over, applied on a magnificently larger scale, and carried to their ultimate conclusions—or to absurdity. The political organization of Italian Fascism began with a meeting called by Mussolini in Milan on March 23, 1919. Those present—the numbers given vary between thirty and one hundred and fifty—were later to become famous as "Fascists of the first hour." In their ensuing campaign, the Fasci di Combattimento, as Mussolini called them, employed a modified "cell system" (see below), setting up "sessions" of twenty members as organizing units in every locality, with professional groups and squadre di combattimento, "fighting" or, as the modern phrase goes, "storm detachments" at their side. After the March on Rome, Il Duce del Fascismo (the leader of Fascism) became Capo del Governo (head of the government) and the functions of the Party changed. Its organization became completely centralized, exchanged its early democratic features for a strictly hierarchic and authoritative structure, and put in place of the independent battle formation of the squadristi the unified, centralized and disciplined body of the Fascist Militia. Comparatively soon the Party itself closed its doors—the élite group must not be allowed to grow too large. Its recruiting, from then on, was only to be done from its own youth bodies. Other organizations, however, were created and held open to everybody: the Fascist trade unions—later chosen to serve as the basis of a new economic system—received a monopoly to represent employees; associations of civil servants, journalists, lawyers were formed and directed on Fascist lines without requiring membership in the Party as such. In particular, Mussolini had two ingenuous organizatory ideas. First, the youth of the country was guided into the most comprehensive official youth movement since the mythical Lycurgic system in Sparta. From six to eighteen years, as Balilla and Avanguardisti (boys from six to fourteen and fourteen to eighteen, respectively) and Piccole and Giovane Italiane (girls from six to fourteen and fourteen to eighteen, respectively) the Opera Nazionale Balilla undertook to train Italian youth for the Fascist state. Second, the Opera Nazionale Dopolavoro was organized to provide recreational facilities for workers after hours. Membership in it was not compulsory, but the enormous advantages at practically no cost made it quickly popular. Today it is one of the strongest ties between Fascism and the Italian people.

The organization of the National Socialist movement in Germany was something to marvel at. It was built up underground inside of a scant four years, out of the remnants of several miniature political parties, shattered by repeated unsuccessful attempts at a coup d'état, ridiculed, and more than once on the verge of bankruptcy. At the end of those four years, in 1932, it could list among its assets not only a trained, uniformed, and minutely disciplined army of more than a million men with regular and élite troops, cavalry, air corps and motorized units with splendid technical equipment, but also a system of labor unions with rapidly growing cells in every trade or industrial plant in the country, a youth movement that already had an enormous influence on German children, and groups in every branch of business, art, science, or profession, each completely prepared to run the whole show in its particular field at a moment's notice. The main point in the National Socialist organizing campaign during the "years of struggle" was the "cell system." Priority in this method of political work probably belongs to nineteenth century Socialism—particularly to the Russian revolutionary movement—and the Italians had also worked along the same lines, but the system was certainly never before employed so efficiently nor so successfully. Its essence is the establishment of "cells" of trusted followers in every given central point of human relations, each cell at the beginning consisting only of one or two members whose exclusive task is conversion of their own strictly limited realm. There will be cells of the party as such in every building, of the workers' organization in every plant, of the lawyers' organization in every local bar association. Cells are grouped into somewhat larger units—buildings into blocks, other cells into local or district divisions, and so forth. All are authoritatively led and strictly disciplined, and in the case of Germany have served to convert, in an incredibly short time, nearly half of the population to a Fascist movement violently opposed by every legitimate government.

Since Hitler's ascent to power, the Party organization has been greatly enlarged and remodeled very much after Italian examples. The military bodies have been used as emergency police and in various other official capacities. The Hitler Youth is rapidly following the way led by the Balilla towards a monopoly, against which only the Catholic youth organizations are still fighting an apparently losing battle. Labor unions as well as employers' associations have been welded into the "German Labor Front"—in the words of Hitler "the organization of all Germans working with fist or brow." The Party's hold on Labor is additionally strengthened by the Labor Front's subsidiary, the after-work organization Kraft durch Freude (meaning "strength through joy") which is repeating the feats of the Dopolavoro with enormous success. But the Germans went further than the Italians. The ambitions of Nazism, to end four hundred years of dissension by unifying the German churches in behalf of the state, are known and discussed the world over. There is no office, no profession, no artistic or literary occupation, whether free-lancing or in employ, that does not require membership in some organization avowedly established for the sole purpose of keeping its individual members under the immediate influence of the National Socialist movement and constantly in line with its general policies. There is no sport or game, whether athletics, football, ping-pong, or bridge, that can be played in competition by someone not a member of an association dominated by the Party, which in turn is only fulfilling its function to provide for the thorough and durable National Socialism of the country.

(B) ECONOMIC:

The substance of the *Italian* mode of economic organization is outlined in the gospel of corporate theory, the Carta del Lavoro of April 21, 1927. It may be helpful here to quote the highlights of that document and to comment (in parenthesis) briefly upon their dogmatic significance:

Art. I—"The ancient and powerful Italian nation, as an independent organism of superior value with superior purposes and means, stands above the single or combined individuals composing it. Its final realization, as a spiritual economic and political unit, is the Fascist state."

(This is the collectivist basis of Fascism as a whole.)

Art. II—"*Labor,* in all its forms, mental, technical or manual, executive or subordinate, *is a social duty;* and only as such is it under the protection of the state.

"The process of production is, for the nation, an indivisible whole; its purposes, without distinction, are one and the same: individual well-being and the furtherance of state power."

(This marks the end of the individualist notion of production and labor as private activities. In full accord with the organic conception of the state, production becomes a communal interest, and its advancement by work—no matter in what capacity—becomes a national duty. Labor, therefore, is protected by the state only as the fulfillment of this duty—neither as a class, nor as an individual right. So far, it is to be noted, no dogmatic difference is yet apparent between this and Communist collectivism.)

Art. III—"Professional and labor organization is free, but only the legally recognized and communally controlled organization has the right to speak for the entire category of employers and employees for which it is established, to represent their interests before the state and against other organizations, to make collective agreements binding upon all members of the category, to collect dues from them, and to exercise all public functions conferred upon it."

(This marks the authority of economic organization as not derived from the individuals constituting it, but from the state which recognizes and controls it. Individuals can no longer simply get together and, by declaring their consent, empower their association to act for them and collect dues from them. Under Fascism such authority is void—it can be granted only by the state.)

Art. IV—"The collective agreement serves to express the solidarity of the different factors of production, by compromising the conflicting interests of employers and employees and subordinating them to the higher interests of production."

(This replaces the old significance of a collective labor contract—that of mutual concessions by sovereign individuals—with a new collectivist meaning, featuring the totalitarian concept and the subservience to the state common to the most opposed interests.)

Art. V—"The Labor Court is the *organ employed by the state* to decide labor conflicts. . . ."

(Affirming the superiority of the whole over any or

each of its parts; the state acts no longer as conciliator or arbitrator by common consent, as under democracy.)

Art. VI—"The legally recognized corporations assure the *legal equality between employers and employees,* maintain discipline in production and labor, and aid in its improvement.—

"Since the interests of production are national interests, the corporations are legally recognized as organs of the state."

(Affirming (a) the principle of equality of all Fascist citizens, whether employers or employees, and (b) the principle of economic totalitarianism—"everything in the state, nothing without the state.")

Art. VII—"*The corporate state considers private initiative in production the most valuable and most effective instrument for the protection of national interests.*

"Private organization of production is a national function of the employer; he is therefore responsible for it to the state.—Employees are active collaborators in the economic enterprise, the management of which is the employer's function and responsibility."

(Now comes the parting point of Fascist and Communist economic doctrine: where a Communist government pursues the national interest of production by operating it itself, a Fascist government prefers to let the individuals do the job for it. Emphatically repudiated, *in both cases,* is the individualist theory of the productive process being carried on by virtue of *individual right*—Fascist private production is a purely national function, though conferred upon individual citizens, and altogether part of the organic structure of the state.)

Art. VIII—"It is the duty of employer associations to direct all their efforts toward an increased and improved production and toward a decrease in prices."

(This is the—theoretical—*reason* for Fascist capitalism; it is believed that the national interest in both production and consumption will be served better by private initiative and competition than by public ownership and management.)

Art. IX—"State interference in economic affairs takes place only where private initiative is lacking or insufficient, or where political interests of the state are affected. Such interference can take the form of supervision, aid, or direct assumption of control."

(Here, finally, the Carta lays down the *limits* of capitalism in the Fascist state, and they are quite definite: Capitalism will be maintained as long as it (a) serves its purpose to serve the state, and (b) does not otherwise conflict with state interests. The word "political" is really superfluous, since to a Fascist community *all* interests are political. The pronouncement shows clearly that capitalism, an *original element* and a *policy* of Fascism, is not considered one of its *essentials*—it will never be allowed to stand in the way of the superior interest.)

Historically, the evolution of the Corporate State can be traced to ideological tradition as well as to practical expediency. The ground for it had been prepared before the War; the Guild-Socialist theories of the Nationalist Party, and the emphasis placed upon social conscience by the Catholic Church (Encyclica De Rerum Novarum, 1891) served to make economic organization for purposes of social justice a main topic of pre-War Italian political thinking. Thus the idea came very naturally to the Fascists to transmute into instruments of economic policy their early "syndicates"—employer and worker groups in the various trades and industries—which, like the later German "Plant Cells Organization," were at first intended as mere channels of political expansion. The change was facilitated when, after the March on Rome, the old Socialist unions became hotbeds of anti-Fascism and had to be destroyed—and the bulk of their members joined the Fascist syndicates.

At that time Edmondo Rossoni—American unionist who had organized Mussolini's labor groups—pushed a plan for a comprehensive organization of workers and employers "within the state," something closely approaching the eventual German Labor Front set-up; but Mussolini, whether because of employer resistance or on dogmatic grounds, side-tracked the idea. In 1925, the so-called Palazzo-Vidoni Agreement provided for mutual recognition of the Fascist syndicates and the Confederation of Italian Industries as sole representatives of, respectively, employers and labor. On that basis, a succession of laws and regulations established the formal outline of the new structure, as the "moral substance" of which, in 1927, the then as yet unofficial Grand Council of Fascism proclaimed the Carta del Lavoro. From then on the Carta—although itself not of legal nature—exercised a decisive influence upon the application of business and labor law in general; but the actual progress of corporate development was extremely slow. Eventually, after the Fascists had been repeatedly accused of using their corporate theory as a screen for a definitely unsocial practice, a new burst of speed began in 1934: the establishment of the twenty-two corporations was followed by the abolition of parliament, and the substitution of the National Council of Corporations.

Today, the structure is completed substantially as outlined from the beginning—the Italian Corporate State can be complained of as a nuisance, but not as being non-existent.

The essence of the *German* scheme is embodied in Articles 1 and 2 of the Law for the Organization of National Labor:

Art. 1—"In a business enterprise, the owner, as leader, and the employees, as followers, shall work together to further the purposes of the enterprise, and for the common good of the Nation and of the State."

Art. 2—"As between the leader of an enterprise and his followers, the leader shall make all decisions concerning the enterprise.

"He is to take care of the welfare of the followers. The followers are to keep faith with him in the spirit of solidarity in a common enterprise."

For a student of the historical roots of the Fascist leadership principle this formula will provide an auspicious point of departure—but it can easily prove misleading. The comparison with feudalism strongly suggests itself. Feudalism, however, was something essentially connected with the disposition of property; it was an entire system based upon differences in the ownership of land. In the National Socialist scheme, the "enterprise leadership," though it is conferred upon the owner of a business, is not concerned with property rights in the business but solely with its operation. Not the disposition of economic resources is of moment—only their use.

What the Nazi—and the generally Fascist—concept of leadership really goes back to, is not the feudal but the *pre-feudal* German system—the organization of the nomad Germanic tribes. There a band of free men—for the sake of a better utilization of their collective strength—chose one out of their midst to lead them, and vowed to follow him. The "heretoch" was by no means legally or substantially different from his followers—he was no "lord" yet. But within the tribal collective unit, *his function was to command, theirs to obey. This* relationship is the conceptual origin of Fascist authority—and in the "economic leadership principle" it has probably been most clearly preserved.

The organizational development of the Nazis' authoritative economy was made comparatively easy by the nature of the economy they found preceding them. Prevailing in post-War, pre-Nazi Germany was a trend toward "individualist collectivization"—collective economic action by individuals for the purpose of protecting their individual interests. Trusts and cartels abounded in industry, and trade associations exercised vast regulatory powers. The public made increasing use of consumer co-operatives. Labor relations were completely dominated by the principle of collective bargaining. An overwhelming majority of workers was unionized in the Social-Democratic "Free Unions," a small percentage in the Catholic "Christian Unions." Over ninety per cent of trade and industrial employment was covered by collective agreements— mostly of the "closed shop" variety so strongly objected to in this country—which, as a rule, were not concluded between unions and individual businessmen, but "industry-wide," between industrial unions and the representative bodies of employers of entire industries.

Before the Nazis came to power, they campaigned among workers not by setting up rival unions, but by establishing "plant cells" in every business enterprise in the country. After they seized the government, this "National Socialist Plant Cells Organization" (N.S.B.O.), "took over" the existing unions—that is to say, they ousted the old union officials and seized their offices and funds, without, however, assuming their function of collective bargaining. To safeguard the wage structure—and, at the same time, to rivet governmental control— a law of April, 1933, appointed regional "Labor Trustees." The bulk of organized labor was slowly transplanted into a new, and during 1933-34 yet rather vague organization, the German Labor Front. In January, 1934, the "Law for the Organization of National Labor" laid down the principles which henceforth were to govern labor relations: the unit character of the business enterprise, to be conducted according to the leadership principle—with the employer as "leader" under social responsibility; the supervisory power of the state to be exercised by the labor trustees, and a system of "honor courts" to deal with violations of social duty. In November, 1934, the Labor Front was officially constituted as the "Organization of all Germans

working with fist and brow"—which indicated the intention to
extend it beyond the concept of a labor organization into an
equivalent of the Corporate State, covering employers as well
as employees. Business, in the meantime, had been organized
under the Ministry of Economics into two separate structures—
one on industrial lines, with thirteen "main divisions," and
one on regional lines, through the local Chambers of Commerce—both of which led up into the head agency of the
"Reichs Chamber of Economics" which is run according to
the leadership principle by governmental 'appointees. This
set-up, like the Labor Front, was substantially completed in
the winter of 1934-35; and in March, 1935, the leader of the
Labor Front and the Minister of Economics entered into an
"Agreement," under which the Reichs Chamber of Economics,
as a body, was incorporated into the Labor Front as the "Economic Department" of that institution. There have been no
major structural changes since that time, and the system appears to have reached a certain degree of stability—but the
increasingly difficult international economic position of the
Reich may at any moment compel the leaders to use the newly-
established centralized machinery for the enforcement of more
stringently collectivist policies.

For observers of Fascist *farm policy* the most arresting phenomenon is the difference between the German and the Italian
approach. As in the case of industry, the Italians were interested primarily in getting practical results, while the Germans
insisted on first setting up a structure in accordance with National Socialist dogma. Mussolini's farm program, by and
large, consisted of only two measures, but those of vast material economic significance: "Bonifica Integrale," a large-scale
land reclamation undertaking, and the "Battle of the Grain,"
a drive to raise the wheat output. Organization of agriculture
was carried on insofar as it appeared necessary or desirable
for the purposes of those campaigns—the main thing in the

mind of the responsible Fascist officials was quite obviously to provide more arable land and to grow more wheat on it. In Germany, the entire initial emphasis was placed on the creation of the *instruments* for a National Socialist farm policy —by establishing the "Reichsnährstand," an agricultural coverall structure similar to the Labor Front in business, and by forging an enduring bond between the soil and the peasantry by means of a farm inheritance law designed to keep the balance of German agriculture in a broad layer of small and medium-sized peasant holdings, tied to peasant families of "racially" preferable stock. What actually should be done, what policies should be pursued in practice, was left to the experts in the organization and in the controlling governmental agencies.

However, we are again in danger of mistaking differences, based on temperamental contrasts between two nations, for essential dissimilarities. Fundamentally, no matter how it came to pass, the position of the farmer is exactly the same in Italy as it is in Germany. Material policies, of course, vary with the requirements of the different economic situation of the two countries. But the structural tendencies are alike; in either case the farming population is raised to the position of a favored instrument of state policy, its interests receive increased protection in exchange for increased loyalty to communal purposes, its economic activities are being, as far as possible, "decommercialized." Agriculture, from a business pursuit, becomes a special service to the community. In Germany this change was expressed and regulated in specific laws. In Italy it took place as an incident to the effectuation of material policies. But in both countries the complete abandonment of the concepts governing a capitalist agriculture is unmistakable.

This, as has been pointed out in the text, is the significant phenomenon noticeable in every concrete Fascist economic evolution: how capitalism, always an essential point of departure, rapidly becomes a trait of secondary importance in the course of Fascist progress. Finance, agriculture, and special fields like utilities and foreign trade are instances of the past. As this book goes to press, the German Second Four-Year-Plan, under General Goering's direction, seems about to make an example of all German business—too indeterminate, as yet, to submit it to analysis, but apparently presaging the eventual doom of orthodox capitalism throughout the National Socialist state.

INDEX

Page numbers in italics indicate a detailed discussion of the subject; pages listed in roman type indicate mention of subject only.

313

314　　　**INDEX**